CHARLES IVES

Charles Ives, 1947

CHARLES IVES

The Ideas Behind the Music

J. PETER BURKHOLDER

YALE UNIVERSITY PRESS
New Haven and London

Designed by Margaret E.B. Joyner
and set in Baskerville type.
Printed in the United States of America by
Edwards Brothers, Inc., Ann Arbor, Michigan

Acknowledgment is made for permission to quote from the following:

Charles Ives, *Essays before a Sonata, The Majority, and Other Writings.* Selected
and edited by Howard Boatwright. New York: W.W. Norton & Company, Inc.
Copyright © 1961, 1962 by W.W. Norton & Company, Inc. Reprinted by
permission of the publishers and Calder & Boyars, Ltd.

Letters and diaries in the Charles Ives Collection, John Herrick Jackson Music
Library, Yale University. Copyright © 1985 by American Academy and
Institute of Arts and Letters. Reprinted by permission.

Charles Ives, *Memos.* Edited by John Kirkpatrick. New York: W.W. Norton &
Company, Inc. Copyright © 1972 by American Academy and Institute of Arts
and Letters. Reprinted by permission.

Library of Congress Cataloging in Publication Data

Burkholder, J. Peter (James Peter)
Charles Ives, the ideas behind the music.

Bibliography: p.
Includes index.
1. Ives, Charles, 1874–1954.   2. Composers—United
States—Biography.   3. Music—Philosophy and aesthetics.
I. Title.
ML410.I94B48   1985   780'.92'4 [B]   85–2469
ISBN 0–300–03261–7
0–300–03885–2 (pbk.)

The paper in this book meets the guidelines for permanence
and durability of the Committee on Production Guidelines
for Book Longevity of the Council on Library Resources.

10   9   8   7   6   5   4   3   2

dedicated to the memory of

KATHLEEN LINDA BURKHOLDER

5 February 1953 – 15 June 1981

Contents

ILLUSTRATIONS

All illustrations, unless otherwise noted in parentheses, are from the Charles Ives Papers, John Herrick Jackson Music Library, Yale University.

Preface

Understanding Charles Ives's music is no easy task. Its diversity is unrivaled, ranging from band marches to avant-garde experiments and from Victorian church anthems to some of the most complex orchestral music ever written. Within a single work, Ives may mix banal chord progressions with tone clusters and quarter tones, high comedy with spiritual profundity, and the old and familiar with sounds never heard before. It is hard to know when to take Ives seriously and when to laugh, which "wrong notes" and novel effects are intended and which are copyists' mistakes or Ives's own miscalculations, which pieces should be heard as art music and which are private jokes or studies. It is not clear how to listen to this music, what is important in it, or how to interpret it.

Making sense of Ives's music has not been made any easier by the way we have come to know it. Ives is the only major composer whose works have come to light in approximately reverse chronological order, beginning with his latest, most difficult, and most idiosyncratic pieces. When his music began to appear in print and in performance in the decades between the world wars, after he had virtually ceased composing, the first major works to be published or played were the *Concord Sonata* for piano, the *Fourth Symphony*, and the orchestral set *Three Places in New England*, all composed between 1908 and 1916. The more accessible *Second* and *Third Symphonies* and the *Variations on America* for organ were not edited and played until the 1940s and 1950s, half a century after they were written, and the major works of Ives's early years, including the *First String Quartet* and the *First Symphony*, products of the mid-1890s, were not available for performance and study until after Ives's death in 1954. This history of publication and performance has almost completely obscured the logic of Ives's development, distorting our picture of the music itself.

Our confusion has been compounded by attempts to view all of Ives's music through the filter of his writings, which date from near the end of his composing career. The mistake is natural: without knowing the early pieces as a context for the radical later works, musicians before the Second World War encountered Ives's mature music in a vacuum and sought to understand it through the words Ives himself had offered in explanation of his intentions. As the earlier works gradually were edited and performed, the same ideas were applied to them, no matter how different they were from the mature compositions in style and original intention. Thus, the early works were interpreted in the context of the later ones, rather than the other way around, and both were approached through the extramusical programs and theories Ives had advanced for a few of his mature pieces. The predictable result has been a critical literature weighed down with myths, misconceptions, and half-truths.

Ignorance of Ives's development has distorted our view of all the music, early and late, and the unwarranted assumption that the aesthetic philosophy articulated by Ives at the very end of his career as a composer applies equally well to music from every stage of his life has reinforced our ignorance by masking the many twists and turns of Ives's professional career. Indeed, it is precisely in the evolution of his aesthetics that the key to his development as a composer is to be found, and it is only through understanding his development, his changing intentions and methods, that we may hope to understand his music fully.

The aim of this book is to clear our vision by offering the first detailed history of Charles Ives's aesthetics, showing how his aesthetic views and artistic aims changed over time, offering a periodization of his creative life, highlighting the major influences on his music and his conception of music, and demonstrating that changes in Ives's musical aesthetics in turn influenced the genres in which he wrote, the musical styles he adopted, and the new techniques he developed. This study lays the groundwork for a companion volume, *The Evolution of Charles Ives's Music*, which will be the first full account of the development of Ives's musical method. Taken together, the two books offer a fundamental reinterpretation of Ives's career, his music, and his position in music history.

Acknowledgments

No one has given me more encouragement or influenced my thinking more than Charles Ives himself. I started work by listening to his music, playing and singing through what I could, and analyzing many individual pieces. Only then did I turn to his writings and to the secondary literature. As I read and wrote, I continually returned to the music itself and was revived many times by Charles Ives's joy and exuberance. If anything I have written sends the reader back to Ives's music with new enthusiasm or new understandings, I will have repaid a small part of my debt to him.

I have been blessed with the warm personal support of the whole faculty of the University of Chicago Department of Music, where I began this book as a student, and of my new colleagues at the University of Wisconsin at Madison, where I finished it as a member of the faculty of the School of Music. From the start, Robert P. Morgan has been a hard and careful critic and a warm personal friend, sharpening my prose and constantly prodding me to write. Ellen Harris provided fresh insights and new enthusiasm as I was preparing the final revisions, and her sense of fun renewed mine when my sense of humor had temporarily left town. Peter Lefferts caught several questionable choices of phrasing that masked points of fuzzy thinking. I am also grateful to Howard Mayer Brown and Philip Gossett of Chicago and Joseph Straus, Alexander Silbiger, and David Rosen of the Wisconsin faculty, in whom I have found insightful critics and faithful friends.

The community of Ives scholars and enthusiasts is clearly still a community. I have felt welcomed and cheered on by all I have contacted. My deep personal thanks go to John Kirkpatrick, not only for his writings about and editions of Ives's works, both musical and literary, but for freely sharing his knowledge and opinions, reading and commenting on the manuscript at several stages, presenting me with his editions of *Study #20* and the *Five Take-Offs* in manuscript, "playing at" *Emerson* for me, driving me up to Bigelow Ives's home in a wild Connecticut fog, making available his transcriptions of the Ives family letters and granting permission for short passages from them to be printed here, and a thousand other favors. Ives's nephew, the late W. Bigelow Ives, opened his home to me twice, first for an interview with John Kirkpatrick to clarify my rather wayward view of the early Transcendentalist influence on his uncle, and again for an afternoon of cataloguing the Ives family books in the old secretary now in his home. William Brooks has been enthusiastic and encouraging, reading and severely criticizing the early drafts and helping to catalogue the Ives books in Bigelow Ives's home. Carol Yaple arrived in New Haven the same day that I did, shuffled through some of the same manuscripts, and read and critiqued the first draft, letting me know through her enthusiasm that I might be on the right track after all. Vivian Perlis graciously provided me with a copy of the catalogue of books in the Redding house that her students had made. Sidney Cowell and Howard Boatwright both clarified for me their published discussions of Ives's early contacts with the ideas and writings of Emerson and Thoreau. Lucille Fletcher Wallop cheerfully granted permission for me to quote from her unpublished article on Ives. H. Wiley Hitchcock, Clayton Henderson, Stuart Feder, and many others have encouraged and supported my work as it progressed. What is most rewarding about my experience is that I feel a very strong sense of mutual support among Ives scholars, even across disagreements, as if here, at least, the idea of the community of scholars is alive.

Outside of the Ives community, James Miller, chairman of the Department of English at the University of Chicago and an expert on Emerson and Whitman, helped me to clarify my impressions of Emerson's central ideas.

The staff of the John Herrick Jackson Music Library at Yale, home of the Ives Collection, has been most helpful. I would particularly like to thank Kathleen Moretto, Reference Librarian, and Peggy Daub, Rare Book Librarian, for their help during my visit in October and November of 1981. I am grateful to John Kirkpatrick for permission to quote from his transcriptions of letters from Harmony Ives to Charles Ives, and to Lucille Fletcher Wallop for permission to quote from her unpublished article, "A Connecticut Yankee in Music."

The Danforth Foundation, the William Rainey Harper Fellowship from the University of Chicago, The Martha Baird Rockefeller Fund for Music, Inc., and the Marc Perry Galler Prize in the Humanities Division of the University of Chicago all provided financial assistance at various stages along the way. Joel Mambretti of the University of Chicago Computation Center and Jerry Tutsch of the Madison Academic Computing Center helped solve the problems of electronic storage and transmission of the manuscript. Computer costs were borne in part by the University of Chicago Computation Center, Department of Music, and Division of the Humanities, and by the University of Wisconsin Graduate School Research Committee. Michael Pepper and his associates at Yale University Press were helpful technical consultants. My editors at Yale, Edward Tripp, Channing Hughes, and Jean van Altena, have been splendid.

Personal acknowledgments traditionally come last. Most important are my parents, Donald and Jean Burkholder, whose constant faith in my abilities has helped me to achieve more than I imagined I could. I could not have started writing without the friendship and support of Bob Rueter, my housemate for my last year in Chicago. Nor could I have finished without Allen Poor, my host during my many visits to Chicago to consult with my readers and burn the late oil at the computer center. Other friends I must mention are Bob Currier, whose support has been constant, even over great distances; Linda Lorenz, who has shared my enthusiasm for Ives from the beginning; Jeffrey Kallberg, Jim Brokaw, Jeffrey Dean, Andy Budwig, and Mary Pacquette-Abt, for their commiseration and support as we moved together through the dissertation mill at Chicago; and my brother, Bill Burkholder, who has refused to take any of this very seriously, providing a wonderful tonic for my over-earnestness. I realized the true nature of my accomplishment when I heard that Bill was using his bound copy of my dissertation to prop up his living-room couch.

Personal acknowledgments come last, and the most personal last of all. A week after I submitted the proposal for the dissertation from which this is adapted, my sister Kathy died of a sudden brain hemorrhage. Two years later, I defended the final version on the anniversary of her burial. She was sixteen months older than me and was my constant companion and rival during our childhood. In her last years, we had come to know one another again as adults and had become very close, as we discovered how much we had in common, how spiritually at one we were, and how much our lives were following parallel paths. I am thankful that we had enough time to heal all our old wounds together and to realize how much we shared. In many ways, she was my oldest and most constant friend. We grew up in a world that hardly exists anymore, we came from a place and a spirit no one else shares, and I knew her in ways I will never know anyone again. This book is filled with her love and colored by my grief. It has been dedicated to Kathy since before the first word was written.

CHARLES IVES

CHAPTER ONE

The *Essays*, the Composer, and the Music

In 1920, Charles Ives launched his second career in music with the private publication of his most ambitious solo composition, the *Second Piano Sonata*, subtitled "Concord, Mass., 1840–1860," and an accompanying book that he called *Essays Before a Sonata*.[1] The book was originally written "as a preface or reason" for the sonata itself and intended to be printed with the score but was published separately because of its length. Taken together, sonata and prefaces were, in Ives's words, "an attempt to present (one person's) impression of the spirit of transcendentalism that is associated in the minds of many with Concord, Mass., of over a half century ago . . . undertaken in impressionistic pictures of Emerson and Thoreau, a sketch of the Alcotts, and a *scherzo* supposed to reflect a lighter quality which is often found in the fantastic side of Hawthorne" (page xxv).

By the time they were published, the *Essays* took up more pages of print than the *Concord Sonata* itself, having expanded from an attempt to explain the character of each of the four movements of the sonata to include what was to be Ives's most definitive statement of his aesthetic philosophy and purposes. In the Prologue, the essays on each movement, and particularly the Epilogue, the longest of the six essays, Ives stressed the spiritual values, the moral strengths, and the religious impulses he was trying to represent, and thus to teach, in his sonata. In the eighteen years since Ives had abandoned his first career in music, as a fairly successful church organist, vernacular musician, and versatile composer of music in a wide variety of styles and genres, to become a businessman who composed music primarily for his own enjoyment during his leisure time, his compositions had taken such a radical turn that he apparently felt it

1

necessary to justify and defend his music as he introduced it to the world at large, as if afraid that he would be misunderstood. He hoped, perhaps, to deflect criticism of his unorthodox music by arguing that his radical means were necessary to fulfill his radical expressive ends; this was the apparent purpose of the long Epilogue and of the distinction he makes there between *substance*, the inner "reality," "conviction," or "spirit" of a work, and *manner*, its execution or outward form. Ironically, while the *Essays* would indeed serve as a pathway into the music for many, they would also lead to misunderstandings of Ives's music and its genesis.

It was an extraordinary opening salvo for what was to become one of the most extraordinary careers in the history of music. No other composer had inaugurated his career in the public eye only *after* finishing most of his music, including all of his major works, in virtually complete isolation. No other composer had introduced himself to the musical public by publishing on his own what would eventually become recognized as his masterpiece and sending it out virtually at random to friends, performing musicians, composers, teachers, critics, conservatories and schools of music, publishers, and the musical press.[2] And no other composer had been so concerned with the ideas behind the music that he insisted on accompanying his music with a program note at least as long and as difficult to understand as the music it attempted to explain.

Ives followed his first two self-publications with a third, a book of *114 Songs*, "thrown, so to speak, at the musical fraternity" in 1922.[3] After that, Ives did little more to promote his own music, beyond subsidizing publications and performances that others had arranged. His career as "the great American composer" was just beginning, but his part in it was all but done. Of course, no composer has won a place in the classical repertoire without the advocacy of performers, critics, and fellow composers fighting for the cause of his music. What is astonishing in Ives's case is how little he promoted his own music, how dependent he was on his advocates, and, as a result, how thoroughly their conception of his music colored the way it was understood—or misunderstood—by the musical public.

When the *Concord Sonata* caught the interest of the writer, pianist, and academic Henry Bellamann, who praised it in an insightful review and included it in his lecture-recitals on modern piano music, Ives's music found its first real champion.[4] The next three decades brought many more. At first, Ives's supporters were drawn from the ranks of the musical avant-garde, who saw him as one of their own: E. Robert Schmitz, whose society for the performance of new music sponsored the premieres of

Ives's *Three Quarter-tone Pieces* for two pianos in 1925 and two movements from his *Fourth Symphony* in 1927; Henry Cowell, composer and founder of the periodical *New Music*, who published many of Ives's works (starting with the second movement of the *Fourth Symphony* in 1929), sponsored or arranged for performances and recordings, and promoted his music among avant-garde composers and performers; and Nicolas Slonimsky, who conducted the first performances of *Three Places in New England*, *The Fourth of July*, and *Washington's Birthday* in both the United States and Europe in 1931 and 1932.[5] Throughout this period, Ives had a reputation as an innovator, an experimental composer, a member of the far-out avant-garde: that was the side of Ives's work that interested Schmitz, who inspired Ives to write the frankly experimental quarter-tone pieces; that was how he was seen by Henry Cowell, an avant-garde composer himself and Ives's most enthusiastic promoter; and by and large, that was how he was viewed by the public and by the musical establishment.

In the next decade, musicians closer to the mainstream of musical life began to notice that some of Ives's works were not simply radical experiments with new musical resources but finished masterpieces in their own right with a distinctively American character. Among these musicians were Aaron Copland, whose well-received presentation of seven of Ives's songs at the Yaddo festival of contemporary American music in the spring of 1932 marked the beginning of widespread interest in Ives's music; the eminent critic Paul Rosenfeld, who wrote warmly and often of Ives's music in the 1930s and 1940s; John Kirkpatrick, who premiered the complete *Concord Sonata* in New York in early 1939 and was ultimately to become Ives's musical and literary executor; and Lawrence Gilman, music critic for the *New York Herald Tribune* and among the most influential voices in the American musical community, whose review of Kirkpatrick's recital lauded Ives's *Concord Sonata* as "exceptionally great music . . . indeed, the greatest music composed by an American" and brought Ives to national prominence almost overnight.[6]

Success followed success. Compositions that had long gathered dust in the disorderly piles of manuscripts in Ives's music room were gradually resurrected, edited, and performed: two of the violin sonatas in 1939 and 1940, the *Third Symphony* and the *First Piano Sonata* (both reconstructed by Lou Harrison) in 1946 and 1949, the *Second Symphony* in 1951 by the New York Philharmonic under Leonard Bernstein, and many more works after Ives's death in 1954, climaxing in the 1965 premiere of the complete *Fourth Symphony* under Leopold Stokowski. And Ives himself began to garner recognition from the musical establishment: election to the National Institute of Arts and Letters in 1945, a Pulitzer Prize for the *Third Symphony* in 1947, feature articles in *Harper's*, *Time*, and *The New York Times Magazine*, glowing reviews in major newspapers, and performances by major orchestras.[7]

More than any other single event, it was Gilman's review of Kirkpatrick's concert that established Charles Ives as a legitimate composer, perhaps even a composer of great genius. Not everyone was to agree with Gilman's assessment, but the weight of his opinion made it impossible any longer to dismiss Ives as a tinkerer, a crank, a musical illiterate, or an amateur without craft or sense. Thus the *Concord Sonata* launched Ives's career as a composer not once, but twice: its publication in 1920 sparked the first interest in his work, and its performance, or Gilman's review of that performance, established his national reputation almost two decades later.

At both times, the *Essays Before a Sonata* were part of the package. Published alongside the sonata, they were sent with the score to John Kirkpatrick when he requested a copy of the sonata in 1927, and Kirkpatrick studied them in preparing his performance.[8] Gilman prepared conscientiously for his review, requesting and receiving a copy of the sonata from the Iveses, and was sent additional materials as well.[9] These must have included the *Essays*, for almost half of Gilman's review consists of long quotations and paraphrases from Ives's program notes on each movement. The review opens with several paragraphs on Ives's background and his experimentation, apparently gathered from published writings on Ives. But the focus is not on the music, not even on its novelty. What little discussion there is of the music itself describes its feel, its effect, and the literary world it evokes, rather than its sound or structure. Thus Gilman writes that the Emerson movement contains passages "in which the expressional power of musical speech is mysteriously extended and released"; "the Hawthorne movement is a Scherzo of unearthly power and intensity, transcending its subject"; the Alcotts movement has pages of "enamoring, subduing charm and sweetness"; and "in the Thoreau movement, there is music of a poetic fervor and exaltation in which the essence of Thoreau's imagination is imagically captured and conveyed." As Ives's biographer, Frank R. Rossiter, has pointed out, what enchanted Gilman was the sonata's powerful extramusical imagery, its triumphant, inspiring vision of the world of Transcendentalism, a world that Americans had only recently rediscovered.[10] Having asked for the score to study, Gilman ended up studying the *Essays* more thoroughly than the music, coming to the music through the filter of words. Having come to hear a musician, Gilman had encountered instead "a great adventurer in the spiritual world, a poet, a visionary, a sage, and a seer."

Gilman's review established the pattern for later approaches to Ives's music, even as it established his reputation as a great American composer. Ives's music has continued to be viewed through the lens of his writings, particularly the *Essays Before a Sonata*. His obvious concern that the *Concord Sonata* be approached only together with the *Essays*, and his insistence that even such sympathetic musicians as Kirkpatrick and Gilman play and hear the music in terms of the extramusical ideas discussed in his prose, have led subsequent performers, critics, and listeners to assume that these writings are the key not just to the *Concord Sonata* but to all of Ives's music. As a result, the aesthetic program set forth in the *Essays*, intended solely as an explanation or defense of the musical language and expressive aims of the *Concord Sonata*, has been applied indiscriminately to works from all periods of Ives's life. The concepts of manner and substance and the ideas attributed to the Transcendentalist writers Emerson and Thoreau, all of which Ives developed in the *Essays*, have been repeatedly taken as touchstones in the analysis and interpretation of all aspects of Ives's music in every genre or style. From program note to textbook, from scholarly study to radio broadcast, discussions of Ives have habitually treated him as a philosopher in music, America's Transcendentalist composer.

In the process, Ives has been deprived of his history and his diversity. His aesthetic philosophy is commonly taken to be the same from the beginning to the end of his activity as a composer. In fact, however, Ives's aesthetic program and compositional intentions varied widely, not only at different stages of his development as a composer, as one might expect, but also between different pieces worked on simultaneously. The high ideals of the *Essays* are not the whole story; the matter is far more complex. For in the *Memos*, written in the early 1930s, where Ives briefly discusses the genesis and composition of most of his important works in a blend of program notes and reminiscences, it is clear that each piece was written for a specific, sometimes unique purpose that determined the piece's shape, language, and character. To sort out Ives's reasons for writing a piece requires a careful attention to its origin and expected use and an awareness of the dichotomies that characterized Ives's musical life: between vernacular and learned music, between public concert music and private exercises, between finished, professionally copied pieces and those left in sketch, between massive, all-inclusive mature masterpieces and tiny "memos in notes" that try out one idea at a time, between pieces calculated to please a chosen audience and those written out of rage at the musical establishment.

Behind the diversity lies a history that existing studies of Ives's aesthetic thought have only obscured. By concentrating on the *Essays* (begun about 1916 and published in 1920)[11] and slightly later writings in much the same spirit, such as the composer's Postface at the end of *114 Songs* (drafted in 1920–1922) and the article *Some "Quarter-tone" Impressions* (1924), scholars have strongly emphasized Ives's views as formulated in the last phase of his career as a composer, after all of his major works had been completed. The *Essays* are undeniably relevant to the *Concord Sonata* (worked on primarily from 1910 to 1915),[12] as they explain specifically what Ives intended to portray in that work. They also shed light on many other works written between 1908 and 1918, such as *Three Places in New England*, the *Second Orchestral Set*, and the *Fourth Symphony*, although each of these pieces has a musical purpose sufficiently different from that of the *Concord Sonata* to require caution in applying to them Ives's statements in the *Essays*. But the *Essays* certainly do not pertain to the whole of Ives's output, for the philosophical position they articulate is Ives's final, hard-won synthesis of the many conflicting views of music he had either held or encountered during his lifetime. Earlier works do not fulfill the artistic program of the *Essays*, for the simple reason that it had not yet been formulated.

Our understanding of Ives's music must be based on the music itself and his own conception of it as he worked on each piece, rather than on the reputation his work has gained because of the way we have come to know it and the ways it has been interpreted to us. Ives has been seen as an avant-garde composer by members of the avant-garde, a Transcendentalist composer by those who like their music to have mystical overtones, and an American composer by those searching for a native-born champion. Each of these views is incomplete, a partial appraisal of a complex musical mind, and each has promoted misunderstandings of Ives's music. The key to understanding Ives's creative work lies not in the Transcendentalism of the *Essays* or the experimentalism testified to in the *Memos*, but simply in knowing Ives's history and in recognizing how his thinking changed as his methods and purposes for music evolved.

What is most valuable about the *Essays*, beyond their direct relationship to the *Concord Sonata*, is the view they provide of Ives's mature aesthetic stance. When we have bent them to explain compositions to which their subtle philosophical concepts do not and were not intended to apply, they have confused and misled us. Perhaps as compensation for

that, the *Essays* offer us valuable clues for reconstructing Ives's evolution as a composer, particularly the development of his thinking about music and his conception of his own roles and purposes. When one examines Ives's development as a composer while viewing the *Essays* as a set of conclusions rather than a point of departure, the diversity between and within Ives's compositions and the radical changes in style and method at different stages of his career suddenly begin to make sense.

It is the aim of this book to rediscover that evolution. Ives left no statements of his views before the first drafts of the *Essays*; his recollections of his own development in the *Memos* and his correspondence from the 1930s, while invaluable, are often mutually contradictory, confusing, and incomplete. But an analysis of Ives's thinking in the *Essays*, like that in Chapter 2 below, can show us not only his mature aesthetic position, but also the problems he sought to solve and the assumptions from which his discussion proceeded. Once we discover those problems and assumptions, we can examine his education, his music, and the attitudes of the important people in his life, tracing his fundamental concerns and his characteristic habits of thought to their origins and uncovering in the process the development of his artistic philosophy from the earliest stages of his career as a musician to the writing of the *Essays* themselves.

Charting the course of Ives's thought will allow us to recognize the stages of his journey, to place each piece of music in relation to others composed at the same time and to Ives's emerging musical aesthetic, and to sort out the different purposes and traditions represented in his diverse creation, so that the logic behind each work and the logic of Ives's odyssey as a composer may begin to emerge. Ultimately, we may discover not just what Ives believed and when, but also why he believed what he did. With that insight, we will be much closer to understanding both the music and its composer.

CHAPTER TWO

The Aesthetic Stance of the *Essays*

THE FOUNDATIONS OF IVES'S THOUGHT IN THE *ESSAYS*

There are three major foundations for Ives's thought in the *Essays* and most of his other writings from the 1910s and 1920s: (1) a dualistic approach to issues, (2) a personal and social idealism, and (3) a reliance on personal intuition and experience rather than external authority. These are interwoven throughout his writings, sometimes explicitly stated and sometimes having the character of "premises which he . . . took for granted instead of carrying them around with him."[1]

Dualism

In his *Essays*, Ives rarely introduces a concept without immediately pairing it with its opposite, a juxtaposition that helps to define what he means. Some pairs clearly contrast traits that he values with traits he rejects, such as "the activity of truth" with "the love of repose" (pages 16, 82–83, 85), "imagination" with "automatic, ready-made, easy entertainment" (page 47), "reality" with "make-believe" (pages 72–73), "artistic strength" with "moral weakness" (page 75), or "the majority (the people)" with "the minority (the non-people)" (pages 28–29). Others, however, concern poles that must in some sense be integrated to be whole. Ives sees as essentially false the distinctions between abstract and program music (pages 4–5), private and public life (pages 56–57), conservativism and radicalism (page 13), revealed and natural religion (page 19), the moral and the intellectual (page 86), and art and life (pages 80–82, 88–89, 93)[2]—arguing that these need not be experienced as separate. The most interesting set of distinctions pairs concepts that are perhaps equally

8

necessary but not of equal value: soul and intellect (page 24),[3] music and sound (page 84),[4] and the related separation of substance in art from manner (e.g., page 75).[5] Ives's discussion of this last dichotomy occupies most of the Epilogue, and we will return to it below.

It would not be an exaggeration to say that the argument in Ives's *Essays* depends entirely upon such distinctions. But Ives does not follow in the tradition of Hegelian dialectics, nor is he entirely like Emerson, who viewed his paired opposites as necessary poles within an overarching unity. Rather, each of Ives's dichotomies is laid out to make a moral point: that this is good and that is weak; that either of these without the other is unbalanced; or, as in the case of manner and substance, that the lesser ideal must always serve the greater. Ives's dualisms more nearly lie in the Christian traditions of moral opposition (God versus the devil, redemption opposed to damnation) and of paradox (for instance, the death of Jesus on the cross as the price of eternal life). Without these contrasts, Ives's idealism would be much less sharply focused. Further, this dualistic thinking is essential, as both cause and effect, for understanding the oppositions Ives experienced in his musical life and his attempts to achieve integrity. His dualistic approach and the ways his concepts differ from those of the Transcendentalists will be discussed further in subsequent chapters.

Idealism

The *Essays* are shot through with references to idealism, morality, and spirituality. The distinctions listed above are ample illustration. Indeed, the whole book is an effort to justify idealism itself, the portrayal of idealism in music, and an idealism about music.

Ives refers several times to his belief in the innate goodness of humankind, which he calls "the greatest and most inspiring theme of Concord Transcendental philosophy" (page 35), and he writes in the essays on the sonata's individual movements of the idealism of each of his four literary figures.[6] This innate goodness is divine: "In every human soul there is the ray of the celestial beauty; and therefore every human outburst may contain a partial ray" (page 97). It is this divine goodness that brings about progress in the world, as individuals learn to follow the "universal mind" rather than political leaders "with skins thick, wits slick, and hands quick with under-values":

> The main path of all social progress has been spiritual rather than intellectual in character. . . . The majority [is coming] to recognize the true relation

between the important spiritual and religious values and the less important intellectual and economic values. . . . The people are beginning to lead themselves—the public store of reason is slowly being opened—the common universal mind and the common over-soul is slowly but inevitably coming into its own [pages 34–35].[7]

From this same "universal mind" comes a unity within diversity, a healing of the bifurcations of human existence. Ives paraphrases Bronson Alcott: "All occupations of man's body and soul in their diversity come from but one mind and soul!" (page 96). The concept of the universal mind is at the root of all of Ives's idealism, in the worlds of his insurance business and his politics as well as in his art.[8]

A consequence of this belief, and inseparable from it, is Ives's acceptance of intuition as the surest teacher, an aspect of the universal mind which guides each of us in spiritual seeking and in daily life, as it guided Emerson (pages 14, 18). Ives appeals to intuition most strongly in drawing the distinction between substance and manner—the most critical duality for Ives's aesthetic—for it is intuition that allows us to recognize the substantive:

> Substance in a human-art-quality suggests the body of a conviction which has its birth in the spiritual consciousness, whose youth is nourished in the moral consciousness, and whose maturity as a result of all this growth is then represented in a mental image. This is appreciated by the intuition, and somehow translated into expression by "manner." . . . [Substance] is practically indescribable. Intuitions (artistic or not?) will sense it—process, unknown. Perhaps it is an unexplained consciousness of being nearer God or being nearer the devil—of approaching truth or approaching unreality. . . . Substance is higher than manner—because substance leans towards optimism, and manner, pessimism. We do not know that all this is so, but we feel (or, rather, know by intuition) that it is so, in the way we know intuitively that right is higher than wrong [pages 75–76].

This distinction between substance and manner provides the means for Ives to apply his idealism to his art, although he comments later that his theory "may find illustration in many, perhaps most, of the human activities" (page 89). If substance is a hard-to-define idea of "conviction" or "truth" and manner is its form or technique, Ives's theory considers ideal music to be that in which the manner does not exceed the substance, in which there is a more spiritual purpose than amusement, entertainment, spectacular tone-painting, or the display of craft. He contrasts the high spirituality of Bach and Beethoven, whose symphonies are "perfect truths" (page 85), and "the wholesomeness, manliness, humility, and deep spiritual, possibly religious, feeling" of Franck, Brahms, d'Indy, "or even Elgar" (page 73), with Debussy's overemphasis of "parfume" and "manner" (pages 81–82), the "make-believe" of Wagner (page 72), Richard Strauss's striving for effect (page 83), and the "rest, commodity, and reputation" of virtuoso composer-performers such as Vieuxtemps and Paganini (pages 84–85).[9] This spirituality in music in turn depends upon a close relationship between one's art and the rest of one's life, as an aspect of that "spiritual sturdiness" which "shows itself in a close union between spiritual life and the ordinary business of life, against spiritual feebleness, which shows itself in the separation of the two" (page 93). As Ives comments in the Postface to *114 Songs*, "An interest in any art-activity from poetry to baseball is better, broadly speaking, if held as a part of life, or *of* a life, than if it sets itself up as a whole—a condition verging, perhaps, towards a monopoly or, possibly, a kind of atrophy of the other important values, and hence reacting unfavorably upon itself" (page 124; emphasis original).

Art for art's sake breeds an overemphasis on manner, and Ives rejects this emphasis as both unreal and unspiritual, separated from both life and spirit. But it would be a mistake to read into his *Essays* a rejection of manner itself. While preferring Emerson, who "seems to be almost wholly substance," to a highly mannered author like Poe, Ives does not declare Poe to be without value: "The measure in artistic satisfaction of Poe's manner is equal to the measure of spiritual satisfaction in Emerson's substance. The total value of each man is high, but Emerson's is higher than Poe's because substance is higher than manner" (page 76). Similarly, Hawthorne is not condemned for his artistry, which is greater than Emerson's or Thoreau's, but rather is praised for his subordination of it to the substance of his writings (page 39). The problem for a composer with Ives's ideals is one of "recognizing and using in their true relation, as much as one can, these higher and lower dual values" (page 100). In other words, manner is necessary for art—one could argue that it *is* art, although Ives does not say as much—but must assume its true relation to substance, proceeding from and depending upon the spirit.

Self-Reliance

Many of Ives's lines of thought seem circular. Indeed, a linear presentation of his thinking is extremely difficult if not impossible, as many concepts are interdependent and need to be discussed simultaneously, and much the same could be said for discussions of his music. The relationship between idealism and reliance on intuition is one such circular path, for Ives's idealism seems to stem as much from his reliance on intuition as the other way around. This reliance naturally led Ives to oppose unreasoning obedience and to affirm the individual's search for truth, guided—as was Emerson—by "the divine in human reason" (page 18). Ives believed strongly in progress, referring to it at many points in his writings. This progress comes about not through deference to authority but rather through individual inspiration and a willingness to learn through experience and experiment.

In the realm of music, Ives claimed for the composer the right to search for new modes of expression rather than perpetually following the rules: "The humblest composer will not find true humility in aiming low—he must never be timid or afraid of trying to express that which he feels is far above his power to express, any more than he should be afraid of breaking away, when necessary, from easy first sounds" (page 96). Ives had an absolute faith that no aim or technique need be rejected out of hand, and certainly not because the authorities declare it invalid. Rather, each artist has the freedom and the duty to try things out: "Eclecticism is part of [a composer's] duty; sorting potatoes means a better crop next year" (page 79).

This insistence on freedom of technique would seem to contradict Ives's earlier emphasis on substance over manner, but it does not: substance still determines technique. What is important is that the manner not be restrained by external rules but be formed entirely in response to the substance the composer is attempting to realize in his music. Nothing is rejected because it is not "beautiful," for music that is judged to be beautiful may be entirely lacking in substance: "Beauty in music is too often confused with something that lets the ears lie back in an easy chair. Many sounds that we are used to do not bother us, and for that reason we are inclined to call them beautiful" (page 97). Nor is any technique rejected because it cannot be catalogued by musical taxonomers, if it is required by the substance behind the technique:

> If Emerson's manner is not always beautiful in accordance with accepted standards, why not accept a few other standards? . . . The rules of thorough-bass can be applied to his scale of flight no more than they can to the planetary system. Jadassohn [author of the harmony text Ives had studied as a young man], if Emerson were literally a composer, could no more analyze his harmony than a Guide-to-Boston could [page 24].[10]

Common standards of beauty and the normal rules of harmony, form, and counterpoint are suspect for Ives, and he often mocks them. All the same, the revolutions in musical technique made by Debussy, Wagner, or Richard Strauss (discussed on pages 81–82, 73, and 83, respectively) seem superficial to Ives, since they betray a preoccupation with manner over substance, which Ives also rejects.

IVES'S ARTISTIC AIMS

With these fundamental beliefs and the issue of the relation of his ideals (substance) to his musical technique (manner) ever in mind, Ives formulated one principal aim for the works of his maturity: the representation in music of human experience (frequently his own experience) in all its drama, difficulty, awe, emotional power, and confusion. The orchestral movements *Decoration Day* and *The Fourth of July* evoke the impressions and memories of those holidays as Ives remembered them from his Connecticut childhood, while *From Hanover Square North, at the End of a Tragic Day, the Voice of the People Again Arose*, the last movement of the *Second Orchestral Set*, is based on Ives's experience on a commuter train platform the day of the sinking of the *Lusitania*, when everyone spontaneously joined in singing the gospel funeral hymn *In the Sweet Bye and Bye* over the noise and pulsation of New York. These can serve as examples for others; what they share is a closeness to life, a life that embodies deep spiritual values, so that its representation in music will satisfy Ives's requirements for a music rooted in substance.

The *Concord Sonata* and the accompanying *Essays Before a Sonata*, taken as a whole, were intended "to present (one person's) impression of the spirit of transcendentalism that is associated in the minds of many with Concord, Mass., of over half a century ago" (page xxv).[11] In the essays on individual movements, Ives makes very clear that giving such an impression means writing a kind of program music, where specific events, sounds, atmospheres, and even idiosyncrasies of literary style are evoked. He presents programs for the Hawthorne and Thoreau movements in rather explicit detail. While listening to the Thoreau movement, program in hand, one may "follow his thought on an autumn day of Indian summer at Walden," with alternating moments of restlessness and meditation. Perhaps the gentle ostinato on page 62 of the sonata (1947 revised version) illustrates the "broader rhythm" of nature, "the slow, almost monotonous swaying beat of this autumnal day"; near the end, where an optional flute part is indicated, "the poet's flute is heard out over the pond," playing "a transcendental tune of Concord" (the main theme of the Alcotts movement).[12] On the other hand, there is only a hint of a program for *The Alcotts*,[13] which is more of a character sketch than a programmatic work, and no explicit program whatsoever for the Emerson

movement, although the Emerson essay is the longest of the four. However, the essay includes several comparisons of Emerson's prose style to
music: Emerson is not limited by textbook harmony (page 24), but his
"sensuous chords" are not used with Debussy's "voluptuous" purpose
(page 25); his essays are filled with "flashes that approach as near the
divine as Beethoven in his most inspired moments" (page 30). Even his
incoherence finds a musical counterpart:

> To think hard and deeply and to say what is thought regardless of conse-
> quences may produce a first impression either of great translucence or of
> great muddiness—but in the latter there may be hidden possibilities. Some
> accuse Brahms' orchestration of being muddy. This may be a good name for
> a first impression of it. But if it should seem less so, he might not be saying
> what he thought. The mud may be a form of sincerity which demands that
> the heart be translated rather than handed around through the pit. A
> clearer scoring might have lowered the thought. Carlyle told Emerson that
> some of his paragraphs didn't cohere. Emerson wrote by sentences or
> phrases rather than by logical sequence. His underlying plan of work seems
> based on the large unity of a series of particular aspects of a subject rather
> than on the continuity of its expression. As thoughts surge to his mind, he
> fills the heavens with them, crowds them in, if necessary, but seldom ar-
> ranges them along the ground first. . . . Vagueness is at times an indication
> of nearness to a perfect truth [pages 21–22].

While neither this nor any other part of the Emerson essay presents a
program, clearly the surging incoherence that Ives describes in Emerson's
style is paralleled in the Emerson music. Indeed, if the music represents
anything specific, it would be "Emerson in his unshackled search for the
infinite" (page 18); it apes his prose style in order to achieve a comparable
breathlessness and directness.[14]

Ives's representation in music of human experience went hand in
hand with another goal that evolved out of his beliefs: to create a distinctively American music, neither French nor German in inspiration but
breathing pure American idealism. These two goals are tightly linked. For
Ives, a music based on human experience would be necessarily American.
Further, Ives felt strongly that an American music would have to be based
not just on American tunes (or even on borrowed American tunes at all)[15]
but rather on American experience and American ideals for it to be truly
native. According to Ives, if a composer merely incorporates American
folk tunes without breathing the spirit of the idealism of the American
people, the local color provided by the folk tunes remains superficial, a
mannerism rather than part of the music's substance, and "his music is
liable to be less American than he wishes" (page 79). When the people's

music is brought into a composition, the spiritual and emotional meanings of the music must come along as well:

> But if the Yankee can reflect the fervency with which "his gospels" were sung . . . , he may find there a local color that will do all the world good. If his music can but catch that spirit by being a part with itself, it will come somewhere near his ideal—and it will be American, too—perhaps nearer so than that of the devotee of Indian or negro melody. In other words, if local color, national color, any color, is a true pigment of the universal color, it is a divine quality, it is a part of substance in art—not of manner [pages 80–81].

Here Ives's Americanism blends with his idealism. Indeed, for Ives, the United States is a country founded on ideals and still suffused with idealism. He credits Hawthorne with a deep interest "in the idealism peculiar to his native land," and continues: "Hawthorne's art was true and typically American, as is the art of all men (living in America) who believe in freedom of thought, and who live wholesome lives to prove it—whatever their means of expression" (page 41). Ives comes close to claiming, but for his parenthesis, that a devotion to freedom of thought makes one's art American no matter where one lives, and he certainly claims that art produced in the United States that does not share this devotion is not in fact American. This is an indication of the strength of his identification of the United States with its avowed ideals.

The relationship of these two allied goals—creating an American music and representing human experience in music—will be further discussed in later chapters, with an eye to documenting both their origins and their eventual blending together during Ives's evolution as a composer.

"LITERARY MUSIC" AND OTHER PURPOSES FOR COMPOSITION

Understanding these aims is of central importance in tracing Ives's musical development, for this is the spur that motivated his search for an expressive language. No set of musical techniques, no musical style available to Ives from previous composers, could fulfill these aims, for Ives sought to represent (far more than merely picture) what had never been represented in music before, not even by Bach and Beethoven, his models for spirituality in music.

The foundations of Ives's thinking that underlie his aims are by no means new in music and cannot explain his rejection of earlier styles. Indeed, his beliefs can be as easily traced to his musical models as to his philosophical ones. Dualisms are central to most Western musical styles, as in the tonal polarity between tonic and dominant, the sense of opposition and resolution between stable themes and unstable transitions in sonata form, or the tension between horizontal and vertical dimensions in polyphonic music. Ives's idealism is surely no more demanding than that of Bach or Beethoven, composers he admired deeply for their spirituality and whose spirit he felt he continued.[16] And the willingness to go beyond the rules, to try new forms and harmonies, to rely on the authority of one's own ear rather than on the presumed authority of theorists and critics or on the approval of audiences, is a strong trait shared by most great composers of the last three centuries, whether they have Ives's reputation for rebelliousness or not.

But in aiming to represent human experience as it is, and American experience in particular, Ives goes beyond attempts in earlier music to represent extramusical concepts and events—beyond madrigalism, beyond Baroque symbolism, beyond the idealism of the *Ode to Joy*, beyond the dreamy fantasy-obsession of Berlioz's *Symphonie fantastique*, and beyond the concrete program music of Richard Strauss, high priest of "the extreme materializing of music" that Ives acidly mocks in his *Essays* (page 3):

> Can a tune literally represent a stone wall with vines on it or even with nothing on it, though it (the tune) be made by a genius whose power of objective contemplation is in the highest state of development? Can it be done by anything short of an act of mesmerism on the part of the composer or an act of kindness on the part of the listener?

This kind of program music comes closest to Ives's own intentions—Ives does, after all, try to represent the mists over Walden, if not a stone wall with vines—so his rejection of it is striking. Paramount in this rejection is Ives's understanding that ultimately this program music is not about anything worthwhile, that it holds to no ideals, that what it represents is not spiritually edifying, and thus that it lacks substance and reeks of mannerism, tone-painting done for its own sake and for the sake of sheer technical display.

> [Richard Strauss] has chosen to capitalize a "talent"—he has chosen the complexity of media, the shining hardness of externals, repose, against the inner, invisible activity of truth. . . . His choice naturally leads him to glorify and to magnify all kinds of dull things—a stretched-out *Geigermusik*, which in turn naturally leads him to windmills and human heads on silver platters. Magnifying the dull into the colossal produces a kind of "comfort"—the comfort of a woman who takes more pleasure in the fit of fashionable clothes than in a healthy body—the kind of comfort that has brought so many "adventures of baby-carriages at county fairs" . . . the lure of the

media—the means—not the end—but the finish. Thus the failure to per-
ceive that thoughts and memories of childhood are too tender, and some of
them too sacred, to be worn lightly on the sleeve [page 83].[17]

Ives's own musical recollections of childhood—the *Holidays Symphony*,
Putnam's Camp, *Children's Day at the Camp Meeting* (the descriptive title for
the middle movement of the *Third Symphony* and for the whole of the
Fourth Violin Sonata), and others—are indeed not "worn lightly." The
intensity of experience Ives attempts to evoke in his music goes beyond
the concrete, story-telling program music of Strauss into a world of dream
and memory. Indeed, although Ives himself uses the term *program music*
as if it applied to the *Concord Sonata*, he is not satisfied with it (page 4), nor
is it the conception of a programmed sequence of events that the four
movements have in common.

The term *literary music* much better describes the conception and
execution of the works of Ives's maturity. This is music that is avowedly
"about" something, as indicated by title, marginalia, or program notes,
and that corresponds in its structure and meaning to literary forms,
whether narratives, poems, jokes, essays, or plays. Ives's mature music has
been described as "fictional music," has been compared to James Joyce's
"stream-of-consciousness" writing, and has been characterized as a musical parallel to the language of dreams and memories.[18] This literary
music emphasizes not nouns, as might the pictorial music of Debussy or
Strauss, but verbs: the mists over Walden are not still but rise; Emerson's
thoughts surge; "the circus parade comes down Main Street" in the
Hawthorne music; Beth Alcott plays hymns and a little Beethoven at the
piano. When nouns are important, they most often refer to ideas rather
than things: "the sternness and strength and austerity of the Puritan
character,"[19] the Concord ideal, the Unanswered Question itself. And in
its structure, this literary music is free to follow the prose style of Emerson,
the rhythm of restlessness and contemplation of Thoreau, the "fantastical
adventures" of Hawthorne, a subtle dialogue in *The Unanswered Question*,
or the somewhat irregular rhythm of *The Gong on the Hook and Ladder*
during the annual Firemen's Parade on Main Street. To live up to these
demands, such a literary music needs a vocabulary that will encompass
such varied subjects, and the evolution of Ives's music is in one sense the
development of a language capable of fulfilling that need.

But this representation of personal experience is not the only aim
Ives ever had for his music, and it is a mistake to lump all his composing
together as if every piece, every scrap of an idea, shared the same noble
impulse. Some works are pure experimentation, trying out a technique

(e.g., *Chromâtimelôdtune* or *Processional: Let There Be Light*). Some are screams of protest against "emasculated music" (for instance, *In Re Con Moto Et Al*) or attempts to "strengthen the ear muscles" (such as *All the Way Around and Back* and *Tone Roads No. 1* and *No. 3*). But there are also traditional marches for band, parlor songs and art songs in familiar nineteenth-century styles, symphonies and single movements for orchestra, choral psalms and anthems, and chamber works written for public concerts, most of them written early in Ives's career, which show little more than a glimmer of Ives's ultimate aesthetic purposes. Before arriving at his mature approach, Ives tried his hand at pieces in many very diverse genres and styles, representing several different traditions of musical composition, and his intentions in writing music naturally changed as he moved from one genre, style, or tradition to another, from church music to band music to concert music. What we are faced with in Ives's career up to the writing of the *Essays* is not consistency but instead constant and sometimes dizzying change, so much so that it is sometimes hard to imagine all of Ives's music as the work of one man.

The position articulated in the *Essays Before a Sonata* did not come early or easily to Ives. Rather, he grew towards it, raising his sights for what he might accomplish in music as he developed the techniques that would make it possible. This developing purpose is central to the musical biography to which this study seeks to contribute, for the majority of Ives's compositions cannot in fact be understood if approached as manifestations of his aesthetic ideas as he outlined them near the end of his career as a composer. In short, aims and techniques both changed from stage to stage in Ives's career, progressing in tandem.

One Ives scholar, Charles Ward, has proposed a paradigm for Ives's composing: (1) experiences, both real and visionary, prompt a search for a musical vocabulary to express them; (2) the search is undertaken in small, experimental compositions that serve as the composer's workshop, developing and testing the necessary expressive language, element by element; and (3) the language is then used in large-scale compositions to evoke the experiences that prompted the search.[20] Certainly the mature works required of Ives a new musical language, and clearly that language was developed in part in the experimental works. But it would be a serious mistake to assume that the process was as linear as this paradigm suggests, or that the desire to represent experience preceded the experimentation, for in Ives's career the two run along like parallel streams. There is a continual cross-fertilization between pieces that try out techniques and pieces that are in some sense descriptive. Indeed, many works fall into both categories, as new techniques make possible more daring aims, which may in turn prompt a continued experimentation.

To ignore this parallel development of aims and techniques is to trivialize Ives's musical career, implying a false picture of an easy, straight-line development from Ives's Transcendentalist and experimentalist boy-hood to his Transcendentalist and experimentalist maturity, delayed only by his composition studies in traditional European forms and styles with Horatio Parker at Yale—which Ward, among others, seems to view as a wholly unfortunate episode.[21] In truth, Ives's career had more twists and turns than the career of almost any other major composer, and Parker's influence was both crucial and constructive. Ignoring the interdependent evolution of aims and techniques also creates a phantom paradox in Ives's development as a composer, an apparent contradiction between his clear subordination in the *Essays* of manner (including both experimental and conventional techniques) to substance and the long period of experimen-tation with musical procedures that preceded the development of his mature style, a period—lasting from his boyhood through the radical innovations of the first decades of the century—when many compositions seem to be motivated more by the spirit of technical play than by substan-tive inspiration.[22] This would indeed be strange if composing the *Concord Sonata* had been Ives's aim throughout his life. But, as we shall see in the next several chapters, it is by no means clear that either the lofty theme of Transcendentalism or the sharp differentiation between substance and manner were central to Ives's thinking before the period (around 1907–1915) when the sonata was conceived and written.

The evolution of Ives's musical method is the subject for another book, a companion volume to this one.[23] But before that history can be written, it is vital to understand the artistic purposes behind each piece and to have a sense of the evolution of Ives's thinking about music. The remaining chapters of this book contribute to clarifying these two issues: Chapters 3 and 4 sift through the evidence regarding Ives's relationship to the Transcendentalist writers, to determine when their ideas may be relevant and for which pieces, and the last six chapters consider Ives's aesthetic statements in the *Essays* and trace them back to their sources in his musical training and his encounters with people who were important influences on his thought, thereby establishing a chronological frame-work for his creative life.

CHAPTER THREE

Ives and Transcendentalism:
A Second Look

Charles Ives has been linked with Emerson, Thoreau, and the Transcendentalist movement ever since the publication of his *Concord Sonata* and *Essays Before a Sonata* in 1920. However, the first claims that Ives was himself a Transcendentalist or that he was trying to write music that would convey the philosophy of Transcendentalism did not appear in the critical literature until more than a decade later. Writing in 1933 with the authority of one who knew Charles Ives "intimately," Henry Bellamann described his music as "a musical equivalent of the spiritual values of transcendental philosophy and human experience."[1] Eleven years later, another personal friend of the Iveses, the composer Elliott Carter, wrote that in both the *Essays* and the music, "Ives reveals himself a devout believer in transcendental philosophy."[2] Since these articles appeared, writers on Ives have voiced a gradually growing conviction that Transcendentalism is both the very source of his music and the key to understanding it. Most recent scholarship accepts this view, tending to place most or all of Ives's music within the context of Transcendentalism.[3]

It is revealing that these two close friends of Ives's wrote of his music in terms unlike those of anyone else writing at the time, and indeed unlike those Bellamann himself had used in his first article on Ives's music, his review of the *Concord Sonata*, written in 1921 before he and Ives had met.[4] In the literature on Ives published during his own lifetime, apart from the articles by Bellamann and Carter, the Transcendentalists were cited only as examples of Ives's focus on American subjects, not as the source of Ives's musical "substance."[5] Bellamann and Carter may be assumed to be voicing Ives's own opinions about his music and his beliefs, for they had direct and frequent personal access to the composer, and Ives saw both

20

articles after their publication and apparently approved their statements about the direct influence of Transcendentalist ideas on his music—at least, he raised no objections, which would have been out of character had he disagreed.[6] Moreover, the view Bellamann and Carter set forth of Ives as a Transcendentalist who sought to give voice to his beliefs in his music cannot simply have come from their sympathetic reading of the *Essays* or from playing through the music, for no one writing on Ives's music during his lifetime who was not personally acquainted with the composer made any such claim. If it was not obvious from the music or the writings, the idea must have come from Ives himself. Certainly, it is clear from the testimony of others of Ives's friends and acquaintances in the 1930s, 1940s, and 1950s that Ives, at least in private, was thoroughly immersed in the thinking of Emerson and Thoreau during his later years[7] and considered his mature music, particularly the *Concord Sonata*, to be Transcendentalist in inspiration and aspiration.[8]

What is not at all clear is when and how Ives developed his enthusiasm for Transcendentalism. If we knew the answer to this question, we would at least know which pieces Ives considered to be expressions of his Emersonian ideals, even though we would be left with the virtually insoluble problem of deciding exactly how to balance musical and extramusical approaches to individual works in our attempts at interpretation. Ives never spoke or wrote about this issue directly, and none of the studies that were shown to him for review or were published during his lifetime address this question at all. The consensus of opinion since Ives's death, based on virtually no hard evidence, has been that Ives developed his enthusiasm for Transcendentalism at a very young age, learning about Emerson, Thoreau, and Transcendentalist ideals from his family, and consequently that all of his music is suffused and inspired by Transcendentalist thought.

This consensus seems to date from the first book-length biography of Ives, completed just after his death in 1954 and published the following year. In it, Henry Cowell and Sidney Cowell strongly implied that Ives was drawn to Emersonian Transcendentalism as a boy and that his later aesthetic ideas grew naturally from his boyhood experiences—that, for as long as he could remember, Ives's world had been dominated by the Concord school.[9] The Cowells' book was the first study to place Ives's aesthetic ideas wholly within the context of Transcendentalism or to suggest that the influence of the Concord writers could be traced back to his childhood. Howard Boatwright relied on the Cowells' book for the biographical material in his Introductory Note to the *Essays*, where he suggests that "Ives must have come into early contact with the Concord writers whose work was to affect him so deeply."[10] Perhaps following the Cowells' lead, many scholars have subsequently huddled all of Ives's ideas about music under the umbrella of "Transcendental Aesthetics"[11] or have claimed that his entire oeuvre may be understood in Transcendentalist terms.[12]

The picture of Ives's aesthetic and personal philosophy as thoroughly Transcendentalist and unchanging from his childhood to his old age appeared to be confirmed with the publication of Ives's *Memos* in the early 1970s. John Kirkpatrick's edition includes in two appendices brief mention of the enthusiasm for Emerson's writings on the part of Ives's grandmother, Sarah Hotchkiss Wilcox Ives, and eldest paternal uncle, Joseph Moss Ives, and of the "family tradition" that Emerson visited the Ives house on the occasion of a lecture in their home city of Danbury, Connecticut, during the 1850s.[13] This so completely conformed to the accepted view that Laurence Wallach, writing not quite two decades after Ives's death, could cite this information in his dissertation and proceed immediately to state without further supporting evidence that Sarah Ives passed on her enthusiasm for Transcendentalism to her son George Edward Ives and that George passed the spirit on in turn to his son Charles, particularly in and through the realm of music.[14] This view seems eminently logical, suggesting a direct and unbroken line of influence from Emerson himself through the Ives family to the *Essays Before a Sonata*. But there are links missing: there is no evidence to support the assumptions that enthusiasm for Emerson continued unabated in the Ives family from the 1850s until Charles Ives left home to enter college nearly half a century later, that Ives was himself directly affected by it, that the importance of Transcendentalist ideas for Ives remained constant from his youth to his old age, or the even more sweeping assumption that the essential elements of Ives's aesthetic philosophy originated in Emerson and Thoreau.

If Ives was a thoroughgoing Transcendentalist at the time he wrote the *Essays*, if none of his ideas derived from non-Transcendentalist sources, and if he learned his Transcendentalism completely at home, then there would be no need to trace his aesthetic development or demonstrate what the influences on his thinking were; his thought would begin and end with Emerson and Thoreau, and what changes could be detected in his views over time could be credited to a natural process of maturation. This seems to be the common view: it regards Ives's philosophical evolution as easy and straightforward and his aesthetic as internally consistent.

But as I will show in the remainder of this study, none of these three conditions is the case: he was never solely Transcendentalist; most of his important ideas—especially about music—come from sources outside the Transcendentalist tradition; and his all-consuming passion for Emerson and Thoreau seems to be of relatively late origin, deriving not so much from tutoring within his family or at school as from his own reading as an adult.

While the influence of the Transcendentalists, particularly Emerson and Thoreau, is vital for understanding Ives's thought and the way he articulates it in the *Essays*, it is too simplistic to imagine that all of his ideas stem directly from them or are entirely consonant with their thinking. As the evidence linking Ives with Transcendentalism is carefully examined, it becomes clear that the influence of Emerson and Thoreau on Ives's thought and music grew considerably over time. Despite some exposure to both Transcendentalist writers and Transcendentalist views within his family as he was growing up, Ives was not a fully formed philosopher at the time he entered Yale. There is ample evidence of strong non-Transcendentalist influences on Ives from other quarters, in both music and philosophy, from his family, from his mentors in college, and from his wife and her family, and these influences were in many ways equally important in shaping his mature thought.

Definitions of Transcendentalism

Our understanding of the influence of Transcendentalism on Ives's thinking has been muddied by an inconsistent use of the term. *Transcendentalism* may refer either to the literary and philosophical tradition originating in the meetings of the Transcendental Club of Concord and Boston in the late 1830s or to the set of beliefs that are taken to form the core of that tradition. The latter seems to be the more specific meaning, and the meaning more applicable to a study of Ives's music and writings, yet it is not; as we shall see, the Transcendentalists were a diverse group, their central beliefs are hard to define, and Ives's interpretation of these beliefs is his own. Both meanings, therefore, are important for understanding Ives's philosophical links with the Transcendentalists, particularly in clarifying the relationship of his mature philosophy to his experience of Transcendentalist ideas as a child, but the distinction between Transcendentalism as a belief and as a tradition must be maintained if the conception of a Transcendentalist influence on Ives's thought is to be at all useful. Unfortunately, the Ives literature—including, at times, Ives's own writings—is consistent only in confusing these two meanings with each other.

Ives's contacts with Transcendentalism, as tradition or system of belief, were almost wholly through the writings of Emerson and Thoreau. Apart from these, of the many figures associated with Transcendentalism, he mentions in the *Essays* only Amos Bronson Alcott and William Ellery Channing. Alcott (1799–1888), patriarch of the Alcott family and father of the writer Louisa May Alcott, was more a teacher and a talker than a writer, in Ives's view. Ives's allusions to Alcott are brief. The essay on the Alcotts is only a fifth of the size of the essays on Emerson and Thoreau; the discussion of Bronson Alcott fills only two of its four pages and is almost wholly anecdotal, showing no sign that Ives had read any of Alcott's work; and Ives mentions Alcott only once outside the Alcott essay.[15] Channing (1780–1842) was a Congregationalist preacher and a leader of the revolt against Calvinism, especially against the central Calvinist doctrine of the innate depravity of humanity, which resulted in the establishment of the Unitarian Church in early nineteenth-century New England. Emerson and most of the other early Transcendentalists were drawn from the Unitarian ranks, and in many respects Unitarianism paved the way for Transcendentalism. Channing, however, was not himself fully in sympathy with Transcendentalism.[16] The other early Transcendentalists—the Kantians George Ripley and Frederick Henry Hedge, the clergymen Orestes A. Brownson, Theodore Parker, and James Freeman Clarke, the poets Jones Very and Christopher Cranch, the literary critic and feminist Margaret Fuller, even the music critic John Sullivan Dwight—are nowhere mentioned in Ives's *Essays*, *Memos*, or other writings. Ives had probably heard of Fuller and Parker,[17] but otherwise he was apparently as ignorant of the larger Transcendentalist circle as are most Americans today. What interested Ives was Emerson's form of idealism as demonstrated in his essays and poems and in his disciple Thoreau's pilgrimage into the solitude of the woods. For Ives, Transcendentalism meant the tradition of Emerson and Thoreau.

If Emerson was the center both for the early Transcendentalists and for Ives, Emerson's characterization of Transcendentalist belief should suffice for our purposes, particularly since Thoreau, the only other important figure for Ives, offered no definition. Yet Emerson's attempted definition only muddies the water.[18] In his lecture "The Transcendentalist" of 1842, he defines Transcendentalism as "Idealism" in modern form, a reliance on intuition over experience. He credits the word *transcendental*, referring to knowledge that is inaccessible to the senses, to

Kant, yet his own usage is less precise than the German philosopher's had
been. Emerson contrasts this kind of idealism with "Materialism," the view
that one can know only what one has directly experienced. These ideas
and definitions are evocative for Emerson rather than specific. The
second half of this lecture describes and defends those—identified as
Transcendentalists—too full of "the worship of ideas" and of the purest
form of love, "the last and highest gift of nature," to be patient with the
shallow, gossiping, and acquisitive concerns of other people. This kind of
melancholy idealism, involving the pursuit of Beauty as the highest moral
good, a discontent with normal life after an experience of momentary
enlightenment, and a "wish to exchange this flash-of-lightning faith for
continuous daylight" expressed in a withdrawal from human society and a
search for silence and solitude in nature, has almost nothing to do with
Kant's view of a realm beyond the sensual. Indeed, it is entirely played out
within the realm of experience and ends in a plunging into communion
with nature through the senses. However, Emerson's conception of idealism owes a great deal to the idealistic aspirations of Goethe, Wordsworth,
and the other German and English literary romantics of the half-century
between Kant and Emerson. Emerson interchanges these two meanings
of *idealism*, that of Kant and that of the romantics, as if unaware of the
distinction. This great influence of the romantic writers, compounding
Emerson's very subjective reading of Kant, transforms New England
Transcendentalism into a literary tradition rather than a philosophical
school. We are left without a clear definition of the beliefs of Transcendentalism from its principal exponent; Emerson rests his arguments on no
doctrine or dogma, relying instead on a vague, emotional idealism.

   In one sense, then, Transcendentalism is a literary tendency rather
than a coherent philosophy, "an enthusiasm, a wave of sentiment, a
breath of mind that caught up such as were prepared to receive it, elated
them, transported them, and passed on," in the words of a member of the
second generation of Transcendentalists, Octavius B. Frothingham.[19]
This makes Ives's position clearer. As the author of the *Essays Before a
Sonata*, he fits into the literary tradition of which Emerson is the central
figure, a tradition blending philosophical with poetic idealism and empha-
sizing both the intuitive power of the individual and the moral strength of
nature. This is a wide stream, and it closely parallels many other currents
of romantic idealism in the nineteenth century in religion, literature, and
the arts in both Europe and the Americas, most of which, like Transcendentalism, have their source in the eighteenth-century idealism of
Kant. When Ives chooses to speak as a Transcendentalist, he is able to

incorporate all of his previous thinking and ideas gleaned from a great variety of sources into this one tradition, because it has so much in common with these other prevailing currents of thought.

Yet Ives conceived of Transcendentalism not as a literary tradition but as a way of life, and this must not be wholly ignored. In the Emerson essay, he speaks of Transcendentalism in the broadest possible terms, painting it as a universalist view whose central doctrine and "most inspiring theme" is the "innate goodness in man, in Nature and in God" (page 35).[20] Frothingham criticizes Emerson's definition as too vague and offers his own: "Transcendentalism was a distinct philosophical system. Practically it was an assertion of the inalienable worth of man; theoretically it was an assertion of the immanence of divinity in instinct, the transference of supernatural attributes to the natural constitution of mankind."[21] Behind every essay of Emerson's, explicit at some point in it, is the view that the individual has a direct relationship with the divine; one may be self-reliant, one may rely on intuition, because the self is part of the universal soul.[22] This is not the same as a belief in "the innate goodness of man." Although Ives's reading of Emerson was not an uncommon one, and there is no incongruence between what Ives saw as the core of Transcendentalism and what Emerson actually wrote, the idea of man's innate goodness is not as central to Emerson as it is to Ives. The belief in direct access to the divine in oneself, in others, and in nature is an even broader stream than the literary tradition of the Transcendentalists and includes several non-Western religious traditions, George Fox and the Quakers, many radical Christian theologians such as Horace Bushnell (who is discussed further in Chapter 8 below), and possibly Jesus of Nazareth himself. However, Ives credits the belief in the innate goodness of humanity uniquely to the Transcendentalists. As we shall see in Chapter 4, this provides a clue to the origins and importance for Ives of Transcendentalism as both a system of beliefs and an intellectual tradition.

Thus two meanings of the term *Transcendentalism* remain: on the one hand, it represents a literary tradition, limited in Ives's experience to virtually only two writers, Emerson and Thoreau; on the other, it signifies a set of beliefs, centering on the ideas of the divine presence in nature and humankind and immediate access to the divine through intuition, simplified in Ives's view to the idea of humanity's innate goodness. Both meanings may, indeed must, coexist, but they should not be confused with one another.

Non-Transcendentalist Aspects of Ives's Ideas

Temporarily adopting the conception of Transcendentalism as a literary tradition rather than as a distinctive point of view can help to highlight the portions of Ives's aesthetic and philosophical approach as laid out in the *Essays* that do not derive solely from Transcendentalist sources.

First, dualism is vastly more important for Ives than it is for Emerson or Thoreau. While Emerson frequently cites antipodal relationships, or polarities, which provide variety within an overarching unity resulting from the universal presence of Spirit,[23] and sometimes, as in the lecture mentioned above, establishes clear dichotomies in which one aspect is to be preferred over the other, his arguments do not depend for their force on such oppositions. Rather, choices, when made, are made by intuition. For Thoreau, such dualities do not seem to be an issue. Ives's entire argument, however, hinges on establishing what is moral or preferred by contrast with its opposite. Some of Ives's distinctions, such as those between "artistic strength" and "moral weakness" (page 75) or "the majority (the people)" and "the minority (the non-people)" (pages 28–29), clearly imply fullness of Spirit on one side and its lack on the other. This is a far more moralistic and less tolerant attitude than Emerson's conception of polarities within an overarching unity and owes more to Puritan than to Transcendentalist thinking. This strong streak of dualism and its moralistic tinge derive from Ives's experiences as a young man, as discussed below in Chapters 5 and 6, and perhaps from New England Protestantism, rather than from Transcendental sources. Indeed, a large part of Emerson's appeal for Ives must have been as a guide to synthesizing or transcending these dichotomies.

Second, those parts of the *Essays* that conform to Transcendentalist thinking are principally argued in Ives's own terms rather than those of his mentors, suggesting that Ives may have arrived at many of his conclusions independently, before finding support from other writers. For example, although Ives's central distinction between substance and manner to some extent echoes Emerson's differentiation between inspiration and expression, or idea and technique,[24] the terminology is quite different, and most of the argument is original with Ives, buttressed by quotations from Emerson and others. Similarly, Ives finds in Emerson a strong belief in the innate goodness of man, as discussed above, although Emerson in fact never uses those words or expresses the idea so directly.

Third, Ives highlights only those aspects of his literary figures that strike a resonant chord in him. His Thoreau is the author of *Walden*, the contemplative listener, rather than the social rebel of *Civil Disobedience*.[25] His Hawthorne is the comic satirist, conjurer of the fantastic, not the chronicler of sin and guilt.[26] His Emerson is also subtly selected, not distorted, but carefully chosen to make Emerson a supportive model for Ives's own exploring of "the spiritual immensities" (page 11), for his apparent illogic or incomprehensibility (pages 21–22), for his going beyond the rules (pages 24–25), for his eclecticism (page 25), for his emphasis on substance over manner (page 21),[27] and for others of Ives's beliefs and traits as a composer. Sondra Rae Clark has pointed out that what Ives says of Emerson is usually equally if not more true of Ives himself.[28] Here Ives is clearly not changing his own beliefs to fit Emerson's but is using the Transcendentalist as a model to illustrate and justify his own point of view, choosing his Emerson to fit his own circumstances.

Fourth, there is only a superficial resemblance between Ives's aesthetic of music and that articulated by the Transcendentalists. Emerson knew little about music, had no appreciation for its technical aspects (unlike Ives, whose fascination with technique led him to experiment with new musical materials), and thus could enjoy it as "the chief instance among the arts of an aesthetic experience that represents pure escape," as Vivian C. Hopkins has put it.[29] His inability to understand musical form or compositional techniques may have led Emerson to see music purely in evocative and spiritual terms, but the escapist pleasure he found in it has little in common with Ives's ideals for what music might accomplish in spiritual realms if it were tough enough and deep enough. Similarly, although Margaret Fuller (1810–1850, writer, critic, lecturer, and founding editor of *The Dial*, the Transcendentalist journal) saw music as the "all-enfolding language" surpassing other forms of knowledge and art, this exalted view of music and her uncritical admiration for Beethoven above all other composers had no real basis in technical understanding or perceptive clarity. According to one scholar, "music was for her, in spite of pretensions to the contrary, little more than a sensuous pleasure and a stimulant towards free imaginative association with all elevating experiences."[30]

The only Transcendentalist figure with any musical expertise (and that apparently only rudimentary)[31] was the music critic John Sullivan Dwight (1813–1893), essayist, former Unitarian minister, participant in the Transcendentalists' communal experiment at Brook Farm (1841–1847), and editor of *Dwight's Journal of Music*, published in Boston from 1852 to 1881, one of America's most influential musical periodicals.[32] Dwight was a musical conservative, staunchly promoting the European classics, opposing the "moderns" of the second half of the nineteenth century, and measuring the American works he heard against the classical ideal.[33] He suspended publication of his journal in 1881, when he came to feel that he was fighting a losing battle against modernism, and expressed his preferences in a valediction in the final issue: "Startling as the new composers are, and novel, curious, brilliant at times, they do not inspire us as we have been inspired before, and do not bring us nearer heaven."[34] Dwight also opposed sentimentality and had little use for vernacular music. He placed pure music at the pinnacle of the arts, beyond the realm of words, because it was highly abstract, referring to no mundane objects and telling no stories, and therefore embodied the pure essence of nature or the human spirit[35]—precisely the opposite of Ives, who sought in the *Concord Sonata* to express in music spiritual and moral values that were usually expressed in words or in other ways.[36] While Dwight and Ives share a sense of the deep spiritual value of music, their opposing evaluations of vernacular music, modernism, and musical representation indicate that their aesthetic views correspond more in rhetoric than in reality. This is not surprising, since the idea of the spiritual in music can encompass a wide range of aesthetic interpretations, but it suggests that most of Ives's ideas about music came from his concrete experience of music rather than directly from Transcendentalist influences.

The above points make clear that much of Ives's thinking is not accounted for by reference to his Transcendentalist models. Other important influences will be discussed in the course of the following chapters; it is enough here to stress that the dominance of Emerson and Thoreau in the *Essays* has tended to obscure all other sources of Ives's eclectic philosophy. Similarly, the prominence of the *Concord Sonata* in Ives's career, particularly its important role in establishing him as a major American composer, has obscured the non-Transcendentalist aspects of his compositions.

Ives is known as a Transcendentalist chiefly because it was the *Concord Sonata*, and to a lesser extent the *Essays*, that first gained him a measure of recognition. These works overflow with Transcendentalist currents because their subject is the Concord school, just as *The Circus Band* resounds with the sounds of calliopes and marching bands because of its subject. Without prejudging Ives's earlier attitudes through familiarity with the *Concord Sonata* and the *Essays*, it would be difficult to find unmistakable traces of "transcendental propositions" in the music written before the second decade of this century. The first musical work to refer in any way to the Concord authors is the lost, possibly unfinished *Orchard House Overture* of 1904, the model for *The Alcotts*,[37] which has clear links to Beethoven (it quotes the opening motto of Beethoven's *Fifth Symphony*), the Transcendentalists' favorite composer, but no clear relationship to Transcendentalism as a philosophy. Only *The Unanswered Question*, a few other pieces from 1906, and the unfinished *Emerson Concerto* of around 1907–1908 begin to hint of an interest in philosophy of any sort.

Not even the *Concord Sonata* itself is a wholly Transcendentalist work. It is Concord, not Transcendentalism, that is the connecting thread between the four movements; the Hawthorne movement is a fantasy-scherzo, *The Alcotts* more a picture of the Alcott children and the "home under the elms" than of Bronson Alcott's "philosophical raptures."[38] Nor were the sonata's movements originally conceived as a whole. Like the *Holidays Symphony* and *Three Places in New England*, the sonata is a set of previously existing movements, if not complete at least partially sketched at the time of the set's creation. Each movement was first conceived for a different medium from any of the others: the Emerson movement as an overture for large orchestra or a concerto for piano and orchestra (Ives referred to this earlier version as the *Emerson Overture* or the *Emerson Concerto*); the Hawthorne movement as a piece for piano, two pianos, two pianos with four players, or even "a dozen pianos"; the Alcotts movement for organ or for piano with voice or violin, as well as in the form of the *Orchard House Overture*; and the Thoreau movement "in terms of strings, colored possibly with a flute or horn."[39] The orchestral version of the Emerson movement was once grouped with a set based on abolitionist themes, and the Thoreau movement was projected as the last movement of a set entitled *Sounds*,[40] suggesting that Ives did not always see the Transcendentalist aspect of these movements as the most important. Emerson's connection with abolition was apparently quite strong in Ives's mind; the one text of Emerson's that Ives set to music, in the song *Duty* (?1911 for chorus and orchestra, arranged for voice and piano in 1921), was an excerpt from his poem *Voluntaries*, a tribute to the first regiment of black soldiers in the Union army to fight in the Civil War.[41]

Finally, whereas the writings roughly contemporary with the *Essays* (such as the *Postface to* 114 Songs, *The Majority*, *The Amount to Carry*, and

others in Boatwright's 1970 collection) present substantially the same
viewpoint, often borrowing ideas and even passages from the *Essays*, the
Memos, written almost fifteen years later, make almost no mention of
Transcendentalist ideas. In a letter of 1930, Ives notes that he can no
longer agree with some of the ideas presented in his *Essays*.[42] This does
not mean that Ives was no longer a Transcendentalist, for in the 1930s he
was as devoted to Emerson as ever. Indeed, it was his fervor for Emerson
and Thoreau in his later years that seemed to justify the common assumption that he had been equally enthusiastic about them all his life. It does
show, however, that Ives's ideas were fluid even after he had ceased
composing, changing according to his situation, and suggests that to
use the *Essays* as a guide to music from earlier periods in Ives's life is
misleading.

The preceding analysis of some of the disparities between Transcendentalist philosophy and Ives's own thinking, writing, and composing
has demonstrated that, while recognition of the Transcendentalist influences is vital for understanding much of what makes Ives unique as a
thinker and a composer, it cannot fully account for either Ives's views or
his music. Ives has commonly been thought of as a Transcendentalist
composer, and his music has often been assumed to be the music a
Transcendentalist would write. As can be seen from the example of John
Sullivan Dwight, who, although not a composer, was more closely involved with Transcendentalism and the Concord group than Ives himself,
this can hardly be assumed; there is something beyond the Transcendentalist ideas of unity within diversity and the universal immanence of Spirit
that influenced Ives in his musical evolution.

I have not proven, nor do I wish to suggest, that Ives was not a
Transcendentalist, for he was. There is room for a great deal of variety
within a philosophy that speaks of the underlying unity of Spirit, as has
already been shown. But Ives brought to his music not only Transcendentalist ideas, but also two other vital components, which may be called
literary inspiration and memory. The former, the idea that music can
somehow express the spirit of literature, has no equivalent in previous
Transcendentalist thought, although it has many counterparts in nineteenth-century European music. The latter, notable for example in Ives's
attempts to recreate in his music the sounds and moods of holidays in
his boyhood world of Danbury, Connecticut, arises from a completely
different source, one that became important to Ives, as we shall see,
because of the influence of his wife Harmony. Indeed, the celebration of

people and of the experience of shared events such as holidays and camp meetings speaks of a side of Charles Ives's character entirely at odds with the Transcendentalists' celebration of solitude.

Beyond these, the larger concept of imitation, in which music mimics other sounds or creates an analogy with some other kind of motion, and which is at the core of almost all of Ives's mature music, has no place in the writings or thought of any of the Transcendentalists. The Transcendentalists as a group disdained the representation of reality characteristic of fiction—a representation or imitation of life exactly analogous to that in most of Ives's "literary music"—because, while growing out of experience and making use of imagination, it does not force the reader back into experience as does the shared reality of works such as *Walden*. Fiction offers the imagination distance instead of a call to action, severing the direct relationship between thought and life that the Transcendentalists worked to promote.[43] The realistic evocation of actual events in some of Ives's compositions, while not fiction in the strictest sense, is played out in a realm far more removed from daily life than the essays and journals of Emerson and Thoreau. Even the most "documentary" of Ives's compositions are experienced like fiction rather than as a kind of musical journalism. In writing representational music, even music about the spiritual questing of Emerson and the contemplation of Thoreau, Ives was pursuing aims entirely in conflict with this aspect of Transcendentalist thought. Indeed, by this criterion, Dwight's preference for abstract music is as characteristic of the Transcendental school as Ives's sound-photographs are uncharacteristic.

The usual picture of Ives as the Transcendentalist composer par excellence simply cannot account for what is most basic to his music, nor for the origins of his complex aesthetic. That Ives sought to depict Transcendental figures and something of Transcendental thinking in music is obvious. But he did not develop his musical method or conceive his musical aims through or because of Transcendentalist philosophy.

CHAPTER FOUR

The Philosophical Tradition of the Ives Family

The distinction made in the previous chapter between Transcendental-ism as a literary tradition and Transcendentalism as a system of belief is a fundamental clue in our attempt to trace Ives's early contacts with Tran-scendentalism within his family. As we shall see, Ives had some opportu-nity to learn about and to read Emerson and Thoreau at home, but their writings were only part of a broader tradition of interest in religion, philosophy, and social justice. What stands out in Ives's recollections of his family is not Emerson and Thoreau as individual thinkers or writers but rather the broad concept of "the innate goodness of man." When Ives later read Emerson and Thoreau, as a student and as an adult, the attitudes he had learned at home shaped his understanding of their writings. It was because he recognized in their writings issues and ideas that had become central to his own philosophy—ideas he may have absorbed from his family or may have come to through his own reading and experiences—that he developed in his later years an enthusiasm for Transcendentalism sufficiently powerful to obscure other, perhaps equally important influences.

RELIGION AND SOCIAL REFORM

Charles Ives's family was one of the oldest and most distinguished in Danbury, Connecticut, where Charles grew up. His direct ancestor Wil-liam Ives had been one of the first settlers of New Haven in 1638, and the Iveses had been successful businessmen and important citizens of Con-necticut ever since. Isaac Ives (1764–1845), Charles's great-grandfather, graduated from Yale in 1785, began his career in Danbury, made his fortune in New York, and retired to Danbury in 1829. He was soon joined by his son, George White Ives (1798–1862), Charles Ives's grandfather, who spent the latter part of his life as a philanthropist and prominent citizen of the town.[1]

The Ives family had a long tradition of taking matters of religion and related questions of philosophy, ethics, and social justice very seriously, and most of their reading and their books had a religious focus.[2] This is confirmed by what remains of the family library belonging to George White Ives and his wife Sarah Hotchkiss Wilcox Ives (1808–1899), Charles Ives's grandparents. The collection includes several books of psalms and hymn texts, sermons and discourses by preachers such as Jonathan Edwards (an early president of Princeton College), John Newton (a leader of the eighteenth-century Evangelical revival in England), Timothy Dwight (president of Yale College early in the nineteenth century), and many others, a Bible in six volumes (Isaac Ives's family Bible), a Biblical concordance, catechisms and Bible lessons for children, and other religious and philosophical works.[3] There is one work by a Transcendentalist writer: Theodore Parker's *A Discourse of Matters Pertaining to Religion*, his most influential book.[4] Parker (1810–1860) was a Unitarian minister, radical theologian, contributor to the Transcendentalist journal *The Dial*, leading abolitionist, and friend of the Iveses. He inscribed the volume to "Mr & Mrs Ives / With the thanks / of Theodore Parker / [?] 15, 1857." The collection may also have included Sarah Ives's own copies of Emerson's essays and perhaps of Thoreau's writings as well, but these have not yet come to light.[5]

In addition, there are several important abolitionist works, including a much-read paperbound copy of Harriet Beecher Stowe's *Uncle Tom's Cabin* (Boston: John P. Jewett, 1852) and a leather-bound copy of *The Works of John Woolman* (5th ed., 2 vols. bound as one [Philadelphia: Benjamin & Thomas Kite, 1818]), the eighteenth-century Quaker abolitionist, which is rubber-stamped "G. W. Ives" and quite dog-eared, especially the chapter *On Loving Our Neighbors*, which is concerned with the slave trade. Finally, there are several sets of literary works, such as an 1819 pocket edition of *British Classics* in several volumes and a similar collection of *The British Poets* in sixteen volumes, published in 1821. These last two sets of books are rubber-stamped by G. W. Ives. In contrast to the books on religion and social reform, these appear to have been very little read, and it seems safe to conclude that the religious and abolitionist books in the library were of much greater interest to George White and Sarah Ives.

The tradition went beyond merely reading, as members of the Ives family practiced their faith and witnessed to their convictions in their actions as well. According to Bigelow Ives, the composer's nephew, Sarah Ives was "apparently a woman of great energy." His uncle once told him that, after she first came to Danbury, Sarah led a group of women up to New Fairfield, about ten miles away, on a march to rescue a fugitive slave who was about to be returned to the South, and "raised so much hell that they let him go."[6] George White Ives was also a strong abolitionist, according to Charles Ives's own testimony,[7] and so was his eldest child, Joseph Moss Ives (1832–1908).[8]

George Edward Ives (1845–1894), George White Ives's fifth and youngest child and Charles Ives's father, was the only member of the immediate family to serve in the Civil War, enlisting in 1862 as a band-leader attached to a Connecticut regiment.[9] During that time, he befriended a young ex-slave boy, Henry Anderson Brooks, taught him to read and write, and brought him home to Danbury. Charles Ives writes of Brooks in the *Memos* that "Grandmother took him in, brought him up and sent him to school in Danbury. She and Grandfather would take anybody and everybody in, and give them their last cookie or last cent, if their sense of injustice was stirred" (page 53).[10]

These incidents testify to a strong family tradition of tolerance and concern for social justice, a tradition continued by George Edward Ives and passed on to his two sons. Many years later, Charles Ives drew on that tradition not only for subjects for his music—as in *The Anti-Abolitionist Riots* (1908) and *Lincoln, The Great Commoner* (1912)—but for much of his political philosophy as well. While Ives himself was not always consistent, he held up the views and actions of his grandparents as an ideal to follow.

His younger brother Moss (Joseph Moss Ives II, 1876–1939) maintained a similar commitment to social justice, particularly to religious tolerance. In his book on Catholicism in colonial America, Moss Ives argued for the importance of the contribution of the early Catholic settlers of Maryland to the cause of religious liberty.[11] In the public affairs of Danbury, where he returned after his education at Yale to serve as a lawyer and judge, Moss urged the integration of Danbury's growing Catholic population (chiefly of Irish and Italian descent) into the larger community at a time when Catholics were still often feared and reviled.[12]

This family tradition of religious inquiry, tolerance, and concern for social justice, which can be traced back through four generations to Isaac Ives, was a tremendous influence on Charles Ives's character and beliefs. However, the special enthusiasm for Emerson on the part of some members of the Ives family during the years just before the Civil War seems to be only a minor current within this much larger commitment to religious and social concerns. Its importance for George Edward Ives, his wife, and his sons, or indeed for any members of the Ives family in the years after the Civil War, is not yet clear.

EMERSON, TRANSCENDENTALISM, AND THE IVES FAMILY

The main Emerson enthusiasts in the Ives family—indeed, the only ones for whose interest we have any direct evidence—were Charles's eldest uncle Joseph Moss Ives, who met Emerson in 1856, and his grandmother Sarah, who apparently attended at least two of Emerson's lectures, was thrilled to meet Emerson in person when Joseph brought him home, and, according to David Wooldridge, was a "confidante of Margaret Fuller."[13] In a letter to John Kirkpatrick, Ives mentions his grandmother's attending an Emerson lecture on the "New England Reformers": "I remember her saying that she was startled (perhaps somewhat put out) to find that the printed text, which she knew almost by heart, was hardly more than an outline in his lecture."[14] Her memorization of the printed lecture suggests how important Emerson was to her—this topic was particularly dear to her heart, judging from her other interests—although, according to David Wooldridge, her more business-like husband George, "ever since hearing Andrews Norton's attack on transcendentalism, had never quite trusted Emerson's radicalism."[15] We can assume from his report that Ives discussed Emerson with his grandmother, or at least heard her talk about him.

However, it remains unclear what the importance of Emerson and the other Concord writers was for George Edward Ives, Charles Ives's father and most important model, or for Mary Elizabeth Parmalee ("Mollie") Ives (1849–1929), his mother. Indeed, there appears to be no surviving evidence at all that the Ives family's interest in Emerson continued after the cause of abolition had been won. About the Transcendentalists' "most inspiring theme," discussed in the previous chapter, we can be more sure. In an early sketch (from 1919) towards *The Majority*, Ives (speaking through the character George, but clearly for himself) says that his father "brought [him] up on the great transcendental doctrine" of "the innate goodness of man."[16] While this is the only place in his writings where Ives ascribes Transcendentalism to his father, and the ascription even here is indirect, relying on the assumption that George is speaking for Ives, it is probable that George Edward Ives firmly believed in man's "innate goodness" and passed that belief on to his sons. This would certainly be congruent with the strong family tradition of tolerance. Whether or not George Ives considered this doctrine "Transcendental," his son found it in Emerson and Thoreau, and Charles's reading of their works was probably heavily influenced by the beliefs he learned at home.

Beyond this, there is no documentary evidence to indicate that George Edward Ives shared his mother's passion for Emerson or even possessed his own copy of Emerson's works.[17] If Sarah and Joseph Ives first became enthusiastic about Emerson in the late 1850s, as would seem to have been the case, George Ives would already have been old enough to be absorbed in his own interests, particularly music, and may never have been affected directly by the fervor of his mother and his older brother. There is no reason to assume that Sarah and Joseph Ives's enthusiasm for Emerson was shared by Joseph's younger brothers and sisters. Charles Ives's Aunt Amelia Ives Brewster (1837–1918), the third oldest child of George White and Sarah Ives, was an important figure in Charles Ives's life, especially after the death of his father,[18] but there is no hint in her letters to Ives and his wife, in her character, or in Ives's own testimony that she absorbed the least interest in Transcendentalism from her mother, although it is clear from her surviving letters that her concern for religious matters was as strong as that of all the other Iveses.

Nor is there any hint, even from Charles Ives himself, that George Ives encouraged an interest in Emerson on the part of his son. While the childhood diaries of both Charles and his brother Moss record their parents' reading to them on Sunday afternoons, one of the Ives family rituals,[19] when the books read from are mentioned, they are stories or biographies (including a *Life of Beethoven*), never essays or philosophy. In his writings and conversation, Ives did not mention his parents' views of the Concord writers, nor did he ever discuss his childhood and the Transcendentalists in the same context.

Similarly, there is no evidence that Charles Ives read Emerson before entering college. In his early correspondence and diaries, he never refers to Emerson's works or alludes to his ideas. One may imagine that Emerson's books were around the house and his ideas in the air, but the practicality and lack of education of Ives's mother[20] and George Ives's devotion to music and fondness for tinkering do not suggest a household devoted to literature.[21] Further, Charles Ives's commitments to music, sports, and scholastics would seem to have left little room for reading Emerson's works during his adolescence.

Finally, if there was a tradition within the George Ives family of enthusiasm for reading Emerson or Thoreau, it was not passed down to Moss Ives and his children, as were both the family's other particular enthusiasms, George Ives's interest in music[22] and the larger family tradition of tolerance, concern for religious issues, and interest in social

reform. Bigelow Ives has testified that within Moss's family the works of
Emerson, Thoreau, and the other Concord authors were never con-
sulted: "They were simply books on the shelf."[23]

This lack of evidence cannot and does not prove that Emerson, his
followers, and their ideas were unimportant to George Edward Ives's
family; that which is most important may leave the fewest traces, being
absorbed in the fabric of daily life. But it severely challenges the view of
Transcendentalism and its relation to religion within the Ives family
suggested by the Cowells, a view that has been repeated frequently but
never questioned. They write in their biographical sketch of Ives,

> [Ives] has always been a highly articulate man, and he found compatible
> bedrock for his thinking and writing about music in the New England
> Transcendentalists, whose attitude toward life placed so indelible an im-
> print on the developing American character after the middle of the nine-
> teenth century. In his profoundly moral New England environment, the
> counsel of the Concord philosophers was examined right along with the
> Bible and applied literally to every human concern. For his own creed Ives
> drew on Emerson, and on the uncomfortable Thoreau for courage; it is not
> too much to say that all his life he has been closer to these two than to any
> living man.[24]

That Ives "found compatible bedrock for his thinking and writing
about music in the New England Transcendentalists" can hardly be dis-
puted; the vital question is when in his life he found that bedrock. If by
"his profoundly moral New England environment" the Cowells refer to
Ives's upbringing in Danbury, as the context of this passage and its
concluding sentence imply, they exaggerate the influence of the Transcendentalist writers in relation to the larger religious tradition of the
Iveses. The notion that during Ives's youth the words of Emerson and
Thoreau were as well known and literally interpreted as the Bible cannot
be justified by the picture of the Ives family drawn above. The complete
lack of evidence for this level of devotion to the writings of the Concord
school contrasts sharply with the rich existing witness to the involvement
of George and Mary Ives and their children in Protestant and Evangelical
Christianity. Both contemporary evidence and Charles Ives's own later
testimony thoroughly document this participation, which included providing music at religious revivals and for church services, reading the
Bible, and attending church virtually every Sunday, often twice.[25] There
is no evidence, either from contemporary documents or from Ives's later
testimony, for the notion that in the Ives household in Danbury the
Concord authors and the Bible were ever viewed as on an equal footing.[26]
What the Cowells describe here is not Ives's childhood environment, but

that of his retirement years with his wife Harmony in the house in West Redding, Connecticut, where the Cowells visited the Iveses, when Ives would often refer to Emerson or Thoreau in his conversation, and when Harmony would read passages from Emerson aloud, as if they were poetry.[27] Of the intensity of Ives's devotion to his Transcendentalist heroes in these final decades of his life, long after the *Essays* were written, there can be no question.

What little Transcendentalism Ives came to know as a child, then, seems to have been neither Emerson's *Essays* nor Thoreau's *Walden*, but simply his father's strong belief in "the innate goodness of man," which Charles Ives would later call "the fundamental doctrine of transcendentalism."[28] What Ives knew then of Transcendentalism as a set of beliefs can be summed up in that single phrase, and what he knew of it as a literary tradition remains an almost total mystery. When exactly Ives first read or heard about Emerson and Thoreau is by now impossible to trace.

With the larger family tradition to build on, Ives's first reading of these writers, whenever it was, would surely have been sympathetic. It is Kirkpatrick's firm opinion that the Iveses—either Charles's grandmother or his father—would have made sure that Charles read in them.[29] Perhaps the complaint of George, the protagonist in Ives's early draft of the essay *The Majority*, should be taken to provide support for Kirkpatrick's view: "Before I went to college I was interested. I found a pleasure in browsing in my father's library that I never found in college."[30] There is no more concrete evidence than this that Ives read Emerson before his senior year in college, when he submitted an essay on Emerson to the *Yale Literary Magazine*.[31]

Whatever exposure to Emerson's ideas or to the essays themselves Ives had gained at home, which apparently cannot be known for certain, it does not seem that Ives developed his overwhelming passion for Emerson or his habit of quoting him frequently before his mid-thirties, a decade after graduating from Yale. The development of this enthusiasm, virtually simultaneous with Ives's maturation as a composer, is discussed in Chapter 9.

Of his two favorite writers, Ives may have read Thoreau first. He mentions in the Thoreau essay that *Walden* was briefly "sailed over" in a literature class he took before college,[32] which suggests that he may have read parts of it at the latest during his late teens. Howard Boatwright, editor of the *Essays*, interprets Ives's cryptic reference to Thoreau as "that reassuring and true friend, who stood by me one 'low' day, when the sun had gone down, long, long before sunset," to mean that Ives derived comfort from Thoreau at the time of his father's death, a month after Ives had entered Yale in the autumn of 1894.[33] There are other possible and perhaps more likely interpretations: Ives may have been referring to the time of his heart attack in October 1918 or to Harmony Ives's emergency operation in 1909 (which apparently involved a miscarriage or therapeutic abortion and hysterectomy),[34] both of which occurred closer to the time that the *Concord Sonata* and the *Essays* were conceived and written. But if Boatwright is correct, this would seem to demonstrate that Ives was familiar with Thoreau as far back as his teens. Although Emerson is a more important figure for the *Essays* and for Ives's philosophy of art, it may be that Ives read and admired Thoreau at an earlier age, as the above scant evidence would seem to suggest.

Charles Ives mentions Hawthorne and the Alcotts only in speaking of the *Concord Sonata*, and their importance for the Ives family is hard to establish. There is a partial set of Hawthorne's works in Charles Ives's house at West Redding,[35] which may have come from Sarah Ives's collection. There is also a work of Bronson Alcott's, his *Conversations with Children on the Gospels*, in the secretary currently in Bigelow Ives's house with the other books from George White and Sarah Ives's library.[36] However, Ives apparently learned about Alcott chiefly from secondary sources, his discussion of Alcott in the *Essays* relying almost exclusively on anecdotes drawn from works on Thoreau and Concord published in the 1910s.[37] Of the two, Bronson Alcott would have been of greater interest to the Ives family, due to his religious and abolitionist concerns, but there is no compelling reason to assume that Charles Ives was familiar with either author before encountering them in preparatory school or college.

Several avenues of research remain to be pursued before a clearer picture of the influences on the young Ives and his beliefs can be drawn. Among these are an investigation of the sermons and revival preaching Ives heard, an examination of any extant letters or diaries of Sarah Ives, Joseph Ives, Lyman and Amelia Ives Brewster, and other relatives, and a look at the character and beliefs of the Parmalees, Ives's mother's family. The above discussion has shown only that we do not know as much as has been assumed about the early intellectual influences on Ives.

It is clear that Charles Ives's character and ways of thinking were molded to a great extent by his family's tradition of tolerance, concern for social justice (especially for the abolition of slavery), and interest in religion, ethics, and philosophy. Although Transcendentalism, particularly the lectures and essays of Emerson, was an important part of this tradition for Sarah and Joseph Ives in the 1850s, and its influence presumably was passed on in some form to George Edward Ives and his two sons, it remained merely a part of the tradition, not its core. Just as Emerson's was not the sole religious or philosophical influence within the Ives family, so Transcendentalism did not form the core of Ives's personality or world view as a youth or as a mature philosopher, and it cannot explain every facet of Ives's aesthetic. Transcendentalism has been so heavily emphasized as an element in the Ives family history because of Charles Ives's own further development, as he grew closer and closer to Emerson's philosophy as an adult. Ultimately, the whole of his family's tradition and his own thinking became integrated in Ives's mind through his own reading of Emerson and Thoreau, and his ideas attained their apparent Transcendentalist cast as he redefined his childhood influences in Transcendentalist terms. Because of this, and because an interest in Transcendentalism—particularly the idea of "the innate goodness of man"—is undeniably an element in the earlier mix of family interests, it has seemed obvious that Ives's philosophy grew essentially unchanged out of the important influences of his youth.

This static view of Ives's philosophy can no longer be accepted. Charles Ives did not leave Danbury as a committed Transcendentalist. He left having taken only the first steps in his philosophical journey, and his views on religion, music, and Transcendentalism itself changed and developed over the course of his career. His upbringing, in both philosophical and musical spheres, helped to set him on his path, but later influences were equally strong in determining his course and preparing his achievements.

Because Emerson is the central figure in the *Essays*, the key to and virtually the symbol of the philosophy Ives develops there, one of our principal tasks in charting the stages of his aesthetic development will be to explore where, when, and how Ives developed his enthusiasm for Emerson. One aspect of his odyssey was in a sense a return to the Emersonian enthusiasm and commitment to social justice of his grandparents. But that was not all his journey entailed, and the rest of his philosophical and musical evolution can indeed be traced, albeit imperfectly, with the evidence now available. It will become clear that Ives arrived at most of his attitudes about music and his concepts of dualism, idealism, and self-reliance independently of the sage of Concord, in large part at least, but that Emerson's writings played a vital role in the final stages of his development.

Charles Ives at age fourteen

CHAPTER FIVE

Early Musical Training (1874–1894): George Ives and Danbury

AN OUTLINE OF IVES'S CAREER

There are six main periods to Ives's life, distinct from each other in the manner and types of music he wrote, his philosophy of music, his important relationships, and the places he lived, studied, and worked.

1. During his *boyhood* in Danbury, Connecticut (1874–1894), Ives studied music with his father and others, worried about school, kept busy with team sports, and wrote sentimental parlor songs, pieces for his father's band, and organ and chorus pieces—sometimes musically adventuresome—for the churches where he performed regularly as an organist.

2. In 1893, Ives moved to New Haven to attend a preparatory school prior to college, but it was not until he entered Yale in the fall of 1894, began theory and composition studies with Horatio Parker, and experienced the sudden death of his father that November that the next period of his life was to begin. This period of *apprenticeship* (1894–1902) lasted through college and his first four years in New York. Despite his changing locale and his entry into the insurance business in 1898, these years are unified by his steady work as an organist and by the kinds of music he was writing—large romantic works in the mold of his teacher Parker, including his first two symphonies, first string quartet, and first attempt at a violin sonata, and more experimental pieces for chorus, organ, or theatre orchestra.

3. Ives's resignation from his last position as an organist in 1902 marked a break with music as a profession, an acceptance of a growing role in business, and the beginning of an isolation as a composer that was to provide a protective cocoon for the next six years of *innovation and*

synthesis (1902–1908). He returned to vernacular styles, showing an increased interest in ragtime, and began to incorporate into the longer classical forms he had learned from Parker the techniques he had first tried in his experimental and highly dissonant church music, producing a series of chamber and orchestral works based on hymn tunes and on the music he had written for church. In the second half of this period, returning to his earlier experimental approach to musical techniques and encouraged by a new self-confidence gained through his developing relationship with his future wife, Harmony Twichell (1876–1969), Ives began to create what Kirkpatrick has called "a whole world of far-out music."

4.   The next nine years saw the conception and creation of the greatest and best-known works of Ives's *maturity* (1908–1917). His marriage to Harmony in June 1908 marks the beginning of this period, when he was to produce a series of ambitious compositions evoking the past, a personal past Harmony helped him to resurrect, or inspired by his reading, an interest Harmony encouraged.

5.   After the entry of the United States into the First World War in 1917 and Ives's heart attack in October 1918, he began to produce much less and to work mostly in smaller forms, especially songs and pieces for piano, while pulling together his previously scattered, often unfinished works into two self-publications, the *Concord Sonata* and *114 Songs*. This is the period of his *last works* (1918–1926) and his first notice in the musical press since 1902, mostly mocking "reviews" of his two publications. As his name became known among a small circle of the avant-garde, his musical isolation diminished, and, perhaps paradoxically, his compositional powers seemed to fade away.

6.   Ives spent the rest of his life tinkering with the music he had already produced, in some cases making substantial changes and finishing or restoring incomplete or partially lost pieces, but producing no new compositions. This period of *tinkering* (1927–1954) also brought him gradual recognition and finally, by the end of his life, a growing fame through his associations with Henry Cowell (whom he met in 1927), Nicolas Slonimsky, John Kirkpatrick, Lou Harrison, and others who were to become champions of his music.

This brief sketch of the main aspects of these six periods and the landmarks within and between them will serve as orientation for the discussion in the remaining chapters, in which the development of Ives's aesthetic ideals, his philosophy, his compositional purposes, and his conception of musical genre will be the main focus. The story of Ives's development is a confusing one to relate, because in some sense everything about his ideas, his music, and his life must be told simultaneously if his progress is to be understood. His growth was not linear, but dialectic, and his mature thought and music evolved from the combined influences of every period of his life. Further, many of the clues to changes in Ives's thinking about music must be sought in the beliefs of those around him at different stages of his life or through examination of the music itself, as he has left few written accounts of his ideas prior to the *Essays*. For these reasons, the stories of his musical and philosophical progress necessarily intertwine, and both must be placed in the context of his relationships and his careers in music and in business.

GEORGE IVES

Ives began his musical studies with his father, George Edward Ives. George Ives had spent a total of four years in Morrisania, now part of the Bronx, and in New York, studying theory and counterpoint with Carl Foeppl, a German musician and keyboard player, and taking cornet lessons with another teacher.[1] The rigorous theoretical grounding he received was part of the accepted academic training for musicians in Germany, far beyond what was expected of small-town bandleaders in America but useful for the sort of all-around musician George Ives was to become. There is no hint that he ever intended to compose seriously, and in fact he wrote almost nothing. Rather, he used his training in his teaching, his conducting, his arranging, and his acoustical experiments.

Charles Ives credited his father to a great extent with forming his attitudes towards music. Most important were George Ives's reverence for and devotion to music,[2] rigorous discipline in technique as a foundation for performing and composing, exemplified in the exercises in harmony and counterpoint he assigned to his son, and open-mindedness. This last, manifested in both an experimental approach to sound and music and an attitude of intent listening, was the only one of these attitudes that was unusual among professional musicians, and it became extremely important for Ives's development.

TECHNIQUE AND EXPERIMENT

Ives writes in the *Memos*,

> One thing I am certain of is that, if I have done anything good in music, it was, first, because of my father, and second, because of my wife. . . .
> What my father did for me was not only in his teaching, on the

George Edward Ives, ca. 1890

technical side, etc., but in his influence, his personality, character, and open-mindedness, and his remarkable understanding of the ways of a boy's heart and mind. He had a remarkable talent for music and for the nature of music and sound, and also a philosophy of music that was unusual. Besides starting my music lessons when I was five years old, and keeping me at music in many ways until he died, with the best teaching that a boy could have, Father knew (and filled me up with) Bach and the best of the classical music, and the study of harmony and counterpoint etc., and musical history. Above all this, he kept my interest and encouraged open-mindedness in all matters that needed it in any way.

For instance, he thought that man as a rule didn't use the faculties that the Creator had given him hard enough. I couldn't have been over ten years old when he would occasionally have us sing, for instance, a tune like *The Swanee River* in the key of Eb, but play the accompaniment in the key of C. This was to stretch our ears and strengthen our musical minds, so that they could learn to use and translate things that might be used and translated (in the art of music) more than they had been. In this instance, I don't think he had the possibility of polytonality in composition in mind, as much as to encourage the use of the ears—and for them and the mind to think for themselves and be more independent—in other words, not to be too dependent upon customs and habits [pages 114–115].

At other spots in the *Memos*, Ives recalls his father saying, "Every dissonance doesn't have to resolve, if it doesn't happen to feel like it, any more than every horse should have to have its tail bobbed just because it's the prevailing fashion" (page 116); exploring with his son chords made by stacking more than three thirds on top of one another (page 120); introducing nontraditional percussion instruments into the Danbury Band, which he directed (page 124); using the "Humanophone" (different singers taking different notes, like a handbell choir) to sing a melody with extremely wide leaps (page 142); and experimenting with microtones, pure intervals, scales without octaves, and other tunings outside the tempered scale system (pages 44–45).[3] All of these exhibit George Ives's open-mindedness, his willingness to try anything out to see what the results might be and his awareness that the rules of music are fashioned by humans, not by divine law.

Charles Ives responded to his father's theoretical interests with enthusiasm, developing a fascination with musical technique for its own sake—both traditional and experimental—that lasted throughout his life. But George's open-mindedness was always complemented by a sense of discipline, of carefully learning the traditional techniques as well as indulging in "boy's fooling." Towards the end of his time in Danbury,

Charles Ives began to experiment with canons, whole-tone and other nontraditional chords and scales, and pieces in two or more keys simultaneously. George Ives was willing to let his son try these ideas out, even to the extent of allowing him to write four-part fugues in which each new voice entered in a key a fifth or a fourth higher than the previous voice, creating a texture of four simultaneous keys, as long as Charles could prove that he understood the traditional tonal techniques he was seeking to extend.

> Father used to say, "If you know how to write a fugue the right way *well*, then I'm willing to have you try the wrong way—*well*. But you've got to know what [you're doing] and why you're doing it." It was his willingness to have boys think for themselves—within reason—that I looked back on later as quite remarkable, but it didn't seem [so] to me then as a boy. I had to practise right and know my lesson first, then he was willing to let us roam a little for fun. He somehow kept us in a good balance. It was good for our minds and our ears.[4]

The combination of assured, disciplined technique and willingness to try things out that Ives learned as a boy contributed immeasurably to his later self-reliance, his dependence on intuition and his own experience in music rather than on external rules and tradition. This is an important part of his mature musical philosophy, not fully realized until his thirties but originating in his studies with his father. Ives's interest in the technical aspects of composition remained high throughout his life, and his secure knowledge of both traditional and newly devised methods was fundamental to his musical independence. Had he felt that the attacks on his music from professional musicians were based on his technical inadequacy rather than on his aesthetic unorthodoxy, he probably could not have continued to compose in the face of such violent opposition.

Yet Ives did not acquire only an experimental open-mindedness from his father. He absorbed along with it a strict dichotomy between private inquiry and public performance, a distinction that should help us to make sense of the bewildering diversity of styles in his music. Laurence Wallach describes the elder Ives as "above all a public musician, a man whose creative activity originated in and reflected the life around him."[5] In all the documentation about George Ives's musical career that Wallach has gathered from newspaper accounts and other public sources, there is not a word about George Ives's investigations into polytonality, microtones, new chords and scales, or other basic materials of music.[6] These were private concerns, shared with his family, including his son, and his public performances as cornettist and bandleader were another thing altogether.

Charles Ives points out that his father did not have in mind the possibility that his practice in keeping two keys going at once might lead to polytonal composition,[7] and indeed George Ives prevented his son from performing the polytonal episodes in the *Variations on America* (1891) in public[8] and omitted them from the manuscript of his son's work that he copied and submitted for publication.[9] George Ives seems to have regarded his own investigations into musical sound and materials as *research*, having no immediate or even foreseeable application in musical composition. It was left to his son, many years later, to try out in actual compositions the ideas George Ives turned up in his explorations of musical sound.

Most of the references in the *Memos* to George Ives's sound-experiments are offered in partial explanation of Charles Ives's own compositional experiments. And yet Charles Ives continued to maintain until the end of his life the strict distinction between private research and public concert music that he had learned from his father. He referred to his experimental works, most of which are short and very carefully worked out (as an experiment should be, if it is to offer a fair test), as "hardly more than memos in notes" (*Memos*, page 64), designed to explore new technical possibilities. Even the *Three Quarter-tone Pieces* for two pianos (1923–1924, premiered in 1925), the last of Ives's experiments to be written down and perhaps the first of them to be performed in public since his college days, were not intended as "definitely completed works of art or attempts at works of art," but simply as "studies within the limited means we had with which to study quarter tones" (ibid., page 111). Ives later incorporated many of the ideas he had first developed in his "memos in notes" into his music for public performance, first in his church music and then, after 1902, in his sonatas, chamber works, movements for orchestra, and many of his songs. Yet in these pieces, the new techniques were often less rigorously handled than in the experimental works, for in his concert music Ives was concerned not with technique for its own sake but rather with musical and emotional effects. In other words, there was no confusion in Charles Ives's mind between private speculation and public music, any more than there had been in his father's. While there is a direct link between George Ives's sound-experiments and the experimental music of his son, this experimental music remains in a category separate from Ives's concert music, which was intended to be performed in public.

Once the distinction between Ives's concert music and his experimental music is made, the bewildering diversity of his music suddenly becomes comprehensible, and its evolution over the course of his career becomes clearer. Experimental music is by its very nature diverse and unpredictable, since each experiment may try out techniques unrelated to any other or may take earlier experiments to new extremes. If there is a pattern of change over time in Ives's experimental music, it more closely resembles the execution of a successful line of research than the distillation of a coherent musical style. Within Ives's concert music, on the other hand—the symphonies, the string quartets, the piano trio, the sonatas, the orchestral sets, and many of the songs—we may trace a clear and steady pattern of development, as Ives gradually absorbed the various influences on him and his own novel techniques into his mature method.[10]

It is not simply George Ives's experimentation and open-mindedness that made possible the audacities in Charles Ives's music intended for concert performance, however. Indeed, George Ives's clear separation between private speculation and public entertainment would have legislated very firmly against the blend of innovation and tradition that Charles Ives achieved in his mature music. This integration depended, first, on an increased self-reliance on Ives's part, gained only in his mature period through his relationship with his wife and his growing enthusiasm for Emerson and Thoreau, and, second, on a new understanding of the experience of concert music in the European tradition as an essentially private one, a conception he absorbed from his studies with Horatio Parker at Yale. Without these influences, Ives could not have drawn together the conflicting musical traditions and attitudes he first learned from his father.

"HOW CAN THERE BE ANY BAD MUSIC?"

In certain respects, George Ives's open-mindedness approached the Transcendentalist view of the divine beauty in all humans, and in nature as well. Charles Ives wrote of his father,

> He had a belief that everyone was born with at least one germ of musical talent, and that an early application of great music (and not trivial music) would help it grow. He started all the children of the family—and most of the children of the town for that matter—on Bach and Stephen Foster (quite shortly after they were born—always regardless of whether [they] had, would have, or wouldn't have any musical gifts or sense, etc.). He put a love of music into the heart of many a boy who might have gone without it but for him.[11]

At one point in Charles Ives's discussion of his father, George Ives seems to approach a distinction between the actual sounds heard and the spirit or idea behind them, as he defends the spirited but out-of-tune and raucous singing of a Danbury stonemason: "He is a supreme musician. . . . Watch him closely and reverently, look into his face and hear the music of the ages. Don't pay too much attention to the sounds—for if you do, you may miss the music. You won't get a wild, heroic ride to heaven on pretty little sounds."[12] This looking beyond the "sounds" to the "music" is similar to the famous distinction Ives draws in the Epilogue to the *Essays*, in response to a concertmaster's casual suggestion for a change in a violin part to make it "fit the hand" and therefore "sound better": "My God! What has sound got to do with music! . . . Why can't music go out in the same way it comes in to a man, without having to crawl over a fence of sounds, thoraxes, catguts, wire, wood, and brass? . . . That music must be heard is not essential—what it *sounds* like may not be what it *is*" (page 84).[13]

What is most essential in George Ives's view here is spirituality or, more simply, spirit, and what he is concerned with is performance, not composition. The sound—an excessive concern for correct performance—must not get in the way of the spirit expressed. Charles Ives writes of the way his father would lead the singing at the religious revivals outside Danbury that he "would always encourage the people to sing their own way. If they threw the poet or the composer around a bit, so much the better for the poetry and the music."[14] This is very similar to Ives's own later attitude towards performing, as demonstrated in his instructions to Nicolas Slonimsky about the 1931 Paris performance of *Three Places in New England*: "Just kick into the music as you did in the Town Hall—never mind the exact notes or the right notes, they're always a nuisance. Just let the spirit of the stuff sail up to the Eiffel Tower and on to Heaven."[15] In the same spirit, Ives advised Kirkpatrick in playing the Emerson movement of the *Concord Sonata* to "do whatever seems natural and best to *you*, though not necessarily the same way each time."[16]

George Ives's distinction between the "sound" and the "music" has been seen as a source of Ives's later dichotomy between substance and manner, but this ignores an important distinction. Charles Ives certainly incorporated his father's spirit-centered approach to performance, but there is nothing in George Ives's composing, arranging, or musical tastes— except perhaps his commitment to the "great music" of Bach and Stephen Foster—to equal his son's compositional idealism.[17] Most of George Ives's idealistic or apparently Transcendentalist attitudes towards music seem principally to be concerned with hearing, listening with open ears and an open mind, and refusing to judge according to the accepted standards alone. The "unknown philosopher of a half century ago" quoted at the end of Ives's Conductor's Note to the second movement of his *Fourth Symphony* may well be his father:

> "How can there be any bad music? All music is from heaven. If there is anything bad in it, I put it there—by my implications and my limitations. Nature builds the mountains and meadows and man puts in the fences and labels."[18]

This is consistent with George Ives's ideals but not with the careful distinction his son makes in the *Essays* between music with substance and the mannerist music of Strauss, Wagner, and Debussy. George Ives's open-mindedness about musical sound cleared the way for Charles Ives to explore music virtually without limit, and the idealism inherent in his view of music as being "from heaven" similarly predisposed his son to listen to all music with open ears. But George Ives emphasized the responsibility of the listener to sense the spirit behind the sound; by the time of the *Essays*, Charles was principally concerned with conveying spiritual ideas in music, a radically different emphasis.

IMITATION OF SOUNDS

This listening with open ears and an open mind had other important ramifications for Charles Ives's music. Part of George Ives's open-mindedness involved listening to sounds, man-made or natural, and attempting to imitate them with musical instruments. Ives remembered as an adult that his father, while practicing the violin, had joined in with the two Ives brothers in playing railroad in the yard when Charles was about ten, and had "discovered that staccato passages and arpeggios could be made to sound like the clicking of the car wheels."[19] Such imitation was possible only by listening closely to environmental sounds, recognizing their intrinsic interest, and trying to construct a similar sound from musical tones. While originating in an attitude of listening, this kind of imitation of extramusical sounds in music also depended to some extent on experimentation, as nontraditional musical techniques often had to be invented in order to reproduce the sound. In *Some "Quarter-tone" Impressions*, Ives tells of his father's trying to capture at the piano the "chord" produced by a church bell ringing in a thunderstorm. When he failed to reproduce what he was hearing, he built a machine that could produce quarter-tones in an attempt to find the right set of tones.[20] Charles took to this kind of imitation as well, trying to duplicate at the piano the indeterminate pitch of a drumbeat and resorting to complex dissonant chords to achieve the effect, which he referred to as "piano-drumming."[21]

The attitude of intent listening that Charles Ives absorbed from his father's open-mindedness was as important to his musical development as its twin, the experimental approach towards musical sound, although the latter has provoked more comment. Imitation of sounds and of the impressions or feelings associated with those sounds, especially with musical sounds, was to become a very important aspect of his mature style, an aspect almost wholly derived from his early experiences with his father. There is relatively little direct imitation of individual sounds in the music of his boyhood, and that which is present is fairly obvious text-painting of words such as *trumpet*[22] and *bell*.[23] But three early songs imitate or borrow appropriate musical styles or pieces of music: *Slow March* (ca. 1887), a memorial for a dead pet, uses the *Dead March* from Handel's *Saul* for the interludes in the piano; *Waltz* (ca. 1894) is a quick mindless waltz in the manner of Michael Nolan's *Little Annie Rooney*, which it quotes very briefly while the text comments on both the dance and the lady in question; and *The Circus Band* (ca. 1894), while quoting no preexisting marches, evokes the sound and spirit of a circus parade down Main Street, including an imitation of drumming in the piano, the earliest written instance of many uses of Ives's technique of piano-drumming described above. Imitation of sounds, both musical and nonmusical, became more important for Ives in his later music. In his last year at Yale, he wrote a short piece for orchestra, the *Yale-Princeton Football Game* (1898), which included the sound of each school's songs and cheers, the shouts and noise of the crowd, and the referee's whistle. His listening and trying to capture the sounds and feelings of what he heard underlie several works of the period leading up to his major mature compositions, such as *The Pond* (1906), an evocation of the sound of his father's trumpet echoing across a pond, *Central Park in the Dark* (1906), "a picture-in-sounds of the sounds of nature and happenings that men would hear some thirty or so years ago (before the combustion engine and radio monopolized the earth and air), when sitting on a bench in Central Park on a hot summer night,"[24] and the *Country Band March* (1903), an affectionate parody of the mistakes, missteps, and enthusiasms of an amateur band.

This listening with open ears and recording sounds and their related moods in musical form has nothing to do with Emerson's philosophy of art and little to do with his philosophy at all. Emerson's own reaction to amateur players was never so kind or affectionate,[25] and he seems to have found no music in the natural blur of noises. Nor was he interested in music that was descriptive, programmatic, or anything but abstract. But Thoreau entirely shares this intent listening attitude. In the opening pages of his Thoreau essay, Ives pays tribute to this aspect of Thoreau's contemplation:

> Thoreau was a great musician, not because he played the flute but because he did not have to go to Boston to hear "the Symphony." . . .
> Thoreau's susceptibility to natural sounds was probably greater than that of many practical musicians. True, this appeal is mainly through the sensational element which Herbert Spencer thinks the predominant beauty of music. [But] Thoreau seems able to weave from this source some perfect transcendental symphonies [pages 51, 53].

Towards the end of the same essay, Ives quotes (with some alteration) a passage from *Sounds*, the fourth chapter of *Walden*:

> Sometimes, on Sundays, I heard the bells, the Lincoln, Acton, Bedford, or Concord bell, when the wind was favorable, a faint, sweet, and, as it were, natural melody, worth importing into the wilderness. At a sufficient distance over the woods this sound acquires a certain vibratory hum, as if the pine needles in the horizon were the strings of a harp which it swept. All sound heard at the greatest possible distance produces one and the same effect, a vibration of the universal lyre, just as the intervening atmosphere makes a distant ridge of the earth interesting to our eyes by the azure tint it imparts to it.[26]

The interest in both man-made and natural sounds, in how they mix together, and in the effects of distance on sound is an attitude Charles Ives shared with his father—who experimented with the spacing of groups of performers and with playing music from a distance, as well as with imitating sounds he heard—and with Thoreau. It is quite possible that Ives recognized this connection during his teens, if he was in fact familiar with *Walden* at that time. In any case, like his self-reliance, this aspect of Ives's musical personality did not become fully realized before his maturity. Although not closely related to the three principal ideas of dualism, idealism, and reliance on intuition and experience outlined in Chapter 2 above, the attempt to evoke in music the natural and musical sounds he heard was fundamental to Ives's idea of a music that represents life experiences.

It was from his father that Charles Ives first derived his interests in music and in exploring musical technique, both of which flowered into passions. George's ideal of spirit-centered performance stayed with Charles throughout his life, though it was not until later that he began to make similar spiritual demands on himself as a composer—not, indeed, until his mature works of 1908 and after. Perhaps the single most important contribution George Ives made to his son's development was his fascination with sound, leading to explorations of nontraditional techniques, an attention to environmental sound, and attempts to reproduce extramusical sounds through new musical means. His open-minded acceptance of dissonance and disorder paved the way for Charles Ives's later development of new techniques and methods for organizing sound.

LESSONS, SCHOOLS, AND CHURCHES

As a boy, Ives studied piano, drums, and organ with various teachers, in addition to the early lessons in music and continuing lessons in theory and composition that he received from his father, and from 1889 on, he held full-time positions as a church organist.[27] This solidified his musical training as a performer, but it also exposed him to the dualities of music-making in Danbury.

First, art was considered to be separate from life, something frivolous and perhaps a bit unreal. George Ives was never fully respected as a bandleader and musician, and his obituaries emphasized his work in business while slighting his work in music, which took more of his time and most of his commitment.[28] It was against this separation that Ives was later to assert the unity of art and life and the poverty of each when divorced from the other.[29]

Second, both Ives and his father had an interest in musical sound for its own sake, which was not shared by the rest of Danbury. Danbury's music was essentially utilitarian, comprising religious music for church and for revivals, entertainment music for holidays and business promotions, music for dancing or for singing at home, and genteel concerts staged less for the sake of the music than as proof of the town's cultural progress. Musicians did not make music for its own sake, but for a specific purpose, and Ives first learned to write music that served a specific need. Given these attitudes, it is not surprising that few in Danbury responded with any interest to George Ives's experiments with sound. It was not just the strange noises and effects that Danbury could not understand, but the notion that music might be listened to for its own sake, neither for entertainment nor for "self-improvement," but simply for its intrinsic interest. The wrestling in Ives's music between genres and forms that are clearly utilitarian—religious choral works, organ interludes, marches, parlor songs—and the urge to create a music worth listening to outside of its generic context is apparent for at least another decade after he left Danbury.

Third, and related to the above, a split between popular and genteel music divided the musical life of Danbury into two mutually antagonistic camps. What passed for classical or cultivated music—often the least enduring and most sentimental works in that tradition—was seen as entirely separate from popular or vernacular forms.[30] Partisans of each disdained the other, vernacular styles and uses of music being accused of baseness, while cultivated styles were dismissed as pretentious and foreign to American taste and ideals. Although George Ives's musical life was clearly split along generic lines—band music, camp-meeting hymns, orchestral concerts, and so on—he refused to make such a strong separation or to devalue either form of music-making and attempted to preserve the equilibrium of the two streams, in his own career at least.[31] This dichotomy between cultivated and vernacular traditions was one of the great problems of Charles Ives's career, one he ultimately resolved by incorporating the substance and character of vernacular music into works that in form, instrumentation, and aspiration were fully within the cultivated tradition.[32] However, this rapprochement did not happen in Danbury, and probably could not have, as restrictions of genre were too severe.

For the churches where he played, Ives wrote songs and choral works to religious texts and occasional organ solos that might have been performed as interludes during services or in the recitals that the churches' musical directors occasionally staged. For the bands in Danbury, he wrote marches, most often incorporating a familiar tune (such as *Son of a Gambolier, Annie Lisle* or *My Old Kentucky Home*) into one of the strains. For his counterpoint lessons with his father, he wrote canons, fugues, and a few more daring experimental pieces. Beyond these, he wrote only sentimental songs in the popular style. It would have been as impossible for Ives to incorporate band tunes or music-hall ballads into his organ preludes and choral works as to put fugues into his works for band. An integration of the two divergent streams of cultivated and vernacular styles could happen only in music that was intended to be listened to for its own sake, not music that was as closely tied to its function as a servant of church, business, or society as was music in Danbury. This blending of traditions came about for Ives only after he became familiar with the longer genres of European art music in a much more thorough way than was possible in Danbury, and it is primarily this knowledge that Ives gained from his Yale professor of music, Horatio Parker.[33]

Ives moved to New Haven in the early winter of 1893 to study at

Hopkins Grammar School, for the sole purpose of passing the Yale entrance examination. The first period of Ives's career comes to an end with his matriculation at Yale in September 1894, followed little more than a month later by the sudden death of his father on 4 November 1894. His father's death left him without his most important teacher and influence, making the transition into the next phase of his career more abrupt and complete.

CHAPTER SIX

Years of Apprenticeship (1894–1902): Yale and New York

When Ives entered Yale, just before his twentieth birthday, he was an accomplished organist, a skilled composer of band music and church anthems, and a facile songwriter in the popular style. Eight years later, after four years in college and four more in New York City as a full-time office worker and a part-time church musician, he resigned his last position as an organist, never to play music in public again. His resignation marked the end of his years of apprenticeship, years during which the focus of his music-making had almost completely shifted from the civic, utilitarian music of Danbury to the cosmopolitan tradition of classical music made and enjoyed for its own sake. During those years, Ives had written his first string quartet, his first orchestral overtures, his first two symphonies, his first *Lieder* and *mélodies*, his first piece of program music (the *Yale-Princeton Football Game*), his first cantata (*The Celestial Country*), and his first attempt at a sonata for violin and piano. If he had had boyhood dreams of leading a village band like his father, writing marches like David Wallis Reeves and John Philip Sousa, or cranking out hit tunes like Stephen Foster, those dreams were long gone by the end of his apprentice years. Indeed, of all the genres he had practiced in his youth, by 1902 he had abandoned every one but the song.[1]

The period between 1894 and 1902 is often seen as a time of regression, when Ives's creative experimentation, nurtured by his father, was driven underground by an unsympathetic musical establishment represented by Ives's professor of music at Yale, Horatio Parker. But such a view is far too simplistic. These are years not of regression, but of redirection and preparation. What Ives had learned at home, from how to write a march to how to rewrite the rules of fugal counterpoint, could hardly have prepared him to conceive and carry out the great sonatas and orchestral works of his maturity. While he would later reject much of what Parker taught him, his contact through Parker with the aspirations and achievements of the European tradition of classical music made it possible for him to recognize for the first time what was trivial, banal, and shallow in the musical traditions of Danbury. This disenchantment with the genres and attitudes of Danbury's vernacular and devotional music provided Ives with the intellectual distance that was essential for a composer who would later so successfully evoke in his music the sounds and feelings of the music he had known as a child. In order to wax nostalgic about that music, Ives first had to leave it behind; in order to write symphonies and sonatas that took the tunes and marches of his youth as their subject matter, Ives had to stop writing tunes and marches of his own. Ironically, the celebration of innocence required its loss, and paying tribute to the spirit and substance of vernacular music required forsaking its outward forms.

Far from representing a step backwards, then, Ives's experiences at Yale and in his first years in New York were vital in preparing him to choose his own path. During these years, he tried out and subsequently rejected each of the roles available to him within the musical establishment. At Yale, even while studying classical music with Parker, Ives reached the pinnacle of his success as a composer of marches, glees, and popular songs, only to abandon that side of his career almost completely upon graduation. In New York, he tried to make a career as a church musician, modeled to some extent on Parker's own career as an organist and composer, only to give that up as well. Ives continued to test the roles and question the aims of his music for some time before finding his distinctive voice and purpose as a composer a decade after leaving Yale, but his arrival at Yale marked the beginning of that period of testing and thus the most fundamental turning point of his career.

HORATIO PARKER

Horatio Parker (1863—1919), composer, conductor, organist, and professor of music at Yale, exercised the most profound and long-lasting influence on Ives's music of any of his associates in the decade after his father's death. Ives studied music with Parker for four years (1894—1898), first auditing Parker's classes as an underclassman, then registering for two music courses each year as a junior and senior, and probably having private lessons on occasion. Yale underclassmen were not

Horatio Parker

permitted to register for electives (which included all six available courses in music), but Ives showed Parker some of his compositions at the beginning of his freshman year, presumably audited Parker's courses in Harmony and The History of Music, and apparently wrote exercises for Parker throughout his college years.[2] The enrollment in all of these classes was always very small—around a dozen in the harmony and history classes and from one to three students in the courses in Counterpoint, Strict Composition (advanced counterpoint and fugue), and Instrumentation that Ives took as an upperclassman—and both teacher and student must have come to know thoroughly each other's opinions, capabilities, and limitations.[3]

At least two of Parker's attitudes strongly affected Ives: first, his rejection of the untraditional and experimental music Ives brought him, and second, his intense idealism about music. Ives mentions in the *Memos* some of Parker's reactions to his music, such as his calling an unresolved dissonance "inexcusable" (page 116), making a joke of Ives's fugues in four keys (page 49), and early in Ives's first year asking him "not to bring any more things like these into the classroom" (page 48).[4] Ives recognized a lost cause and "didn't bother him but occasionally" with his experiments after the first few months (page 49). However, Ives respected and to some extent absorbed Parker's idealism about music. He comments in the *Memos*,

> I had and have great respect and admiration for Parker and most of his music. It was seldom trivial—his choral works have a dignity and depth that many of [his] contemporaries, especially in the [field of] religious and choral composition, did not have. Parker had ideals that carried him higher than the popular but he was governed too much by the German rule, and in some ways was somewhat hard-boiled [page 49].[5]

These ideals are discussed in William Kearnes's dissertation on Parker and include "beliefs in individualism, personal virtue, duty, sacrifice, and service," "mental discipline, self-reliance, and self-improvement," a "belief in the necessity of progress" whose expression in music is a pragmatic eclecticism,[6] a preference for "strong" over "weak" music,[7] a belief in the spiritual and moral force of music,[8] and a rejection of music that is purely sensual or hedonistic.[9] These beliefs are entirely consonant with Ives's own ideals as stated in the *Essays*.[10] Moreover, Parker endorses a composer's reliance on intuition as strongly as does Ives:

> Music is the expression of feeling and not of [ordinary] feeling, but of musical feeling, and progress is made not by reasoning in the usual sense but

by intuition, instinct, and mostly by practice. . . . Musicians are not good at verbal logic for their support, their refuge and stay [is] on feeling and intuition. But the past has shown that cultivated feeling and educated intuition are not merely safe but the only guides for their essentially unlogical wishes.[11]

It is reasonable to assume that Parker's views made a great impression on the young Ives, as he mentions Parker's ideals almost forty years later in the *Memos*. While there are other sources for his ideas besides Parker, it seems clear, given the similarities between his own later aspirations and those of his teacher, that Ives fully incorporated Parker's high-minded beliefs about both music and personal conduct.

Parker's beliefs were not unique, of course; one reason Ives could accept Parker's ideas so fully was because both men shared the underlying moral assumptions of the time. What role Transcendentalism may have played in either man's thinking at this time is far from clear. Kearnes makes much of Parker's apparent agreement with the Transcendentalist point of view, citing parallels between Parker's statements and those of Emerson or other Transcendentalists,[12] but offers no proof of Transcendentalist influence on Parker. Rosalie Sandra Perry expands on this idea and implies that Parker drilled Transcendentalist ideas about music into his students, including Ives. Citing Kearnes, she asserts that Parker's "lectures often reiterated the dogmas of Emerson and the Transcendentalists. Ives wholeheartedly accepted these beliefs."[13] In fact, what Kearnes says is this:

> Transcendentalism, the American transposition of German idealism, reached its apex nearly two generations before Parker's time; however, its emphasis on spiritual resources, intuition, a priori truths, and individual inspiration maintained a powerful hold on the New England if not the entire American mind for the remainder of the nineteenth century. As much of a conscious philosophical position concerning the place of art in society as Parker managed to put together in the course of his lectures, speeches, and casual observations fits the dogmas of Emerson and his followers, as will be seen [page 8].

Kearnes claims only that Parker was a man of his times, a conformist "in a society certain of its values" (page 8), a society flavored with Puritanism as well as Transcendentalism. There is no evidence that Parker ascribed his ideals to Emerson, mentioned Emerson in his prepared lectures or classroom work, had ever read Emerson, or was in any way directly connected to or interested in the Transcendental school.[14] There is no way to prove that Parker did not mention Emerson or instill Transcendentalist "dogmas" in his students, but in the absence of any evidence one must assume that Ives absorbed at most some of his idealism, but not his Emerson, from Parker.

Perry suggests further (page 8) that Ives derived his ideas on manner and substance from Parker, citing a talk given in 1902 in which Parker objects to program music as exemplified by Richard Strauss and emphasizes "form and substance" as the foundation of music.[15] Ives and Parker agree in seeing Strauss's music as shallow striving for effect; very probably, Ives absorbed his negative view of Strauss directly from Parker, for teacher and student couch their criticisms of Strauss's music and aesthetics in strikingly similar terms. But their concepts of "substance" have nothing to do with each other. For Parker, music with substance is abstract, pure, concerned with form; he rejects extramusical associations entirely. Ives, however, groups form with manner,[16] dismisses the distinction between program and absolute music,[17] and includes in his representational music all the extramusical points of departure Parker sees in Strauss and explicitly rejects: "philosophy, religion, jokes, definite ideas, sometimes even physical happenings."[18] Perry may be right that Parker's point of view stimulated Ives's thinking, and perhaps even that Ives borrowed the term *substance* from his teacher, but he certainly did not derive his central aesthetic tenet, the distinction between manner and substance, from Parker. Instead, as will become clear below, Ives probably owes this dichotomy to an article by John C. Griggs, published more than a decade after Ives left Yale. What Ives did learn from Parker was a conception of music where such idealism could be appropriate; the idea that music might have substance in its own right was all but irrelevant to the utilitarian music for parlor, band, and church that Ives had written in his teens.

The ideals and aspirations for music that Ives shared with Parker were common to most composers of the cultivated tradition and served in part to distinguish the tradition of Bach, Beethoven, and Brahms from both the vernacular tradition Ives had learned from his father and the tradition of sentimental, relatively shallow devotional music pursued by many of Parker's contemporaries and familiar to Ives from his work as a church organist. This high plane of aspiration was of enormous importance to Ives and led to his placing increased demands on his own music, but it is not sufficient to explain Ives's ultimate aesthetic views. The concepts of manner and substance and the incorporation of life experience, chiefly represented by vernacular music, into the cultivated tradition—that is, the ideals that distinguish Ives's music from the tradition of Bach, Beethoven, and Brahms, as opposed to those that place him firmly in that tradition—are part of a later synthesis of Ives's views, not part of his heritage from Parker.

With Parker, Ives reviewed the same harmony textbook and covered some of the same problems of counterpoint as he had with his father, though at a more rigorous level.[19] The compositions from this period that were clearly done for Parker's classes are primarily songs in the severe style of German Lieder, often using German or French texts already famous in other settings (such as *Ich grolle nicht* and *Wie Melodien zieht es mir*), and works for orchestra. The *Postlude in F* (1895), adapted from a lost organ postlude of three years earlier, and the incomplete *Overture in G* (ca. 1895) are Ives's earliest surviving works for the standard symphony orchestra, indeed the first for any instrumental emsemble other than military band or theatre orchestra. Ives's *First String Quartet* (1896), by his own account, was "written for some of the revival services" held at Center Church, New Haven, where he was organist while at Yale,[20] but may also have been shown to Parker.[21] Except for its use of hymn tunes as a source of thematic material, this quartet is certainly of a piece with the instrumental music Ives was writing for Parker. The major work of his four years at Yale was his *First Symphony*, whose first movement was finished, according to the full score, in May 1895, near the end of his freshman year, and whose last three movements were written presumably in Ives's senior year. It is a fine student piece, reminiscent of Dvořák and other late Romantic composers—including Parker himself—and of a completely different mold from the instrumental works Ives had written before college.

In assigning abstract compositions in forms of the European tradition of art music, Parker offered Ives a means to free his music from the limitations of both aspiration and genre imposed by Danbury's cultural life. Even Parker's pieces for church choirs and choral societies, written for the purposes of worship and group singing, asserted in their quality and complexity an ideal of music as an abstract art that was worlds away from the strictly utilitarian music of Danbury. Here is where Parker exercised his most profound and enduring influence on the young Ives. George Ives had maintained an interest in both music and sound for their own sakes, outside their context in community life—an interest probably developed during his musical studies with Foeppl, as it was shared by few musicians in Danbury—but had offered his son no path to follow in composing an intrinsically interesting, personal music. The abstract ideal that Parker pursued offered Ives a new purpose for music, incorporating a conception of musical genre entirely distinct from Danbury's divisions between music for the church, music for entertainment, and music for genteel concerts: music in all forms and for all ensembles could serve the same master, the personal will of the composer, rather than responding to the requirements of the community for whose use it was written. When such music is shared, it is shared as is a book, a poem, a painting, or a conversation, rather than as is a billboard, a speech, or a meeting; even in public performance, the experience remains primarily a personal one.

Ives would eventually reject Parker's idea that music could remain abstract and would bend his compositions to imitation, representation, and moralistic or spiritual purposes. But, even when celebrating the holidays of his boyhood town, he came to adopt wholeheartedly the Romantic vision of music as a private experience, a story shared between a composer with a recognizable personality and an individual listener, rather than as an artifact made by a craftsman working in a common style for all to use together. In this respect, Ives learned not only European forms and techniques from Parker, but the very ethos of the European Romantic composer. Indeed, Ives went far beyond Parker in his Romantic individualism, for Parker wrote in a style that conformed closely to both his European models and his American contemporaries such as Edward MacDowell, George Whitefield Chadwick, and John Knowles Paine, while Ives has become the model for later generations of the individual composer who pursues his own path, speaking with his own voice.

Horatio Parker's strong personality helped to set up a central dichotomy in Ives's musical life, in which Ives's father and his major professor incarnated the opposing camps. This is clear from the ways in which Ives speaks of these two and plays one off against the other in the *Memos*. Part of this dualism can be traced back to Danbury, as it involves the separation between vernacular and cultivated traditions. Although George Ives had attempted to bridge that gap, in retrospect, and in comparison with Parker's strong distaste for popular music,[22] he came to represent vernacular music for Ives. Two new dichotomies were set up as well. First was a dichotomy between following a single path and choosing a kind of eclecticism; Parker's aesthetic rigidly excluded the vernacular tradition from his music, while George Ives, though never mixing cultivated and vernacular music within the same context, provided a model for his son of a musician who could move comfortably in both musical worlds. Second, both figures were theoretically minded—one of the few points of contact between them—but whereas George Ives had integrated his traditional theory with an experimental approach to musical sound and musical materials, Parker (as an instructor, at least)[23] was intolerant of deviations from the norm and uninterested in novel effects. On the one hand, Ives needed the rigorous training in counterpoint and longer musical forms that Parker gave him and was aided further in adopting the classical tradition by Parker's idealism and total devotion to that tradition. On the other, Ives gained immeasurably by preserving the open-mindedness, the willingness to experiment and the Thoreau-like attitude of intent listening, that he had learned from his father. Without the contributions of both of these mentors, Ives would not have had the technique to write the music he did; without the tension created by the dualities they came to represent in his mind, Ives would not have arrived at the aesthetic and musical synthesis he did. His compositional and aesthetic work for the decade after college was devoted to integrating these two major musical influences in his life and incorporating the music and attitudes they symbolized into a single musical and philosophical fabric.

During this period, however, there were other influences, philosophical, career-related, and personal, that helped to determine his course. Two of the principal achievements of that decade—discussed further in Chapters 7 and 8 below—would be a renewal of his self-confidence, a self-confidence seemingly worn away during his lessons with Parker,[24] and a concurrent healing of the deep divisions within his musical life.

VERNACULAR MUSIC AT YALE

The vernacular and experimental sides of Ives's musical personality were also nurtured at Yale, for the most part outside Parker's view. Rossiter sums up Ives's musical contributions to college life as consisting of humorous pieces, sentimental love ballads, and college songs, all of which "had, above all, a utilitarian purpose: the strengthening of the bonds of collegiate fellowship."[25] These included two songs published in the *Yale Courant* (*A Scotch Lullaby* and *A Song of Mory's*, both 1896), songs to words by Rudyard Kipling (for, or at least inspired by, the Kipling Club, one of several literary societies on campus), music for shows by his junior fraternity, Delta Kappa Epsilon (DKE), *The Bells of Yale* for the Glee Club (performed widely and regularly and later published in *Yale Melodies* of 1903), and other works in vernacular genres.

Particularly important for future developments were Ives's exposure to ragtime at Poli's, a vaudeville theatre in New Haven, through its piano player George Felsburg, and performances (or readings) of some of Ives's experimental pieces by the orchestra at the Hyperion Theatre in New Haven, led by Frank Fichtl.[26] Of these pieces, Ives wrote in the *Memos*,

> Some had old tunes, college songs, hymns, etc.—sometimes putting these themes or songs together in two or three differently keyed counterpoints (not exactly planned so but just played so)—and sometimes two or three different kinds of time and key and off-tunes, played sometimes impromptu. . . . The pianist (who was I, sometimes) played his part regardless of the off-keys and off-counterpoints, but giving the cue for the impromptu counterpoint parts, etc. [pages 39–40].

> When other similar things (half in fun, half serious) were tried, as I remember, there were usually one or two, either among the players or the listening students, who would be sort of interested and ask to have it played again. . . . Some said—one was Sid Kennedy—that it made the music stronger and better, after he had got used to it [page 41].

Ives also gained a certain measure of success beyond the walls of Yale. Although neither he nor his father had been able to secure publication for the most important work of his pre-Yale years, the *Variations on America*,[27] Ives arranged for the publication of three vernacular works during 1896: *William Will*, a Presidential campaign song for William McKinley; *For You and Me!*, a song for barbershop quartet or male choir; and the *March Intercollegiate* for band.[28] Perhaps as a reward for the campaign song, the march was played by the Washington Marine Band at McKinley's inauguration in March of 1897.[29] These publications and performances, both on campus and off, demonstrate Ives's substantial success as a musician in the vernacular tradition during his college years. That he turned away from composition in vernacular forms after his graduation, never again producing publishable popular music, is testimony to the influence of Parker and to the rise in Ives's level of aspiration for his music during his four years of studying composition in the European art tradition. Vernacular compositions could serve a purpose in the communities of Danbury and Yale, promoting worship or conviviality and playing a part in entertainment and celebration, but they did not allow Ives the level of personal expression offered by the Romantic conception of music. It would take Ives a decade to find his mature voice, but that journey would take place in the tradition Parker represented, into which the other aspects of his musical personality would be integrated. In vernacular music, that journey was not possible at all.

CENTER CHURCH AND JOHN CORNELIUS GRIGGS

Ives played the organ at Center Church of New Haven for the entire four years he was at Yale, and there he found a supportive colleague in the new choirmaster and baritone soloist, John Cornelius Griggs (1865–1932), who performed some of Ives's choral music and songs.[30] In the *Memos*, Ives described Griggs as "the only musician friend of mine that showed any interest, toleration, or tried to understand the way I felt (or what might be felt) about some things in music. . . . He didn't like all the things I wrote by any means, but he was always willing to listen and discuss anything seriously" (page 116).[31]

Ives particularly needed this open-mindedness after his father's death, as a counterweight to Parker's mockery. For instance, after they had heard Ives's *Prelude and Postlude for a Thanksgiving Service*, the 1897 organ prototype for *Thanksgiving*, "Parker made some fairly funny cracks about it, but Dr. Griggs said it had something of the Puritan character, a stern but outdoors strength, and something of the pioneering feeling. He liked it as such, and told Parker so" (*Memos*, page 39). In a letter to Griggs in 1930, Ives paid tribute to Griggs for helping to "fill up that awful vacuum" after his father's death.[32]

Ives kept in touch with Griggs after leaving New Haven,[33] sent Griggs his *Concord Sonata* and *Essays* when they were printed, and received in return "what may be the most significant critique of the *Essays* he ever received."[34] Griggs praises the Emerson and Thoreau essays in a single sentence, reserving his major criticisms for the Prologue; one must assume that his main interest in the work is in its philosophy of music, rather than in Transcendentalism itself. Griggs focuses on the question of "the translatableness of music," "a direction in which I can see no light."[35] This concern echoes his statement, in an article on Debussy that Ives knew and cited in the Epilogue to his *Essays* (page 81), regretting a rise in the popularity of descriptive instrumental music, whose "full appreciation [is] dependent upon extraneous and non-musical ideas, and a corresponding decrease in the amount of music claiming undivided attention for its intrinsic musical thought."[36] It is interesting that immediately after this passage Griggs defends Debussy's very descriptive music as interesting "more often through its absolute content than through its descriptive value"—words that are perhaps equally true of Ives's music—for to admit

John Cornelius Griggs

that Debussy's music succeeded only in extramusical terms would have been, for Griggs, to condemn it.

Griggs's opinion that music cannot directly represent or describe things or actions remained consistent throughout his life. In an essay entitled *The Literary Work of Richard Wagner*, written in 1887 while a student at Yale, Griggs had argued that Wagner turned to drama precisely so that music could find more definite means of expression, considering music itself to be intrinsically indefinite, an art that "may be interpreted according to every man's individual mood or desire."[37] In his letter to Ives, Griggs writes with passion that music's very nature calls it beyond the material, beyond memory or that which can be put into words, the very places to which Ives is trying to take it.

> Art is a projection into a realm beyond the understandable. . . .
> Music is preeminent (because of its aloofness from spoken word, material form or temporal thought) in piercing this realm and making of this prophecy a definite super realization, a living experience. Why insist on always turning it back to a review of the understood and past experience,— to the commonplaces of reason and intellect? Why demand that it should be always a review of yesterdays, or even of the impressions which yesterdays have brought?[38]

Just as words and memories should not be translated into music, Griggs argues, so music cannot be translated into words, because the words that try to describe musical experience are too vague. "The experience as glimpsed on the higher plane in music is not vague, but explicit, complete, self substantial, as easy of identification and memory as baldest fact or event and to some of us as precious. Only the attempted translation into the terms of more ordinary fact is vague."[39] From these criticisms and from the similar concerns revealed in his published writings, it is clear that Griggs lent no support to Ives's ideas of representing life experience or philosophical ideas in music.

Yet, in his article on Debussy, Griggs poses the question of the relationship of "manner" to "content" in very similar terms to Ives's dichotomy of "manner" and "substance" (page 484), concluding of Debussy that "his novelty of expression is inevitable because of the novelty of his thought" (page 494). Ives does not arrive at the same conclusion about Debussy's music—he suggests that "Debussy's content would have been worthier his manner if he had hoed corn or sold newspapers for a living," or "if his adoration of Nature . . . had been more the quality of Thoreau's" —but he adopts Griggs's dichotomy completely for his own discussion of Debussy in the *Essays*.[40]

If there is one single most important source for Ives's conception of a duality between manner and substance in music, it must be Griggs. The source is most likely to be this article from 1912, and presumably the discussions Ives and Griggs shared in the 1910s, rather than their conversations from the Yale years, for two reasons.

First, the idea of "manner" as opposed to "content" or "substance" does not seem to have been part of Ives's thinking about music in college. As late as the *Second Symphony* of 1900–1902, he was still clearly working within Parker's equation of substance with form, fitting his music into clearly defined genres derived from the European art-music tradition. Indeed, there is evidence in the early drafts of *Essays Before a Sonata*— undatable, but certainly no earlier than the mid-1910s—to suggest that the dichotomy between manner and substance became fixed in Ives's mind only while actually writing the *Essays*. In the fourth page of notes, the words *substance* and *manner* appear in the margin as generic names for categories already roughed out on the page, and in subsequent pages they reappear embedded in the text.[11] Ives had probably been aware of this duality for some time but seems first to name it in these notes, apparently relying partly on Griggs's terminology. Ives found the dichotomy useful in explaining his attempts to portray spiritual values in music, in the context of the *Concord Sonata*, but it is clear that his explanation is retrospective; like Griggs, he uses this dichotomy to examine the content of a musical work separate from its technique, in part as a way to justify the extraordinary techniques used in the sonata. Those who would take the issue of manner and substance as the wellspring of Ives's aesthetic credo and apply it without hesitation to the works appearing before his mature period and before his formulation of this idea may be treading on very shaky historical and theoretical ground.

Second, the other issues Griggs discusses in his articles of the 1910s can be traced back to earlier periods of his life, whereas this dichotomy cannot. Indeed, it seems to have been freshly invented specifically for the troublesome case of Debussy, as Griggs temporarily sought to put aside the issue of Debussy's shockingly untraditional method in order to address the question of musical meaning alone. Briefly, Griggs's principal interests seem to lie in the literary aspects of music. More than half of the article on Debussy is devoted to Debussy's "well-nigh perfect" settings of text and mood in his songs and opera. In his last published article on music, *The Influence of Comedy Upon Operatic Form*,[42] as in his undergraduate essay on *The Literary Work of Richard Wagner*, Griggs concentrates on the dramatic aspects of operatic form, conceiving music as an element contributing to opera's power and unity as drama. His literary efforts in college—his essays for the *Literary Magazine* discuss poetry, literature, and politics as well as music—and his eventual appointment as a professor of English at Canton both demonstrate a lifelong interest and competence in literature. In contrast to these concerns, discussion of the dichotomy between content and manner in music can be found only in the 1912 article on Debussy.

Griggs's concerns for declamation and proper illustration of a text, natural for a professional singer and choirmaster and evident in his writings, must have been an important influence on Ives's vocal compositions during his Yale years, perhaps particularly on the works Griggs performed. His sincere religiosity and interest in music as an element of church worship, demonstrated in his article *The Pastor and His Choir*[43] and in his other writings on religious music, must have reinforced and molded Ives's own quite similar attitudes as a church musician. Further, Ives's insistence that enharmonic equivalents are not necessarily the same, even on the equal-tempered piano—a view that led him occasionally to notate strange chromatic intervals in place of their simple diatonic equivalents— may owe something to Griggs's interest in pure intonation.[44] But in other respects Ives parts company with Griggs, disputing for instance the latter's argument for the naturalness of the major scale,[45] as well as his more positive evaluation of Wagner and Debussy.

It is clear that the two men respected each other's opinions and that Ives learned a great deal from Griggs. It was important to Ives to be able to talk with a fellow musician about theoretical and even philosophical issues in music, though they seem to have disagreed as often as they agreed, judging both by the written opinions each has left and by Ives's impressions of their conversations. Griggs's main contribution during the Yale years may simply have been to have taken Ives's novel ideas and experimental music seriously at a time when no other musician of Ives's acquaintance would do so or would offer him such careful criticism—or listen to them at all without smiling. Finally, it was probably Griggs, through his 1912 article on Debussy and his talks with Ives face to face more than a decade after Ives left New Haven, who stimulated Ives to formulate his dichotomy of manner and substance, a concept that lies at the heart of the aesthetic he presents in *Essays Before a Sonata*.

WILLIAM LYON PHELPS

There was another major influence on Ives during his Yale years, a figure who has received no attention from Ives scholars despite his appar-

William Lyon Phelps

ent importance in shaping Ives's literary interests, possibly including his enthusiasm for the Concord school. This was William Lyon Phelps (1865–1943), who taught Ives English Literature in his freshman and sophomore years and nineteenth-century American Literature in his senior year.[46] Phelps was extremely popular with students at Yale,[47] and, given Ives's choice to study with him more than with any other professor except Parker and Ives's relatively good performance in his classes,[48] it is apparent that Ives respected Phelps deeply and learned a great deal from him. Ives himself paid tribute to Phelps's influence as a teacher and expressed the deep affection he still felt in a letter he wrote to Phelps in 1937, almost forty years after graduating from Yale.

> I can't close without telling you something that I know you know. All Yale men, even those who went to Princeton, have the same feeling of affection and gratitude to you that I have. Mine reaches far back. I can never forget you behind that white teacher's desk (probably once a pulpit) in the little classroom under Old Chapel. It was not only the natural and unusual way you had of stirring the mind and arousing enthusiasm that stands out in my memory, but—you always looked as if you thought everybody knew just as much as you did. Emerson they say had the same way with him.[49]

Ives mentions Phelps in the *Essays* (page 26), and argues at their close (pages 100–101) for reading literature and philosophy in a striking parallel to Phelps's own views as articulated in his *Autobiography*: "Nothing is more essential in the proper furnishing of a man's mind than a knowledge of the world's best literature."[50]

The impact of Phelps's teaching can be judged, in part, from the fact that Ives set to music many of the poets that he had studied or probably studied with Phelps. This includes two late songs, *A Sea Dirge* (1925), to a text from Shakespeare's *Tempest*, and *Evening* (1921), an excerpt from Milton's *Paradise Lost*, both studied in Phelps's sophomore English Literature class,[51] and settings of poems by Keats, Wordsworth, Browning, Byron, Shelley, and Tennyson, the six poets whom Phelps identified in a slender publication as *The Pure Gold of Nineteenth Century Literature*[52] and who were certainly the focus of the study of poetry in his class. Other poets Phelps discusses in print, and presumably discussed in the courses that Ives took with him, include Robert Louis Stevenson, Matthew Arnold, Landor, Kipling, Whitman, and Whittier, all of whom Ives also set to music. One of Ives's most ambitious projects, never completed, was a series of "overtures representing literary men," including Browning, Emerson, Whitman, Arnold, Whittier, and Henry Ward Beecher.[53] Of these, Phelps published essays or books on all but the last.[54] It seems that for much of his music during the thirty years after graduation, Ives continued to be inspired by the parts of his literature professor's reading list that he found most attractive. This is not to imply that there were not other influences—Ives's wife Harmony was a particularly avid reader and an important influence on his taste in books—but simply that Ives's tastes conformed quite closely to those of his teacher.

Some of the roots of the *Concord Sonata* reach back to Phelps's course on American Literature, where Ives must have studied Emerson, Thoreau, Hawthorne, and the Alcotts in depth, some perhaps for the first time in a classroom setting. The essay on Emerson that Ives submitted to the *Yale Literary Magazine* during his senior year, only to have it "promptly handed back," was probably written for this course.[55]

It is tempting to credit Phelps with inspiring or at least rekindling Ives's interest in Emerson and the Concord school. And yet, Phelps was not as devoted to Concord as Ives later became, and cannot have enkindled such a great enthusiasm in Ives solely by his own example. In his voluminous published writings, Phelps wrote only one essay each on Emerson, Hawthorne, and Thoreau, and none on the Alcotts.[56] Although a few passing quotations from Emerson are scattered throughout Phelps's *Autobiography*, it was Robert Browning's poetry that he found "paramount," after reading the works for himself around 1890 with the intensity of a conversion experience,[57] and he cannot in any sense be considered a Transcendentalist. In contrast to Ives, Phelps considered Emerson's poems to be the peak of his achievement, whereas Ives cites the essays almost exclusively and set to music only one brief quatrain of Emerson's poetry (*Duty*, from *Voluntaries*). It is true that in his essay on Emerson, Phelps summarizes the Concord school of literature much as would Ives, adding Margaret Fuller: "Emerson was the Head; his chief disciple was Thoreau, whose fame brightens with the passage of time; Margaret Fuller and the Alcotts (A. Bronson Alcott's chief contribution to the world was Louisa) of course belong here; Hawthorne lived in Concord, and the whole New England galaxy were profoundly influenced by the emanations from the village."[58] But this essay originated as a lecture in 1922, composed after Phelps had reviewed Ives's *Essays* for the *Yale Alumni Weekly*,[59] making it impossible to tell whether Ives got his ideas about the Concord group from Phelps, or the other way around.[60] There is no clear indication, possibly excepting Ives's college essay on Emerson, to suggest that Emerson dominated either Phelps's thinking or Ives's during the time Ives was in college.

What can be assumed is that Phelps taught Emerson with sympathy and passion (his references to Emerson in his *Autobiography* and his essay on Emerson are entirely sympathetic), that Ives read Emerson in the same spirit, that Ives became excited enough about Emerson to submit his essay to the *Literary Magazine*—which may have been a daring step for a generally poor student such as Ives—and that seeds were planted that Ives would eventually develop. If Ives had read Emerson before, his experience with Phelps must have revived his enthusiasm; if he had not, Phelps's importance for Ives's later philosophy is clear. Even if Phelps only encouraged Ives to read as an adult books he had already known about during his years in Danbury, the contact with Emerson's writings themselves was an important step on the road to Ives's later thought. The level of intensity of Ives's enthusiasm for Emerson by the time he graduated from Yale, however, cannot be fully determined, as we lack not only the senior essay, but also any other notes from the period about Emerson, and any clear testimony from Ives himself. Whatever Ives's interest at this time, there is no further hint of Emerson's importance to him for almost a decade.

FIRST YEARS IN NEW YORK (1898–1902)

Upon his graduation from Yale in June of 1898, Ives moved to New York City and took a job in the actuarial department of the Mutual Life Insurance Company, a position he secured through his father's second cousin, Granville White.[61] He worked in insurance for the next thirty-two years, until his retirement in 1930 from his own agency, Ives & Myrick, founded in 1909.

Much has been written about Ives's decision to enter the insurance business rather than make a career of music, beginning with his own self-justifications and the writings of his associates before his death. These either assert the wholeness of existence and the indivisibility of art and life[62] or defend his money-making activities in business on practical grounds, arguing that they allowed him to support his family without compromising his ideals as a composer.[63] Both of these arguments suggest a conscious decision not to rely upon music as a source of income, and most scholars assume that this decision must have preceded Ives's entering business in New York.[64]

Rossiter has made the interesting point that, given the choice of Yale over a professional conservatory, Ives's family may never have intended him to pursue music as a career.[65] This suggestion is supported by George Ives's experience, for despite his rigorous musical training, the elder Ives had never consciously aimed at a full-time career in music[66] and began and ended his adult life in Danbury concentrating most of his time on business.[67] Rossiter's surmise is apparently confirmed by a letter Charles Ives wrote to his father in the spring of 1894, telling of his being turned down for the position of organist at the Baptist church in New Haven and outlining his plans for music lessons over the next few months:

> The first thing I am going to get the best of is the harmony & counterpoint, which I ought to get through with out taking much time to it with Dr. Stoeckel. There is some kind of a music course in college which I will look up. I think it can be taken with out any extra charge and may be substituted with other things. . . . I think that my aim ought to be now to improve in the things that I wouldn't have time to do with the church work, and also to see and look out for some place in N. Y. for next year.
>
> Haven't I enough money in the bank to pay what is necessary for my music lessons next fall?[68]

Ives clearly did not go to Yale with the idea of studying music; if he had, he would have known what the music course included. Even as late as the date of this letter, Ives cannot have known that Parker would be teaching at Yale, for Parker's first term on the faculty was in the fall of 1894. As much as his ultimate musical personality owed to Parker, Ives seems simply to have stumbled upon him as a teacher. It seems clear, too, that Ives's primary prospects in music at this point were as an organist, and that he considered his musical studies separate from his academic course-work rather than intrinsic to it. All of this would tend to confirm the view that Ives studied at Danbury Academy and Hopkins Grammar School with the sole intention of qualifying for entry to Yale, and that he viewed his studies at Yale as having little to do with music.

The family had chosen Yale for Charles not as a preparation for any specific career but as an institution.[69] Yale was a part of the Ives heritage. Charles's great-grandfather Isaac Ives had been the first and only previous member of the Ives family to graduate from Yale, in 1785. Charles's uncle Joseph Moss Ives had been sent to Yale in the 1850s but was taken out after playing a prank in his sophomore year, and the other men of the Ives family, from Isaac's generation down to Charles's, had gone directly into business without going to college.[70] George Ives's two boys were the youngest of their generation and the family's last hope as students at Connecticut's most prestigious college. His intense efforts to get his children into Yale may have been part of an attempt to redeem himself in the eyes of his family, who saw his working in music instead of achieving success in business as "a breach of the traditions" of the financially success-ful Iveses and of the expectations of Danbury society.[71] Both Charles and Moss attended Yale, the latter graduating from the Law School in 1899 after only one year of study, having served previously as an apprentice to his uncle Lyman Brewster.[72]

Qualifying the view that Ives had planned to go into business by the time he entered Yale, however, is Ives's continuing to work professionally as an organist for four years after graduation. He seems even to have secured his first church position in the New York area, at the Presbyterian church in Bloomfield, New Jersey, before graduation and before beginning work at Mutual Life Insurance Company in New York.[73] In fact, Ives made no clear-cut decision to make his career in business rather than in music before April 1902, when he resigned from his last regular appointment as an organist, at Central Presbyterian Church in New York, where he had moved from the Bloomfield church in the spring of 1900. Nor does he seem at any point to have considered trying to make his way solely as a composer of serious music. Although he had submitted pieces for publication from his youth on and had succeeded in publishing a few short pieces while in college, the career in music that he may have seen as an alternative to business, the career he renounced in 1902, was primarily that of a performer, not a composer.

George White Ives, Charles's grandfather, had given each of his first three children music lessons, only to abandon the attempt when they all proved unmusical. However, when his youngest child, George Edward Ives, showed both musical talent and a great deal of interest, he was eager to provide him with good musical training.[74] George Edward Ives, not surprisingly, followed his father's example in giving his children music lessons, teaching them himself. Music theory was included as part of these lessons, but, as in his own case, harmony and counterpoint were considered a foundation for musicianship rather than as the central concern.

Harmony Ives remembered that George's ambitions for his son Charles were in the field of performance rather than composition: "Charlie's father had wanted him to be a concert pianist, but he was much too shy—he couldn't face that being-alone on the stage in front of an audience."[75] Although Charles appeared in recital as a child[76] and remained an excellent pianist throughout his life—as both the complexity of his piano-writing and the assuredness of his solo recordings from the 1930s and 1940s attest[77]—his shyness made performing in public unpleasant for him. As an organist, however, he had no problems playing for an audience, perhaps because he was normally out of sight of the congregation. His talent as an organist was substantial, and he was something of a prodigy; when he was fifteen, the *Danbury Evening News* cited him as "the youngest organist in the state."[78] In Danbury, and later in

New York, he was primarily known as an organist, not as a composer. Indeed, his compositions throughout the time he worked as an organist fall into two principal groups: (1) pieces written as exercises, whether for his studies at home, for Parker's courses at Yale, or as experiments in musical technique, and (2) works for immediate use, usually performances in which he participated. Ives's strong theoretical bent prompted an interest in composing, not just experimenting as his father had done, and this interest was deepened by his studies with Parker, who believed that it was the primary role of university schools of music to train composers and had designed the program at Yale accordingly.[79] Yet, by and large, Ives's composing remained subordinate to his playing, as long as he was performing regularly. It was only after the spring of 1902, when he resigned his last position as an organist, that he turned seriously to composing as an end in itself, writing pieces for their own sakes, not for use in a church or as part of a community celebration, not to please an intended audience, and not as part of a course of study or as a technical challenge. As a result, his compositions gradually came to conform to neither the generic restraints of civic music nor the genres of abstract music he had learned from Parker.

During his first four years in New York, Ives wrote primarily for organ and choir. His works from this period include four choral *Psalms* (100, 14, 25, and 135), the three *Harvest Home Chorales*,[80] other anthems that have presumably been lost, and numerous organ preludes, interludes, and postludes that do not survive, except in adaptations for other instruments, and may never have been written down in final form. These pieces were written for use at the churches where Ives performed, and several were presented either during services or in recital. Outside of his church music, although he was no longer taking composition lessons, Ives kept up the habit of composing in the forms on which Parker had concentrated. During these years, he wrote more than a dozen songs in the serious style he had learned at Yale, six of them in German or French (like many of the songs he wrote for Parker), and worked on two major instrumental works, completing most of the *Second Symphony* and two movements of a projected sonata for violin and piano (called the "Pre-First Violin Sonata" by Kirkpatrick). These share the character of Ives's exercises in composition from his college years, in two respects: they continue the same kind of musical forms and ideas that Ives had learned from Parker, and they were written with no immediate prospects of performance—as it turned out, the symphony did not receive its first public hearing until fifty years later. While they demonstrate some of

Ives's individuality, particularly in his uses of existing music, these works
also show a close adherence to Parker's example, as Ives tried to prove
himself as a composer in the manner of his teacher. These works, then,
are functional in another way: not written for immediate use, they seem to
have been written instead in the hope of gaining a reputation as a composer and employment as a teacher of music as well as a performer.

Ives understood perfectly well the predicament of the composer of
serious music in American musical life. Parker, who was relatively lucky in
being able to teach and to work as an organist and conductor to support
his compositional activities, put it quite bluntly:

> The money rewards of a serious composer are slender at best, and most
> precarious, especially in this country. Excepting a few men who devote
> themselves chiefly to light opera or dance music, the writer knows not one
> composer in America who can possibly live by the exercise of his chosen
> vocation. One who aspires to compose must therefore be prepared to
> content himself with little beyond his work.[81]

For Ives, it was not a question of having his children "starve on his
dissonances," since it was the serious character of the kind of music Parker
and Ives had in mind that made it unpopular and unprofitable, not its
level of dissonance. No one, not even Parker, could make a living as a
serious composer in the turn-of-the-century United States. Although Ives
had achieved some success during his college years with his music in a
popular vein, including securing publication for three of his pieces, and
although popular music offered the chance of a career writing music, Ives
seems to have completely absorbed Parker's commitment to cultivated
music of the highest quality, since he stopped writing vernacular music
entirely when he left college. If he wished to compose in the tradition of
serious music, Ives would have had to support himself through positions
as a performer and—if possible—a teacher, as did Parker. As long as he
did so, he had ready opportunities for performing his works, even though
their high level of dissonance and difficulty might make performances
hard to bring off. But without a position, there was almost no possibility of
arranging performances. Despite the impossibility of surviving as a composer, the idea of a career in music was not unreasonable as long as Ives
had a position to build on and some hope for advancement.

Thus, Ives's resignation in 1902 of his position as organist at Central
Presbyterian Church, the last post in music he ever held, was a major step
in his life. In his *Memos*, he referred to it as the time "when I resigned as a
nice organist and gave up music" (page 57).[82] This is more than an ironic
comment, for this "giving up music" involved not only leaving the church

position but abandoning his aspirations for a career in music as well. Ives took this step in apparent disillusionment, after his attempts to gain recognition or a more distinguished position bore no fruit. His hopes for advancement were apparently pinned on his status as a student of Parker and on his ability to write music in the style and of the quality of his teacher's, however far that may have been from the style of his dissonant and experimental music for church choir, and his failure ultimately led to a radical change in the purpose and style of his music.

Victor Fell Yellin has suggested that Ives wrote *The Celestial Country* (1898–1899), a cantata for organ, chorus, soloists, and orchestra, which was performed at the church only a week before Ives announced his resignation, "in a style calculated to meet the taste and level of his contemporary audience, publishers, critics, and colleagues."[83] Ives had identified himself to the newspapers as Parker's student and had clearly modeled both text and music of his cantata on Parker's oratorio *Hora novissima*, which had helped to secure for Parker his appointment at Yale. The whole production seems to have been intended to establish Ives's reputation as an organist-composer in the Parker mold. If that was indeed its purpose, judging by the pleasant but patronizing reviews, the concert and the work were utter failures, as they made no great impact on the musical public and failed to secure for Ives either publication or a position as a teacher and composer. Yellin implies that it was this failure that finally prompted Ives, days after seeing the reviews,[84] to abandon music as a career and turn all of his attention to insurance, an arena in which he could succeed.

It is very likely that this disappointment led Ives to give up any hope of accommodating himself to the kind of musical life exemplified by Parker and to enter wholeheartedly the life in business that he had already begun—a career in which he had not yet had notable success. But it is also clear that this threw Ives back onto his own resources as a composer, freeing him from weekly performances and casting him into an isolation in which his music needed to conform only to what he wished for it. Ives comments in the *Memos*, "I seemed to have worked with more natural freedom, when I knew that the music was not going to be played before the public, or rather before people who couldn't get out from under, as is the case in a church congregation" (page 128). Only in isolation, away from the needs of a congregation, away from the conformism of the academic tradition of Parker and his contemporaries,[85] and away from the vernacular music-making of the Danbury Band or the Hyperion Theatre Orchestra in New Haven, could Ives integrate the diverse musical influences he had encountered, rethink his artistic philosophy, and begin to write the music we now consider his most characteristic. Beginning in 1902, for the first time, Ives could write music without considering its effect on his career, without having to fit it into a genre or a slot in an upcoming performance, writing only to please himself.

Thus the spring of 1902 marks the second great turning point of Ives's life, as important as his entering Yale and losing his father in 1894, and more so than his graduation from college in 1898. The whole period of 1894–1902, from the time Ives entered Yale to the time he finally quit his last regular church appointment, may be seen as a time of learning and testing, briefly trying out the musical and social role of the vernacular musician while at Yale and subsequently aspiring to a career modeled on that of Parker, the well-established performer, academic, and composer. Simultaneously, while at Yale and in New York, Ives was laying the groundwork for a career in business. When he decided to break his ties with music as a paying profession and make his fortune in insurance, the music he wrote began to take a radically different turn.

CHAPTER SEVEN

Innovation and Synthesis
(1902–1908)

At this point, we may pause to take stock of the twenty-seven-year-old Ives's progress towards the views of music outlined in Chapter 2. Besides a devotion to music and a strong sense of discipline, Ives had absorbed from his father George an ideal of open-mindedness, manifested in a self-reliant experimentalism and an attitude of intent listening. These attitudes had gone underground in his studies with Parker but had been kept alive by his contacts with Griggs and with some of his Yale classmates. After 1902, they came to have increasing importance in Ives's philosophy, the experimental orientation emerging in a renewed interest in trying things out to see how they worked, and the listening attitude revealing itself in a series of pieces evoking Ives's impressions of sounds, chiefly musical sounds in outdoor settings.

From Danbury's splintered cultural life and the dichotomy between George Ives and Horatio Parker, Ives came to a view of music that was thoroughly dualistic, even when he attempted to integrate his own varied experience. In his lessons with Parker, Ives found his idealism about classical music—a typically Romantic high-mindedness—strengthened and shaped, and his command of technique deepened. Unlike the music of Danbury or the vernacular music he wrote at Yale, which always served a specific purpose within a community context, the genres and forms that Parker introduced to Ives were part of a tradition that conceived of music as an end in itself and emphasized the personality of the composer and the individual experience of the listener. Ives adopted both the genres and the attitudes of this tradition and, although he was later to move away from abstract musical forms, he retained the conception of music as a private rather than a community experience for the rest of his life;

indeed, this tendency was intensified during the period of his isolation from 1902 on.[1] After writing his *First Symphony* for Parker and absorbing his teacher's aspirations for what might be accomplished in music, Ives found it philosophically impossible to make his way writing marches and sentimental songs in the manner of the most popular composers of the time, and he abandoned completely the career as a vernacular musician that had still seemed a clear option during his youth. From William Lyon Phelps, Ives drew his fondness for literature and renewed or developed an appreciation for Emerson that grew out of the broader philosophical tradition of the Ives family. After his resignation as an organist, Ives no longer attempted to conform to the pattern set for him by Parker and his musical contemporaries and began to follow his own path.

The integration of both philosophy and musical method that took place over the next several years was aided by two complementary factors: Ives's isolation and his growing sense of reliance on his own intuition and experience. He had been writing music with the expectation that it would be performed in his presence and fairly soon after its composition. With the possibilities of performance greatly diminished and the chance of publication almost nil, Ives turned to different genres and different musical aims.

Vernacular Styles and Fictional Music

Ives wrote no more music for organ solo or church choir after 1902, although he later reconstructed (or recomposed) the lost *Psalm 90* (first version ca. 1894–1901, final version 1923–1924). When he left his position at Central Presbyterian Church, he left behind most of his choral and organ music.[2] Perhaps he realized that he would never have any use for those works again; he was leaving behind not just a position, but also the genres and purposes for music associated with it. Ives also wrote very few songs between 1902 and his collaborations with Harmony Twichell four years later, instead turning his energies primarily to instrumental music. He began to write solo piano music, something he had hardly done since his boyhood marches, and pieces for chamber ensemble with piano, which he had never done at all, except for his first attempt at a violin sonata (the "Pre-First"), of which two movements were sketched by 1901.

At the same time that he chose to write for these combinations of instruments, placing himself firmly within the cultivated tradition, Ives began to turn back to vernacular styles, back to a kind of music he had virtually ignored during his first four years in New York because he had

had no outlet for its performance and no longer had an interest in publishing vernacular works. The switch in keyboard instruments from organ to piano seems to coincide with Ives's abandoning the cultivated church style for the rowdier tradition of ragtime piano, as if each instrument were endowed with the character of the music Ives had heard and had played on it.

But there was a new twist: the *Ragtime Pieces* (or *Ragtime Dances*, 1902–1904), for piano solo or for theatre orchestra with piano, and the *Country Band March* (1903) for theatre orchestra are no longer simply vernacular pieces but are concert pieces that are "about" vernacular styles and vernacular performance, quoting tunes, using familiar ragtime rhythms, and evoking the spirit and atmosphere of performances by amateur musicians, including written-out "mistakes" in the manner of Mozart's *Musical Joke*. These pieces, especially the *March*, begin to approach the character of fiction, operating on more than one level. The audience is presumably aware that the musicians playing for them are "supposed to be" playing these wrong notes, and thus must hear their performance as a description of another performance by a different set of musicians in a different setting for a different audience. These works invite their listeners to imagine themselves in a tavern listening to a ragging pianist—perhaps even a mechanical piano—or at a country fair listening to a band.[3]

These pieces of 1902–1904 fall between the earlier *Waltz* and *The Circus Band*, which remained respectively a waltz-song and a march-song while commenting on their own genres, and the mature symphonic works like *Washington's Birthday* (1909), *Decoration Day* (1912), and *Putnam's Camp* (1911–1912, the second movement of *Three Places in New England*), which are clearly not vernacular pieces yet include barn dances and marching bands in their musical landscapes. The *Ragtime Pieces* and *Country Band March* are still for theatre orchestra, might still find performances as novelty numbers in the vernacular tradition,[4] yet begin to move away from the clear generic classifications of the vernacular music of Ives's Danbury period. What is perhaps most important about these new ragtime-influenced works is that Ives later integrated them into works that were clearly in the tradition of European concert music, deriving movements of the *First Piano Sonata* (1901–1909) and the *Second Orchestral Set* (second movement, 1909) from the *Ragtime Pieces*, and portions of *Putnam's Camp*, the Hawthorne movement of the *Concord Sonata* (ca. 1911), and the second movement of the *Fourth Symphony* (1911–1916) from the *Country Band March*. The clash resulting from the sudden appearance of vernacular tunes, indeed large portions of vernacular compositions, within a work for symphony orchestra or piano solo in the cultivated tradition emphasizes the effect of a fictional music, music in which the audience listening to an orchestra play *Putnam's Camp* in a concert hall is asked to imagine itself outdoors, listening to two bands playing different music in different tempi march towards each other, pass, and separate again. The fictional character of these mature pieces is similar to that of the earlier *Country Band March*, but the contrast between the vernacular elements, including tunes, instrumentation, and performance characteristics, and the symphonic context makes the effect of layers of meaning even more powerful.

This idea of fictional music, or music about music, is a vital part of Ives's successful "literary music," where memories or literary programs are represented in sound. Thus, the integration of vernacular and cultivated styles, which began with Ives's return to popular subjects and styles in these pieces from the years 1902 to 1904, was an extremely important step towards his mature compositions. Ives was never again to write publishable music in a vernacular style, as he had as a boy and at Yale, yet the tunes and moods of the vernacular traditions he had learned were to become increasingly important for his music of the next twenty years.

NEW MUSICAL FORMS

These changes call attention to the question of musical genre, which becomes particularly interesting as we approach Ives's maturity. We have already seen one change in Ives's conception of musical genre in the move from the utilitarian music of Danbury to the art music of Parker. In Danbury, style, instrumentation, and other characteristics of a musical work were all largely controlled by the occasion for which it was composed, and distinctions between categories of music were enforced by a rigid sense of what music was proper for each setting. In the tradition of art music, genres were defined by the medium used, such as orchestra or string quartet, and by formal procedures, such as fugue or sonata, but the parts were more interchangeable and the boundaries not so rigidly drawn. A composer could choose to write in any form for any medium, could recast a movement for a different medium, and could maintain a consistent style across generic lines.

Most of Ives's concert music from the years 1902–1908 continues the classical approach to genre, at least in one sense. The *Third Symphony*

(1904), the *Trio* for violin, cello, and piano (1904–1905), the *First Piano Sonata* (1901–1909), and the *First* and *Second Violin Sonatas* (1902–1908 and 1907–1910 respectively) are distinct from each other primarily in their instrumentation (with the exception of the middle movement of the *Trio*, which is a vast scherzo-medley closer in conception to Ives's experimental pieces than to the rest of his concert music). Beyond some individuality of material, all of these share a common vocabulary and approach to form. Moreover, many individual movements are adapted from pieces originally written for different instrumentation, especially for organ, demonstrating the interchangeability of music written in different genres.

Yet, although they still fit comfortably within the outer genres of absolute art music, these pieces already differ from previous art music in their internal structure. At the same time that he was returning to vernacular ideas, Ives was turning away from the traditional conception of musical form that he had learned from Parker. No movements composed after 1902 would fit comfortably into the received forms of sonata, slow movement, or fugue. Instead, new forms came to predominate, primarily of two types, one associated with his concert music, the other with his experimental music. The first, adapted from Ives's organ preludes and postludes, is a kind of cumulative form that develops motives from a borrowed theme, usually a hymn tune, and often presents important countermelodies over the course of a movement before the theme itself is presented in full, with its countermelodies, for the first time at the end. This is the form Ives used more frequently than any other for his compositions in the traditional genres of concert music during the period 1902–1908, and he continued to use it in much of the music written after his marriage.[5] In his experimental music, Ives often based a piece or a section of a piece on a simple, gradual process of change that can usually be explained in words, presented in graphic form, or associated with an extramusical conception. *All the Way Around and Back* (1906, for four instruments and piano four hands), for instance, builds to a climax by adding instruments and increasing in rhythmic complexity then subsides in a strict retrograde, followed by a brief coda in which the climactic measures are repeated.[6] Each of these experimental forms is unique, yet all have elements in common: they all depend upon the same basic procedures of intensification and release, and none follow traditional patterns. When old forms are used during this period, as in the *Three-Page Sonata* (1905), they are mocked or altered almost beyond recognition.

Ives rejected not just the traditional abstract concept of form for each individual movement but also the received pattern for multi-movement works. After 1902, he wrote no more great cantatas in the manner of *The Celestial Country* nor symphonies in the manner of his first and second. In fact, except for his *Second String Quartet* (1907–1913) and the never-finished *Universe Symphony* (begun 1911), each of which was apparently conceived as a unified tripartite work from the beginning, Ives never again produced multi-movement works from an original grand conception. Instead, by and large, his works with multiple movements, including the sonatas for piano solo and for violin and piano, the *Third* and *Fourth Symphonies*, and the sets for orchestra or chamber ensembles, were assembled from individual movements conceived independently and only later gathered together into sets with varying degrees and sources of unity between movements. While some of these sets, particularly the *Concord Sonata* and the *Fourth Symphony* (1909–1916), achieve an impressive sense of integration, none of them completely conceals its origin as a collection of separate movements. For instance, each of the four movements of the *Fourth Symphony* is scored for an ensemble of different size and composition. As sets, rather than sonatas or symphonies in which relationships of tempo or key are understood or set forth before any of the movements are written, each multi-movement work of the period after 1902 follows its own logic, in some cases corresponding to the traditional patterns, and in some cases new or wholly individual, like the slow-fast-slow sequence of movements in the *Third Symphony* or the four-part scherzo, comprising movements two and four of the *First Piano Sonata*, which is split in two by the slow third movement.

After about 1908, the traditional conception of genre virtually disappears from Ives's music. Except for the *Third* and *Fourth Violin Sonatas* (1913–?1914 and 1914–?1916 respectively), both based on earlier pieces from the years 1901–1906, Ives's mature music no longer falls into clear genres: the *Fourth Symphony* is hardly a symphony in the standard mold, the *Concord Sonata* is hardly a sonata (the first sentence of Ives's *Essays*, page xxv, calls it "a sonata for want of a more exact name"), and the orchestral sets, the pieces for unison chorus and orchestra (such as *Lincoln The Great Commoner*), and the *Holidays Symphony* are all in forms that are Ives's own innovations. Even the *Robert Browning Overture* "was called a Tone Poem, having got somewhat out of the overture shape" (*Memos*, page 76). Yet, while Ives was having increasing difficulty figuring out what to call his pieces, the new musical forms of the years 1901–1908 endured, providing models for the mostly programmatic music of his maturity.

HUMOR AND EXPERIMENT

The importance in this period of pieces that imitate environmental sounds has already been discussed above in Chapter 5, in connection with George Ives's influence. Along with imitation and the reappearance of vernacular musical styles, the most distinctive feature of the years 1902–1908 is a renewal of Ives's experimentation. At Yale, he had written another *Fugue in Four Keys* (1897), this one based on the hymn tune *The Shining Shore*, and while still working at Central Presbyterian Church in New York had composed *From the Steeples and the Mountains* (1901–1902), with its angular, atonal parts for trumpet and trombone against a background of four sets of bells playing descending scales in three different keys, but most of his trying out of musical techniques for their own sake had been confined to music for church, where he had some chance of getting it performed. His *Processional: Let There Be Light* (1901) had included sonorities made of like intervals stacked on top of one another, expanding from seconds and thirds out to octaves through every chromatic interval, and the *Harvest Home Chorales* (1898–1901) had included extreme dissonance and complex rhythmic layering. Now he brought these same techniques into instrumental works and extended them. *Halloween* and *Largo Risoluto No. 2* (both 1906) are based on canons that place different instruments in different keys; the string ostinato in *Central Park in the Dark* (1906) is a virtual catalogue of Ives's favorite possibilities for new chordal structures, including whole-tone chords and chords built of fifths, fourths, and fourths mixed with tritones; *All the Way Around and Back* (1906) has simultaneous divisions of the measure into one, two, three, five, seven, and eleven equal parts, making it one of the earliest of several pieces to incorporate such prime-number series either simultaneously or consecutively; and there are many other examples.

Many of the pieces in which Ives experimented with new techniques were written, or at least conceived, as jokes.[7] Some of the theatre pieces from Ives's Yale years, discussed in the previous chapter, apparently had the character of "take-offs" or "stunts" (the words Ives most often used), but none of these are known to survive. The earliest surviving instrumental "joke" is the *Yale-Princeton Football Game* (1898), already mentioned, which is extant only in sketch. Ives seems to have abandoned "stunting" along with vernacular music during his first few years in New York—at least, he wrote nothing down that had the character of a "take-off"—but in the period between 1902 and 1907 he produced about a dozen musical jokes, most of which relied upon some technical experimentation or rule-breaking as part of the humor. The middle movement of the *Trio* for violin, cello, and piano (1904–1905), entitled *TSIAJ* (This Scherzo Is A Joke) to make sure that no one took it too seriously, throws in familiar tunes, raucous dissonance and bitonality, and furious stops and starts in an evocation of celebrations "at Mr. Yale's School for nice bad boys."[8] *Halloween* and *All the Way Around and Back*, mentioned above, were both begun as jokes, and the fifth of a *Set of Five Take-Offs* (1906–1907), entitled *Bad Resolutions and a Good One* (1 January 1907), puns on New Year's resolutions while illustrating the difference between feeble, slightly incorrect but commonplace dominant-tonic resolutions and a bold, convincing, chromatic resolution from a complex dissonant crash—thoroughly incorrect—to tonic octaves.

It is apparent in all of these pieces that the humorous context provided an excuse for Ives to play with dissonance, complexity, quodlibet, and other technical matters with a freedom he did not have in more serious works or in works that might potentially be played in public. Once techniques had been tried out in pieces that could be justified as mere jokes, experiments, or small descriptive pieces,[9] they could be incorporated along with vernacular styles into the framework of large concert works in the tradition Ives had inherited from Parker. An obvious example of this is the case of the slow trio in the short *Scherzo* for string quartet, begun as a joke in 1903 and later made part of the larger (though still comic) work.[10] Ives says of this trio in the *Memos*, "I made a little practice piece called *Holding your own* as a joke (partly serious). . . . One man plays the chromatic scale and another a diatonic [scale] in different time etc.—we played it over and had a laugh. But the last time I found it, it seemed quite (or partially) musical, and worth playing—and [I] put it, as a slow bit, into a fast Scherzo" (page 34).[11] Later in the *Memos*, Ives comments about the *Yale-Princeton Football Game* that "doing things like this (half horsing) would suggest and get one used to technical processes that could be developed in something more serious later, and quite naturally" (page 61).

Humor in this context had two uses for Ives. First, approaching his work with humor helped to open his own ears to what new technical possibilities existed, without limiting himself with any preconceptions.

Humor explicitly mocks and disobeys the rules, always pushing beyond and testing limitations. No attitude could be more useful in researching new musical techniques. Second, verbal and physical humor was an important part of the sociability Ives had known at Yale and continued to know in New York until his marriage, and the puns and pranks in his music reflect the humor he shared with his friends. For his first ten years in New York, Ives lived in a series of apartments, all known as "Poverty Flat," which he shared with other Yale graduates, many of whom were studying medicine or law.[12] Ives's roommates served as unwilling witnesses to his composing and a captive audience for his finished pieces.[13] In such close quarters, it was safer for Ives to be musically adventuresome if he could appeal to his friends' sense of humor and conviviality; a stern, serious approach to experimentation would have been neither understood nor appreciated. It is no surprise that the bulk of Ives's raucously humorous music was written—or, like *Scherzo: Over the Pavements* (1906–1913) and the second movement (subtitled "Arguments") of the *Second String Quartet* (first sketched in 1907 and completed in 1913), begun—in the period between his resignation as an organist in 1902 and his marriage in 1908. The scherzo movements from the mature period, such as *Putnam's Camp* from *Three Places in New England*, the second movements of the *Fourth Symphony* and the *Second Orchestral Set*, and the Hawthorne movement of the *Concord Sonata*, even when they incorporate music first sketched before 1908, are all pieces of greater length, depth, and seriousness of intent than the jokes of Ives's bachelor years. In these later works, as in Beethoven's scherzo movements, the humor is part of a larger conception, often with a spiritual or literary basis, and no longer merely a justification for breaking the rules.

Taken as a group, these pieces from the years 1902–1908, whether classical, experimental, descriptive, or humorous, are more dissonant, more rhythmically complex, and much more difficult to perform than Ives's earlier works. They are scored for ideal performers instead of being tailored to the skills of available players. Since he was no longer writing for specific performers or performances but only for himself, Ives also found it difficult and not altogether necessary to finish his compositions or to put them in final form. This character of incompleteness and indefiniteness was to become an important aspect of Ives's mature music,[14] but seems to have arisen during this period of transition out of a lack of concern for presenting a finished product. The compositions of these six years became harder to understand aurally as well, as Ives moved away from the common assumptions underlying the music he knew, gradually approaching a new personal vision of what music could aspire to.

ISOLATION AND SELF-CONFIDENCE

In this process, his isolation was a definite asset. The *Memos* are already sprinkled with sour comments from professional musicians about his music. It would have been impossible to create the works for which he has become famous if Ives had been surrounded by the enforcers of public taste in his daily life, instead of entertaining them at home only every now and then. However, even his hermit-like work habits would have been insufficient if he had not become convinced of the importance and rightness of his own thoughts, for the extreme negative reactions of virtually everyone to whom he showed his music could easily have destroyed his resolve.

During one visit by Franz Milcke, a well-known violinist and concertmaster in New York, to Ives's summer home on a farm near Redding, Connecticut, in 1914, his visitor snorted at the *First Violin Sonata* (1902–1908), "This cannot be played. It is awful. It is not music, it makes no sense. . . . I cannot get those horrible sounds out of my ears" (*Memos*, page 70). Ives comments about the incident,

> After he went, I had a kind of a feeling which I've had off and on when other more or less celebrated (or well known) musicians have seen or played (or tried to play) some of my music. I felt (but only temporarily) that perhaps there must be something wrong with me. Said I to myself, "I'm the only one, with the exception of Mrs. Ives (and one or two others perhaps, Mr. [Francis] Ryder [the Ives's neighbor in Redding], Dr. [John Cornelius] Griggs), who likes any of my music, except perhaps some of the older and more or less conventional things. Why do I like these things? Why do I like to work in this way and get all set up by it, while others only get upset by it and it just makes everybody else mad, especially well known musicians and critics— . . . Are my ears on wrong? No one else seems to hear it the same way. Perhaps I'd better go back to Mr. Jadassohn" [page 71].[15]

Indeed, Ives notes later in the *Memos* that incidents like this

> had something of the effect on me of a kind of periodic deterrent, something approaching a result of a sedative. . . . So I'd have periods of being good and nice, and getting back to the usual ways of writing, sometimes for

several months, until I got so tired of it that I decided I'd either have to stop music or stop this. . . . But more often, after these instances, nothing happened, good or bad, which is good [page 126].

It was in large part his wife, Harmony Twichell Ives, who gave Ives the self-confidence to carry on. In the *Memos*, at the same time that he pays tribute to his father's influence, he acknowledges the debt he owes his wife:

> One thing I am certain of is that, if I have done anything good in music, it was, first, because of my father, and second, because of my wife. What she has done for me I won't put down, because she won't let me. But I am going to put this down at least:—After any of these musical friends of mine (mentioned above, and others) had left, she never once said or suggested or looked or thought that there must be something wrong with me—a thing implied, if not expressed, by most everybody else, including members of the family. She never said, "Now why don't you be good, and write something nice the way they like it?"—*Never! She* urged me on my way—to be myself! *She* gave me not only help but a confidence that no one else since father had given me [page 114].[16]

Kirkpatrick credits Ives's courtship with Harmony, which began in 1905, with giving Ives "a new self-confidence" to create "a whole world of far-out music,"[17] including the experimental works cited above. As Ives had apparently been in something of a composing slump during the first half of 1905 and wrote the *Three-Page Sonata* in a single burst while on vacation with Harmony and her family in September, Kirkpatrick is almost surely correct in stressing Harmony's importance. The initiation of this courtship subdivides the third major period of Ives's career; their marriage in June 1908 marks the beginning of Ives's mature period, the nine years during which most of the music that lies at the center of his work was conceived and composed.

Harmony Twichell Ives, ca. 1916

CHAPTER EIGHT

Years of Maturity (1908–1917)

Harmony Twichell (1876–1969) was the daughter of the liberal Congregationalist minister Joseph Hopkins Twichell (1838–1918), whom Ives had heard preach while at Yale, and the sister of David C. Twichell (1874–1924), one of Ives's best friends from his college years and for a time a resident of Poverty Flat. According to Bigelow Ives, Ives had taken Harmony to the junior prom while at Yale,[1] but the friendship did not turn into a romance until 1905, although Ives had kept in touch with Harmony's family through Dave Twichell. Their courtship was drawn-out and careful, but when commitment came, it was complete and life-long. The gravest ordeal Ives seems to have suffered was having to pass muster before Harmony's "Uncle Mark" Twain, her father's close friend.[2]

Harmony's importance for Ives's development went beyond providing support and reassurance for his unorthodoxy. The most important aspects of his mature period, following the dissolution of genre that can be traced to his "giving up music" in 1902, are the representation of life experiences and of literature in music, a conscious celebration of America and American music, and high spiritual and moral aims for music, and all of these aspects owe much of their intensity to Harmony Twichell Ives. Although Ives rarely told her what he was working on[3] and she evinced little understanding of his compositions, Harmony's confidence in and commitment to her husband's music seems never to have wavered, even when his own self-confidence flagged. Ives wrote to his wife in the fall of 1910, just before the third anniversary of their engagement, "How much I love to work when you're by me & how hard it is to without you."[4] The truth and the inner meaning of that statement are illuminated by the impressions of Barbara MacKenzie, who got to know the Iveses in 1944 through her husband. She said of Harmony, "People might have thought her prosaic, but she wasn't. She opened doors, she sewed seams, and she was never in doubt that Charles Ives was a genius, and so he was never in doubt."[5] Because they shared the same ideals for what music might accomplish, Harmony could believe completely in what her husband was doing, even without a technical understanding of the music. For the same reason, Charles Ives looked upon his wife as "his greatest source of inspiration"[6] and conceived and wrote his largest, greatest, and most characteristic compositions in the first decade after their engagement.

REPRESENTATION OF EMOTIONAL EXPERIENCE

In a letter to Ives in the late winter of 1908, a few months before their wedding, Harmony wrote about her ideas of artistic inspiration, making clear her belief that music concretely represented emotional experience, most often as it is remembered.

> It seems to me too . . . that inspiration ought to come fullest at one's happiest moments—I think it would be so satisfying to crystallize one of those moments at the time in some beautiful expression—but I don't believe it's often done—I think inspiration—in art—seems to be almost a consolation in hours of sadness or loneliness & that most happy moments are put into expression after they have been memories & made doubly precious because they are gone— I think that is what usually happens tho' I don't see why it should. I think, as you say, that living our lives for each other & for those with whom we come in contact generously & with sympathy & compassion & love, is the best & most beautiful way of expressing our love—and the Bravest way too . . . but to put it too into a concrete form of music or words would be a wonderful happiness   wouldn't it? I think you will & that will be doing it for both of us.[7]

The idea that music represents feelings is of course hardly unique. Harmony here adds support to the Romantic conception of music that Ives had absorbed from Parker, picking up on and reinforcing the idea of music as an embodiment of individual experience. This support was of great significance, for throughout his career, Ives remained a Romantic composer in his conception of the role of music as personal expression, extending to a new extreme the idea of individuality in music for both composer and performer. Yet Harmony's letter goes beyond the typical emotionalism of both cultivated and vernacular nineteenth-century music, in two respects. First, she focuses on "putting into expression" not merely emotions but specific moments or events, moments that are individual, indeed unique, and irreplaceable. Second, she recognizes that writing words or music about "one's happiest moments" is normally done after the moment is over, through memory. Artists rarely separate themselves from a happy experience in order to write about it; to do so will almost certainly end the mood, leaving one to rely once again on memory. Harmony asks directly for Ives to try to write about their love while still in the midst of it, which, except in the most general sense, he did not do; the closest he came to this may be *The Housatonic at Stockbridge*, the third movement of *Three Places in New England*, inspired by a walk along the river the Iveses shared soon after their marriage. But from this time forward, many of Ives's compositions tried to capture the feelings and sounds of specific events, most often remembered ones.

A few works depict recent events, as did Harmony's poem *Autumn*, about the day of their engagement.[8] Among these are *The Housatonic at Stockbridge* and *From Hanover Square North, at the End of a Tragic Day, the Voice of the People Again Arose* (1915), the third movement of the *Second Orchestral Set*, which evokes the sound and feeling of a crowd of commuters singing the gospel hymn *In the Sweet Bye and Bye* on a train platform the day the *Lusitania* was sunk. But most of the works that represent real or archetypal life experiences depend upon memory, harking back to the events and styles of living of Ives's childhood. These include the first three movements of the obviously nostalgic *Holidays Symphony* (*Washington's Birthday*, 1909; *Decoration Day*, 1912; and *The Fourth of July*, 1911–1913),[9] celebrations of the music of Stephen Foster, ragtime and revival meetings, and military bands (in the first and second movements of the *Second Orchestral Set*, both 1909, and *Putnam's Camp*, 1912, from *Three Places in New England*, respectively), and pictures of a Civil War regiment marching (in *The 'St. Gaudens' in Boston Common*, 1911–1912) or four Yankees— perhaps war veterans themselves—talking and arguing (in the *Second String Quartet*).

Evocations of the sounds and ideas of his youth were not new to Ives in 1908, of course. There were already several movements based on the hymn tunes he had known all his life; there was the *Country Band March* of 1903, which celebrated the small-town bands he had heard as a child; and in 1906 he had written *The Pond* in memory of hearing his father play his cornet from across a pond. But a work such as the *Third Symphony* (1904), subtitled "The Camp Meeting" and therefore usually assumed to be in some sense a musical picture of the revival meetings Ives had participated in as a young man, contains virtually no musical description of anything— motion, character, or even the sound and spirit of the singing. Instead, each of the three movements works with its main themes, which are paraphrased from popular hymn tunes, in an intrinsically musical way without any suggestion of extramusical meaning, just as the organ pieces on which they were based had developed the hymn tunes in chorale-prelude fashion. Putting a descriptive title on such a movement or on similar movements in the violin sonatas does not narrow the gap between this more abstract music, concerned with both traditional and new methods of manipulating thematic material, and the sequence of events that unfolds, for instance, in describing Danbury's celebration of Decoration Day through the imitation of musical performances, other sounds, motion, and the feelings these events produce.

NOSTALGIA

If Ives had any predisposition towards nostalgia, Harmony certainly encouraged it. She particularly supported and strengthened his feelings towards his father, sharing his regret at George's early death and reassuring Ives that he was leading his life in a way that would have satisfied his father. Within days of their engagement, Harmony wrote to Charles, "What do you think? in church I thought all of a sudden of your father so intensely that the tears came into my eyes . . . actually as if I'd known him."[10] After a visit to Danbury, where she met the surviving Ives relatives, Harmony wrote on the train back to Hartford, "It has been very sweet to me to be in your home & be so happy there. They all love you . . . your Uncle Joe [Joseph Moss Ives] said how proud your father would be of you two boys if he were here now. . . . I feel sure that your father knows your lives & sees what his love & thought has meant to you."[11]

It has been said of the Iveses that "the son has written his father's music for him,"[12] but this is scarcely true of the music written before Charles's courtship with Harmony, except perhaps for some of the frankly experimental works. What is clear is that several of the mature compositions are in a sense memorials for George Ives, as Stuart Feder has suggested about *Decoration Day*: they recall Ives's Danbury childhood, even the Civil War experiences of the young George Ives himself, and often include the town or regimental band as a major actor in the pageantry.[13] Feder raises interesting psychological issues which need not be considered here, beyond noting that in his mature works, as in his later life, Ives was obsessed with his father and his own childhood, and that Harmony encouraged this retrospection. This presented Ives with new subject matter, new programs, for his composing. It also renewed his links to the musical world of his father, above all to George Ives's open-

mindedness, love of small-town vernacular music, attentive listening to
environmental sounds and attempting to reproduce them, and self-
reliance. None of these connections had entirely disappeared during the
fourteen years since his father's death, but each had been attentuated at
some point along the way, and Harmony's admiration for George Ives—an
admiration first evident in the fall of 1907, after their engagement—
helped Charles Ives reestablish contact with his father's ideas.

    Along with her interest in George Ives, Harmony wanted very much
to know Ives's childhood home of Danbury. On the Christmas Eve after
their engagement, she wrote of wanting to learn about his hometown and
his family: "I know what pleasure it gives for you to be at home—Charlie,
give my love to all that home—I want so much to see & grow familiar with
the places you grew up in & love from happy association—I shall feel
more then that I have a part in the years before I knew you."[14] Harmony
visited Danbury in the winter of 1908, met the surviving Iveses, including
Charles Ives's mother, Mollie (Mary) Ives, his aunt Amelia Brewster, and
his uncle Joseph Ives, and felt welcomed into the family. Harmony was
pleased to find in the Ives family echoes of the religious family life she had
known as a minister's daughter, and the comfort she took in the old-
fashioned morality of the Iveses increased her sense of nostalgia for Ives's
childhood family as for her own. "I have been writing Dad & thinking how
good a thing it is that this new way of life that shows so plain to me is just a
continuation of the old way that has been familiar & fondest & best to
me."[15]

    While Ives had surely admired the members of his family from the
time of his youth, Harmony's interest seems to have increased his own. It
was around the time of their engagement and marriage that Ives wrote
out *The Anti-Abolitionist Riots* (1908), a short piano piece memorializing his
grandfather's participation in the abolitionist movement, and began to
write other works about abolition and the Civil War, including the
unfinished *Emerson Concerto* (ca. 1907–1908); *The 'St. Gaudens' in Boston
Common* (1911–1912), on a statue by Augustus Saint-Gaudens commemorating Colonel Robert Shaw and his regiment of black soldiers, the first in
the Union army;[16] *Lincoln, The Great Commoner* (1912), based on the poem
by Edwin Markham; and a projected but never written movement on
Wendell Phillips's speech at Faneuil Hall.[17] Ives had written no previous
works on Civil War themes. Harmony commented after Ives's death that
she had of course never known any of the older generations in the Ives
family, but that "the amount I can tell you about them is just a gauge of
how much he talked about them."[18] Since Ives had talked about his

family very little to his business associates or to his male friends at Yale or in Poverty Flat, if one may judge by their reminiscences of him, it is safe to conclude that Harmony's interest in the Ives family rekindled his own, and that memories of the Danbury Iveses were a rich part of the private life they shared.

LITERARY SUBJECTS IN MUSIC

Harmony stimulated Ives to write program music of another sort as well: music that took literature as its inspiration. The importance of William Lyon Phelps for Ives's choice of authors has already been demonstrated, but if Ives had kept up the habit of reading literature in the decade after his graduation from Yale, there is no evidence for it from his collection of books or his recollections. Reading had long been a regular habit for Harmony—her letters are full of her recent reading—and was a shared and intense activity that she planned to keep up in her married life. She wrote to Ives in February 1908 of her "horror of fitting into things in N[ew] Y[ork] . . . & of having no quiet hours & solitude" and described her plans for their life together: "We must plan to have times for leisure of thought & we must try & read a lot, the best books—we can live with the noblest people that have lived that way—& we will have your music."[19]

Harmony's plans bore fruit, as Ives separated himself from his bachelor friends and joined her in the companionship of reading. Simultaneously, he began to write music that tried to capture the character and spirit of a particular author, beginning with the *Emerson Concerto* of 1907–1908 and including the *Robert Browning Overture* (1908–1912), the *Matthew Arnold Overture* (sketched in December 1912 but never completed), the *Concord Sonata*,[20] the projected but never written overtures from the "Men of Literature" series, and the choral song *Walt Whitman*, to words from *Song of Myself*. In at least two cases, Harmony's direct influence seems likely in his choice of author as well. One of the two books of Matthew Arnold's poetry in the Ives Redding house was Harmony's before their marriage,[21] and it was probably Harmony who gave Charles a volume of Browning, including the dramatic poem *Paracelsus*, for his thirty-fourth birthday in October 1908, just before he began composing the *Browning Overture*.[22] Presumably, the *Emerson Concerto* was the first of these literary compositions because of Ives's earlier interest in Emerson from Yale and his relatives. Harmony's interest in the Ives family may have rekindled his enthusiasm for his grandmother's favorite lecturer at the same time that her devotion to reading brought him back into direct contact with Emerson's *Essays*. The importance of Emerson for Ives's development at this stage will be discussed further in the following chapter.

AMERICANISM

Both the nostalgic pieces and the most important of the works inspired by literature (excepting only the *Robert Browning Overture*) are also thoroughly American, consciously celebrating the life, music, literature, and history of the United States, particularly of New England. Here, too, Harmony seems to have inspired Ives to move in a new direction.

The question of an American music had been one of long-standing concern for Ives and for each of his musical mentors. The issue was partly one of the opposition between native, primarily vernacular styles and the European-oriented, "rule-bound" cultivated music imported into the United States during the nineteenth century. While participating in music of both types, George Ives had expressed his preference clearly; Charles Ives recalled his father commenting, "The best American music is the worst & the worst is the best"—meaning that cultivated music, which had more status, was moribund, whereas vernacular music was vital.[23] Both Parker and Griggs were concerned about establishing a native cultivated music, but neither saw writing music on American subjects or using native tunes as the best road to follow. Parker avoided such Americanism altogether in his compositions, looking to the advent of a great American composer to establish a distinctly American school,[24] while Griggs saw the influence of the church choir as the most important distinctive feature in American musical life and left the development of a native school of composers as an open question.[25] Ives had written compositions incorporating American tunes all along, from the *Variations on America* for organ (1891) and the *March* (1892) with Foster's *My Old Kentucky Home* in its second strain, through the *Second* and *Third Symphonies*, whose American character depended in large part upon the tunes Ives paraphrased in their themes rather than upon a peculiarly American form or subject.

But Harmony had a sense of idealism about what it meant to be an American that seemed to hit a responsive chord in Charles Ives, and his music from the period of their engagement to the end of his career as a composer is both more directly about American life and literature and more idealistic at its core. During their courtship, the Iveses planned to collaborate on an opera set in North America, and Harmony wrote at one point: "Charlie, of course the place for the Good man in our drama to come from is our country ennobled—our own country as our forefathers planned her & as Mr. Lincoln desired her in his Gettysburg speech & as we hope she will be in the good process of time—don't you think so?"[26] The opera libretto was never written, but Harmony's picture of the ideal American seems identical to the idealistic concept of America Ives later laid out in his *Essays Before a Sonata.*

Ives was drawn to his subjects from American literature and American history primarily because of the ideals they embodied, ideals he identified with his own experience as an American. It can be no coincidence that soon after this letter Ives set out to memorialize the noble, moral, and democratic New England of his youth and forefathers, to celebrate the philosophical quest of Emerson and Thoreau, and to depict the simple heroism of Colonel Robert Shaw and his Black Regiment. Nor is it surprising, remembering Ives's renewed self-confidence as well as his American idealism in this period, that he returned in the first years of his marriage to the *Second* and *Third Symphonies,* among the most American of his earlier works, put them into final form, and had professional copies made of them.[27] Harmony's faith in the idealism underlying her country deepened and intensified Ives's similar feelings and led him to represent instances of that idealism and events from American life in his music. Before 1907, Ives's Americanism had consisted primarily in his willingness to use native tunes as musical material, as in his movements based on hymn tunes, while in his mature music, he moved on to tackle distinctively American subjects as well.

IDEALISM IN THE TWICHELL FAMILY

As Harmony had found confirmation for her own beliefs in the idealism of Ives's family, rekindling her husband's interest in his father and grandparents, so too Ives found his ideals deepened and strengthened through contact with Harmony's family, particularly her father, the Reverend Joseph Hopkins Twichell, and through Harmony herself.

At the time of his engagement, Ives looked to Joseph Twichell as a partial replacement for his own dead father, an older man to whom he could turn for advice and encouragement.[28] Like Ives's father, Twichell had served in the Union army during the Civil War, enlisting as a chaplain in his early twenties, and had been changed by his experiences.[29] Twichell almost certainly told his son-in-law tales of his wartime service; in the *Essays* (page 85), Ives mentions in passing one characteristic incident that must have been a familiar family anecdote.[30] It may be that Twichell's Civil War experiences helped to rekindle Ives's memories of his father's own service. As has been noted already, there are no compositions on Civil War subjects and relatively few quotations of Civil War tunes before 1907, and a sudden rush of both during the years just after Ives's engagement. In addition to Harmony's interest in Ives's father and family, Twichell's own memories may have inspired Ives to take up the Civil War as a theme.

Ives very probably found support for his own beliefs in Twichell's optimism, liberal religion, belief in progress on both spiritual and physical planes, and humanitarian concerns. The last of these was exemplified in Twichell's wishing his parishioners to lead Christian lives rather than follow a "correct" doctrine.[31] It was probably through Twichell, who had been deeply influenced by Congregationalist preacher Horace Bushnell's controversial brand of theology,[32] or through Harmony herself that Ives came to know the thinking of Bushnell, whose sermons he read and whom he cites in the *Essays*.[33] During her first visit to Danbury in January 1908, Harmony wrote to Ives that she and Ives's Aunt Amelia Brewster "went & heard about Dr Bushnell—some things I was very glad to have explained about his theology—I can see so plainly the more I hear of him, how much he has been my father's teacher and leader."[34] Bushnell's belief in the presence of the divine in all human beings and in nature[35] and his stress in the sermon on "Unconscious Influence" on the importance of character are strikingly similar to Ives's own views in his writings.

Similarly, both Harmony Twichell and her father clearly contributed to Ives's religious beliefs and to his ideals of progress and service. On the occasion of her graduation as a Registered Nurse in 1900, Harmony read an essay in which she praised the privileges of a profession whose constant work is helping others, "for it is proved that the fullest development individually comes from altruistic effort, and fullest development means in the end the greatest usefulness and happiness."[36] This concept of service to others as a source of intrinsic rewards is a liberal Christian sentiment quite untypical of Transcendentalism, which is oriented not towards service but towards contemplation. From this liberal Christian root, from the ideals of worship Ives learned at revival services and Harmony learned in the much more staid but still theologically adventurous sermons of Bushnell and her father, the Iveses evolved their own private spiritual mysticism, and it is this religious current that underlies the most worshipful of Ives's pieces: the *Fourth Symphony* (particularly its finale), the final movement of the *Second String Quartet*, and *From Hanover Square North*, the last movement of the *Second Orchestral Set*. Kirkpatrick has noted of the Iveses that their married life showed "a unity that had to be witnessed to be understood,"[37] and goes on to describe their significance for each other:

> Having unusual capacities in different ways—but being alike in setting devotion to ideals above convenience or expedience—their own devotion to each other enlarged their perceptions into what amounted to a mystical vision of reality. The exalted perorations of the *Second String Quartet* and the *Fourth Symphony* are probably not more from transcendentalist sources than from this source.[38]

Elsewhere, Kirkpatrick has observed that

> Ives's adventurousness in philosophic thought went even beyond Emerson, but one of the many paradoxes in Ives was the contrast between his radically adventurous self and his churchgoing self. His churchgoing self was conservative almost to the point of what's called Fundamentalist. He was almost in a state of "Give me that old-time religion, it's good enough for me."[39]

This same kind of mixture of apparent conservativism and apparent radicalism is evident in Ives's compositional methods. Yet, in his philosophy as in his music, the mixture is less of a paradox than it at first appears to be. The radical strand grows out of the traditional, and they intertwine; the two are inseparable. Ives's adventurousness, musically and philosophically, springs directly from his faith in his own inspiration, a faith that was nurtured by his father, his wife, and Emerson's writings and that was rooted ultimately in the religious idealism of the Ives and Twichell families. That idealism, as we have seen, was founded in Christianity; even the Transcendentalists were important to Sarah and Joseph Ives principally as part of the religious life of the family, subordinate to reading the Bible and going to church.

There is a strong tradition of liberal, almost heretical Christian thought in both families, but there is also the revivalism of the camp meetings of Ives's boyhood, and there are hints that Harmony Twichell may have been theologically more conservative than her father.[40] Ives seems never to have been disturbed by contradictions between Bushnell and Thoreau on the one hand and revivalism and genteel churchgoing on the other. What seems to have mattered most for him is sincerity and depth of conviction, not adherence to any particular creed, and in this his attitude towards religion is like that of his father-in-law. Ives derived support for his religious outlook from both the fervency of gospel singing[41] and the erudite insights of Bushnell. That Bushnell and the prayer-meeting evangelists would have disagreed on doctrine seems neither to have upset him nor even to have occurred to him.

CHAPTER NINE

The Importance of Transcendentalism

In the preceding four chapters, every important aspect of Ives's point of view as he articulates it in the *Essays Before a Sonata* has been successfully traced to its origins *without* reference to Transcendentalism. Ives's dualism arose from the dichotomies of music in Danbury and was reinforced by the conflict between his father's views of music and those of Parker; his idealism had religious roots in the Ives family and received new impetus from Harmony; his self-reliance and open-mindedness, both of which were essential for his experimentation and for his emerging mature approach to music, derived from his father's attitudes towards music, again with renewed support from Harmony; his conception of manner and substance in music was taken chiefly from Griggs's article on Debussy and imbued with his own idealistic beliefs; and his aims of representing in music personal emotional experiences, particularly memories, and of creating a music that is American not only in its themes but in its idealism and subject matter were evolved in his conversations and letters with Harmony, with roots deep in the nineteenth-century Romantic conception of music as an embodiment of emotion and national feeling.

The one aspect of the *Essays* that remains to be explained is Ives's enthusiasm for Transcendentalism itself. If Ives was not solely a Transcendentalist, if his ideas and ideals about music and life came from many different sources, what then was the role of Emerson and the other Concord writers in his thought? Where does the intense influence of Emerson in the *Essays* arise, and why? Why did Emerson and Thoreau remain so important to Ives throughout the rest of his life?

We have seen that Ives's devotion to Emerson does not derive from his father, despite the enthusiasm of other family members, nor from

Parker, despite Parker's own ideals for music; not from William Lyon Phelps, who apparently introduced Ives not only to Emerson (if Ives still needed an introduction) but to much of the other literature Ives knew and loved during his life; not from John C. Griggs, nor from the Twichells, father or daughter. The influence of Emerson must have come directly from reading Emerson for himself at a time when the latter's essays had particular meaning for him. This seems simple and obvious, but it wholly contradicts the common assumption that Ives was raised on Emerson's essays and derived his mature philosophy of life and art from that one source.

In all probability, Ives returned to Emerson during his courtship with Harmony, for it seems to have been Harmony who urged Ives to withdraw from his friends and who stimulated him to read as avidly as she.[1] Ives began to sketch the *Emerson Concerto* around the time of his engagement to Harmony, and wrote the *Concord Sonata* over the next few years. It was about this time, too, that Ives began to choose texts to set to music of a more spiritual and often Transcendentalist tone, including some of Harmony's poetry (*Autumn*, from 1907, and *Mists*, 1910), his own words (*Soliloquy*, 1907, and *The Innate*, first version for instruments from 1908, version for voice and piano from 1916), fragments from Emerson (*Duty*, on four lines from Emerson's *Voluntaries*, ?1911 for unison chorus and orchestra), Thoreau (*Thoreau*, to a text adapted from *Walden*, 1915), and Walt Whitman (*Walt Whitman*, from *Leaves of Grass*, version for unison chorus and orchestra from 1913), and other texts in the same vein (e.g., Kipling's *Tolerance*, ?1909).

Ives's Transcendentalism has long been linked with his political beliefs, and it was likewise soon after his marriage that he began to express strong populist or progressive political ideals in his memos, in his music on the subjects of abolition and the Civil War era, and in topical political songs such as *Vote for Names* (1912), about that year's election; *The New River* (choral version from 1911), about noise pollution and the peril posed to the human spirit by runaway technology; *Sneak Thief* (unfinished sketch for chorus, from October 1914), on Germany's invasion of the Low Countries; and *Majority* (first version for chorus, 1914–1915), a testament to Ives's faith in the masses and the song that perhaps comes nearest to expressing his political credo. Before 1911, the last time Ives had expressed a political sentiment in song was in 1896, with his campaign song for the Republican presidential candidate William McKinley, *William Will.*

This is circumstantial evidence, but it is very strong: in the first years of his marriage to Harmony, there is a clear shift of topic in Ives's chosen texts towards spiritual, Transcendentalist, and later populist or progressive political ideals, coinciding with the composition of the *Concord Sonata* and the beginning in the 1910s of Ives's application of Transcendentalist thinking to his concerns in the insurance business and to larger political issues.[2] This combination of circumstances suggests strongly that, whatever Ives's earlier contact with Emerson's writings, he returned to them in earnest around the time of his engagement to Harmony, and their influence grew to affect every aspect of his life.

Thus, instead of assuming that Ives's ideas derive primarily from a lifelong familiarity with the Transcendentalists—a picture of Ives's thought that has never been more than an untested assumption—we may come nearer to the truth by understanding his enthusiasm for Emerson as a point of arrival rather than a point of departure. It seems most likely that Ives recognized in Emerson's essays, at first in his senior year in college and then much more fully ten years later, the articulation of his own thoughts and the solutions to problems with which he had long struggled.

We have already seen that Harmony provided a bulwark of self-confidence for Ives when his music was attacked or dismissed by professional musicians. In the same spirit, it must have been an enormous comfort to Ives to read the opening pages of Emerson's *Self-Reliance*, including the following words:

> To believe your own thought, to believe that what is true for you in your private heart is true for all men—that is genius. Speak your latent conviction, and it shall be universal sense. . . . In every work of genius we recognize our own rejected thoughts; they come back to us with a certain alienated majesty. Great works of art have no more affecting lesson for us than this. They teach us to abide by our spontaneous impression with good-humored inflexibility then most when the whole cry of voices is on the other side. Else to-morrow a stranger will say with masterly good sense precisely what we have thought and felt all the time, and we shall be forced to take with shame our own opinion from another.[3]

The last sentence is suggestive. As Phelps comments in his essay on Emerson, "Our foremost American individualist always spoke to individuals, never to men in the mass."[4] It seems highly unlikely that Ives, or anyone, could be molded and shaped to agree with Emerson's point of view, whether as a child or as an adult. Indeed, the revivalist Christianity he had learned as a boy, the pressure to conform at Yale, and the limited room for eccentricity in business (at least before Ives had his own agency) gave Ives little impetus towards sharing such a view. But as a radical composer virtually without support in his field, Ives could recognize in these words his own experience, reaffirm through them what he had himself "thought and felt all the time," and, most important, reclaim the reliance on his own intuition and experience that had been worn away by criticism and doubt. This self-reliance, instilled in Ives by his father, supported by Harmony's faith in him, and given new energy and purpose by the integration of idealism and individualism that Emerson made possible, was a necessary precondition for the creative torrent of Ives's middle years, particularly for the sudden appearance of so many ambitious and novel works in large forms.

The oppositions in Ives's music between the musical material of his
Both Emerson and Thoreau provided Ives with a philosophical justification for his artistic isolation, Emerson in his emphasis on individual intuition and Thoreau in his retreat from society into a solitary communion with nature and with his own thoughts. Equally important, Emerson's world view provided a framework for resolving the dichotomies of Ives's life and art—including the separation between life and art that he had learned in Danbury and practiced during his business career— through a magical alchemy where differences were transcended by an overall unity and Ives could integrate his father's open-mindedness, Parker's model of an idealistic and private musical experience, and his own social and religious ideals (deeply influenced by Harmony's) into one Transcendental ideal for both music and life as a whole.

The oppositions in Ives's music between the musical material of his vernacular upbringing and the formal and compositional assumptions of his classical training are resolved through a similar alchemy, a process of mixing in which nothing is compromised and the unity of diverse human experience is asserted. Unlike such European nationalist composers as Dvořák or Smetana, Ives did not smooth out or "house-train" the popular elements in his mature music to fit them into classical forms; instead, the surface incongruities are treated as unimportant in light of an overarching spirit of unity. Ives's mature music is completely dependent on his achievement of this mix, which is a product of the years after 1902 and particularly of his works after 1908. Before then, in the works that incorporate vernacular music, such as the *Second Symphony*, popular elements are subservient to the form and texture of the cultivated tradition, as often hidden in the texture as out in front. This mixing together of disparate elements in his music seems to predate Ives's mature enthusiasm for Emerson, but the temporal relationship between technique and philosophy is not at all certain. What is clear is that Emerson provided a philosophical justification for Ives's vast eclectic approach, an approach that has roots in his early music, long before his enthusiasm for Emerson developed.

Emerson is the capstone of Ives's philosophy, not its foundation. That so much of the *Essays* is written in Transcendentalist terms, and that Ives remained so enthusiastic about Emerson and Thoreau during the years after writing the *Essays*, is because the Transcendentalist writers offered a framework in which all of Ives's views could be integrated and all of the outstanding problems in his philosophy of art could be resolved. Viewing Emerson's essays as a source of solutions to problems that were already of central importance to Ives, rather than imagining that it was Emerson who set out the problems in the first place, should change our sense of Emerson's influence on Ives and our estimation of his role in and importance for Ives's development.

In their book *Wittgenstein's Vienna*, Allan Janik and Stephen Toulmin seek to correct the prevailing perception of Ludwig Wittgenstein as a disciple of Bertrand Russell. They comment that "a thinker of Wittgenstein's profundity, independence and originality, does not adopt his characteristic intellectual and moral beliefs, simply on account of the historical influence of some stronger-minded predecessor or contemporary."[5]

The same could be said for Ives. Both Wittgenstein and Ives were already wrestling with problems of fundamental importance in their respective fields *before* coming into close contact with their supposed mentors. Both, in fact, became interested in their predecessors' ideas precisely because those ideas offered a new direction for work that was already under way. Understanding their own backgrounds and interests makes clear why Ives and Wittgenstein chose to emphasize what they did in their elders' work while ignoring other aspects, and why and how interpreting their own works solely in the context of Emerson's essays or Russell's theories of logic, as the case may be, will produce a fundamental misunderstanding of their goals and achievements. Ives and Wittgenstein came to Emerson and Russell because the older philosophers offered ideas and tools that they found useful. That is both an obvious and a sufficient reason for the younger men's devotion.

CHAPTER TEN

The Writing of the *Essays* and After

Ives's integration of his views into a unified philosophy probably happened over time, beginning with the vernacular-inspired and experimental pieces of 1902 to 1908, incorporating Emerson around the time of the *Emerson Concerto* (1907 or 1908), and finally coming to completion only during the late 1910s when he was working on the *Essays*. Both Howard Boatwright and the Cowells point out that Ives read widely in the literature on Emerson and Thoreau during the period in which he was composing the *Essays*,[1] and his perceptions of the Concord writers must have deepened even then, after the *Concord Sonata*, which the *Essays* were intended to explain, was already complete. Thus, the very act of writing the *Essays* provided Ives an opportunity for contemplation and for summing up his mature philosophy and artistic stance.

It is not clear when Ives started making notes towards the *Essays*, but we know from a diary he kept during the first few months of 1919, which the Iveses spent in Asheville, North Carolina, during Ives's convalescence from his heart attack of the previous fall, that he finished the Prologue around the twentieth of January and wrote the Thoreau essay in the next two and a half weeks.[2] After this, he copied out at least three of the movements.[3] The Epilogue, although not mentioned explicitly in the diary, was almost certainly written at Asheville or very shortly thereafter, certainly not before, because of the high proportion of references in it to books and authors that Ives read while at Asheville.

The list of Ives's reading at Asheville appears on page 206 of the diary, and is of some interest in its own right; Harmony's list is on the facing page.

Read in Asheville
Jan-Mar. 1919

C.E.I.   Comic Tragedians [rightly, Tragic Comedians]
          [George] Meredith
          Thoreau—reread "Walden"
          Northanger Abbey   [Jane Austen]
          Sense & Sensibility   [Jane Austen]
          Pride & Prejudice   [Jane Austen]
          Scottish Chiefs   [a romance by Jane Porter from 1810,
                                                    in print in 1919]
          parts of Marcus Aurelius
          Contemporary Composers (reread)   [Daniel Gregory Mason,
                                                    New York, 1918]
          Emerson's Essays
               first & second series
          Bushnell's Sermons (4)   [four books?]
          Middlemarch   [George Eliot]
          [The Confessions of] Henry Lorrequer   [novel by
                                                    Charles James Lever,
                                                    1806–1872]
          Last Chronicles [rightly, Chronicle] of Barset
                                              [Anthony Trollope]
          Matthew Arnold's Essays (2)
          Letters of [Sidney] Lanier   [New York, 1899]

That Ives was rereading *Walden* and reading (or rereading) Emerson's *Essays* is hardly surprising, since he was simultaneously working on his own *Essays*. For the Thoreau essay, he was also referring to two recent books about Thoreau published in the previous three years, which he had presumably read before going down to Asheville.[4] Beyond these, much of Ives's other recent reading also found its way into his *Essays*, principally in the Epilogue: he mentions Bushnell on page 76, *Scottish Chiefs* on page 79, Meredith and Lever on page 87, Mason and his book on pages 87 and 94–95, Lanier's *Letters* on pages 95–96, and Marcus Aurelius on page 100. All of these references are asides, apparently woven into the text because they were on Ives's mind as he wrote, examples close to hand. In all likelihood, Ives wrote the Epilogue at Asheville soon after finishing the essay on Thoreau.

Since the early sketches for the *Essays* are primarily concerned with the essay on Emerson,[5] we may conclude that at most the Emerson essay was sketched before Asheville, that the Prologue, the Thoreau essay, and

the Epilogue were all written there, and that the whole book was revised
and put into final form during the next year and a half, prior to being
published in late 1920. The diary does not mention the Hawthorne and
Alcotts essays—they are very brief in comparison with the others, and
probably cost Ives little effort—but the surviving drafts suggest strongly
that they were written at the same time as the other essays.[6]

There are two important aspects of this summing-up. First, the
Essays mark the point of Ives's final integration of the various influences
on his thought, as he arrived at as successful a solution as he was ever to
find to the philosophical and musical problems with which he had been
grappling. It is not only in reading Emerson and rereading *Walden* as an
adult that Ives found his solutions; it was in the act of writing itself, the act
of putting down his point of view in words. After the *Essays*, there seem to
be no further fundamental changes in Ives's conception of music or his
beliefs in other areas. While there is no later aesthetic statement with the
scope of the *Essays*, Ives's later comments and memos conform in general
to the views set forth in the *Essays*. This very fact is in part responsible for
the assumption that Ives's approach to music was consistent before writing the *Essays* as well as afterwards. With 1919, then, the story of the
development of Ives's artistic aims is complete.

The second important aspect of Ives's summing-up is that it marks
the end of the most productive phase of his career as a composer and the
beginning of a period of setting his house in order, leading ultimately to a
long decline into silence as a composer. Sometime in 1916 or 1917, Ives
apparently stopped writing music, or at least slowed down his amazing
pace of the preceding several years, in order to gather notes for the *Essays*.
The *Concord Sonata* and the *Second Orchestral Set* were finished in 1915, the
Fourth Violin Sonata early in 1916, the *Fourth Symphony* in 1916 or early
1917; after these, Ives was to finish no more major works. He wrote very
little in 1917 beyond a handful of war songs, and the only work from 1918
is the prototype for the song *Premonitions*, composed in January of that
year. It was not his heart attack in October 1918 that stopped his composing, for he had already all but ceased to compose.

During his recovery, Ives set about the actual writing of the *Essays*,
publication of the *Concord Sonata* and the *Essays*, and gathering material
for *114 Songs*, for which he wrote almost forty songs during the years
1919–1921, some newly composed but most adapted from earlier works
in other media. Ives was unable to finish the more ambitious music that he
sketched during this period, including the projected *Third Orchestral Set*,
begun in 1919. After 1921, Ives completed seven more songs, some piano

pieces (largely transcriptions or adaptations of previous works), the *Three Quarter-tone Pieces* for two pianos, themselves partly adapted from earlier works, and a reconstructed version of *Psalm 90*, which had been lost. In 1926, perhaps while trying to breathe life into his unfinished *Third Orchestral Set* (worked on for the last time in that year), "he came downstairs one day and with tears in his eyes said [to Harmony] that he couldn't seem to compose any more—nothing would go well, nothing sounded right."[7] In 1928, Ives tinkered one final time with his *Universe Symphony*, begun in 1911 and left unfinished. In 1929, he rescored *Three Places in New England* for chamber orchestra, for a performance to be conducted by Nicolas Slonimsky; Elliott Carter witnessed Ives at this work, and has said that Ives not only rescored the work for a smaller ensemble but added new dissonances.[8] During the 1940s, Ives added a new text to the 1917 war song *He Is There* to update it for the Second World War and changed the closing tonic chord of the *Second Symphony* to an eleven-note crunch.[9] Ives continued throughout his life to improvise and spontaneously rearrange his works as he played them to himself.

There is no one dividing line. Rather, like the endings of so many of his pieces, Ives's composing gradually fades, from larger forms to smaller, from new works to tinkering with old ones. It seems most sensible to draw the major divisions at about 1918, during the period of silence after he had completed his last major works, and at 1926, when he completed his last new work, the song *Sunrise*. Together with the changes in 1894, 1902, and 1907–1908, these mark the major turning points of Ives's career.

There have been numerous theories put forward to explain why Ives gradually stopped composing. None so far has completely accounted for Ives's gradual decline. Harmony Ives blamed his broken health and creative exhaustion.[10] John Kirkpatrick attributes that exhaustion to Ives's "double life" as a daytime businessman and a leisure-time composer.[11] Colleen Davidson has suggested that the advent of World War One was a devastating disillusionment for Ives the idealistic progressive,[12] a notion that seems to be supported by Ives's own statements in the *Memos*.[13] This suggestion seems the most reasonable offered so far to explain Ives's hiatus in 1917 and 1918 and his renewed output in preparation for *114 Songs* but doesn't really explain his ultimate decline. Frank Rossiter has suggested that the mocking reviews of Ives's *Concord Sonata* and *114 Songs* in the musical press, combined with the resounding indifference of the musical fraternity to his music, "may well have been more crushing for him than the preceding period of utter neglect" and hints that the ridicule may have undermined Ives's self-confidence and crippled his will to compose.[14] Stuart Feder has argued that Ives's music was part of his process of mourning for his father, and that his creative impulse was essentially spent by the age of forty-nine (1923), the age at which his father had died.[15] Perhaps the most radical theory is that of David Wooldridge, who has speculated that Ives must have "quit composing sometime in 1916 to make money" in the stock market: "No man can accumulate the kind of wealth that he had, by 1919, without. . . . And there has to be a better reason for him stopping composing than simply having written himself out."[16]

Each of these may be partly correct, and the problem is perhaps ultimately insoluble. But surely a great part of Ives's energy after 1917 was consumed in reading for and writing *Essays Before a Sonata* and then continuing to express his views in short articles. For the first time, Charles Ives was writing words more than he was writing music. It may be that the exalted ideals and purposes for music that Ives outlined in the *Essays* became impossible for him to live up to, once he had made them explicit in writing. Except for a few new songs and a great many rearrangements of earlier music, where what was demanded of him was relatively minor in comparison with conceiving and executing an orchestral movement, Ives could perhaps no longer meet the standards he had set for his art. Perhaps the very act of summarizing his musical credo choked off any possibility of further development; perhaps the explicit idealism of his writings diverted his energies from the implicit idealism of his instrumental music.

The evidence suggests that Ives stopped growing musically at about the time he wrote the *Essays*, and growth and change had always been essential to his work. The later history of his attempts to write music is one of perpetual dissatisfaction. Perhaps it was partly the internalized criticism of all the Franz Milckes in his life; certainly his isolation had something to do with his exhaustion. But the isolation was what had produced his great works in the first place, isolation plus his wife's absolute belief in what he was trying to do. Overwork, the heart attack, growing older, all of these are contributing factors—but he did not stop trying to compose until the day he said that nothing seemed to go well anymore. He had not run out of ideas, and he had not run out of starting points. His artistic aims had exceeded his grasp, and it was easier for him to express those aims in words than to fulfill them in music.

Whatever the cause of his later loss of powers, the writing of the *Essays* marks the close of Ives's mature period, the decade that saw the composition of his biggest, finest, and most characteristic works. It is the music of this decade that most closely conforms to the aesthetic laid out in the *Essays*, and it is this music that still most intrigues, excites, and engages us.

Ives's path to that music and to the ideas in the *Essays* covered a lot of ground, twisting and turning between the genres, styles, and purposes of the utilitarian music of Danbury, the European classical ethos he learned at Yale, innovations in musical technique, and the dream of a music that might combine them all in a unified, transcendent vision. His individuality grew from his multiplicity, his willingness to be influenced by any and all, his insistence on gathering everything in and refusing nothing. The complexity of his history is the key to his character. His path was not that of the Transcendentalist or the experimentalist, but of the eclectic, the empiricist, the willing student of experience, for whom both experimentation and transcendence are but forms of experience.

Ives warns in his *Essays* against the narrowness of composers who find their style and stick to it, mining the same vein long after it has been essentially depleted or giving up their independence to seek fame or to follow a school. In offering the alternative of the eclectic artist, who limits himself to no categories but seeks the true and the useful wherever he can find them, Ives reminds us of his own history: his abandonment of the well-traveled paths of the tunesmith and church musician, his resulting isolation, and his discovery that all of his experiences contributed to a musical aesthetic and a musical language that made it possible for him to say things that had never been said in music before.

> It may be that when a poet or a whistler becomes conscious that he is in the easy path of any particular idiom—that he is helplessly prejudiced in favor of any particular means of expression—that his manner can be catalogued as modern or classic—that he favors a contrapuntal groove, a sound-coloring one, a sensuous one, a successful one, or a melodious one (whatever that means)—that his interests lie in the French school or the German school, or the school of Saturn— . . . then it may be that the value of his substance is not growing, that it even may have started on its way backwards; it may be that he is trading an inspiration for a bad habit, and, finally, that he is reaching fame, permanence, or some other undervalue, and that he is getting farther and farther from a perfect truth. But . . . if he (this poet, composer, and laborer) is open to all the over-values within his reach—if he stands unprotected from all the showers of the absolute which may beat upon him—if he is willing to use or learn to use (or at least if he is not afraid of trying to use) whatever he can of any and all lessons of the infinite that humanity has received and thrown to man, that nature has exposed and sacrificed, that life and death have translated—if he accepts all and sympathizes with all, is influenced by all . . . —*then* it may be that the value of his

substance, and its value to himself, to his art, to all art, even to the Common Soul, is growing and approaching nearer and nearer to perfect truths [pages 91–92].

Ives is so difficult to understand at times because he tried so hard to be true to his experience, however confusing and contradictory. But part of the power of his music lies in its ability to assert the unity of one man's experience in the face of a world that seems to grow more turbulent with every passing year. One of the lessons Ives has to teach us is that what has been separated can be brought back together, that truth is to be discovered not on any one path but on every path at once. His life, like his music, is a model of reconciliation.

NOTES

CHAPTER ONE. THE *ESSAYS*, THE COMPOSER, AND THE MUSIC

1. The sonata was engraved and printed privately at Ives's expense by G. Schirmer in 1919–1920 and mailed out in 1920. G. Schirmer's name appeared nowhere on the score, and Ives did not copyright the work, as he wished the music to be freely available to anyone without charge and without profit accruing to himself or anyone else. *Essays Before a Sonata* was printed for Ives by Knickerbocker Press of New York in 1920, again at his own expense. Excerpts from the *Essays* were printed with the revised edition of the *Concord Sonata*, published by Arrow Music Press in 1947 and later reprinted by Associated Music Publishers. The whole book of essays was edited by Howard Boatwright in 1961 and printed in a limited presentation edition in 1962. It was subsequently published along with the essays "Some 'Quarter-tone' Impressions" and "Postface to *114 Songs*" as *Essays Before a Sonata and Other Writings* (New York: W. W. Norton, 1964), and finally gathered together with many of Ives's writings on both musical and nonmusical subjects as edited by Boatwright in *Essays Before a Sonata, The Majority, and Other Writings* (New York: W. W. Norton, 1970).

Essays Before a Sonata consists of six essays related to the *Concord Sonata*, a Prologue, an Epilogue, and an essay on each of the four movements of the sonata and its associated literary figures: Ralph Waldo Emerson, Nathaniel Hawthorne, Amos Bronson Alcott and his family (including Louisa May Alcott, his daughter), and Henry David Thoreau, all of whom lived in Concord, Massachusetts, in the two decades before the Civil War. References to this work, given in shortened form as *Essays*, are to Boatwright's edition; the 1964 and 1970 collections have the same pagination (except that p. 1 in the earlier edition is p. xxv in the later edition). References to the other writings in Boatwright's 1970 publication will refer to it by the shortened title *Essays, Majority*, in order to make clear that the works cited are not integral parts of *Essays Before a Sonata*.

2. Frank R. Rossiter, *Charles Ives and His America* (New York: Liveright, 1975), p. 183.

3. From the composer's note at the end of the original edition of *114 Songs*, reprinted as "Postface to *114 Songs*," in *Essays, Majority*, p. 130. Once again, the book was printed privately at Ives's expense by G. Schirmer, whose imprint did not appear on the work, and was not copyrighted.

4. On Bellamann and his writings on Ives, see Henry Cowell and Sidney Cowell, *Charles Ives and His Music*, 2nd ed. (New York: Oxford University Press, 1969), pp. 99–100 and 102; Rossiter, *Ives and His America*, pp. 197–200; and the articles cited at the beginning of Chapter 3 below, notes 1 and 4.

117

5. On Schmitz, see Cowell and Cowell, *Ives*, pp. 101–103; Rossiter, *Ives and His America*, pp. 206–212; and Vivian Perlis, ed., *Charles Ives Remembered: An Oral History* (New Haven: Yale University Press, 1974; reprint ed., New York: W. W. Norton, 1976), pp. 124–130. On Cowell and Slonimsky, see Cowell and Cowell, *Ives*, pp. 103–111; Rossiter, *Ives and His America*, pp. 212–238 and 251–254; and Perlis, *Ives Remembered*, pp. 146–155. On Cowell and *New Music*, see Rita H. Mead, "Cowell, Ives, and *New Music*," *The Musical Quarterly* 66 (October 1980): 538–559; and idem, *Henry Cowell's New Music 1925–1936: The Society, the Music Editions, and the Recordings*, Studies in Musicology, no. 40 (Ann Arbor: UMI Research Press, 1981).

6. See Cowell and Cowell, *Ives*, pp. 109–113; Rossiter, *Ives and His America*, pp. 238–242 and 277–283; Perlis, *Ives Remembered*, pp. 213–226; and Gilman's review, "Music: A Masterpiece of American Music Heard Here for the First Time," *New York Herald Tribune*, 21 January 1939, p. 9.

7. Rossiter, *Ives and His America*, pp. 288–310. Cowell and Cowell, *Ives*, pp. 113–118, take the story up to 1954.

8. John Kirkpatrick, Appendix 8, p. 198, of his edition of Ives's *Memos* (New York: W. W. Norton, 1972). Kirkpatrick's letter to Ives of 28 September 1935, printed in part on that page, makes clear that he was studying the *Essays* along with the music.

Kirkpatrick's edition of the *Memos* includes not only the *Memos* themselves, an informal series of notes from the early 1930s that combine program notes for most of Ives's important pieces with personal reminiscences about their creation and his creative life, but also many appendices containing other fragmentary writings by Ives and much useful information compiled by Kirkpatrick. References to this book are to Ives's own words and to the main body of the *Memos* unless otherwise indicated.

9. Letter from Gilman to Harmony T. Ives, 19 January 1939, in the Ives Collection at the John Herrick Jackson Music Library, Yale University: "I am greatly indebted to you and to Mr. Ives for your kindness in sending me the copy of the 'Concord' Sonata and the other material." Part of the letter is printed by Kirkpatrick in *Memos*, Appendix 7, p. 185.

10. Rossiter, *Ives and His America*, p. 283. The revival of interest in the Transcendentalist writers dates to the publication in 1936 of Van Wyck Brooks's Pulitzer-prize-winning *The Flowering of New England*, which viewed the members of the Concord school as the founders of the American literary tradition, the natural ancestors of modern American writers. Gilman's review of the *Concord Sonata* refers to Brooks's book, remarking that Ives chose to celebrate the same figures as Brooks but more than two decades earlier.

11. *Memos*, Appendix 7, pp. 186–188, includes an early memo on the sonata, dated 1913 by Kirkpatrick, which is unrelated to anything in the *Essays*. Cowell and Cowell, *Ives*, p. 53, state that the *Essays* were begun soon after the sonata itself was completed in 1915. Ives himself says that they were mostly written in 1919 and finished in 1920 (*Memos*, p. 82). The evidence cited in Chapter 10 below suggests that, at most, parts of the Emerson essay were drafted prior to 1919, although Ives had apparently been jotting down ideas for these essays for years.

12.   Because Ives's pieces written after 1902 often waited decades before being performed or published, because of his habit of revising old works or of incorporating passages from previous works into new ones, and because he worked on several of his most important compositions, including the *Concord Sonata*, over many years, assigning a precise date of composition to a work is often next to impossible. In this study, I have followed Kirkpatrick's datings in his list of Ives's works in "Ives, Charles E(dward)," in *The New Grove Dictionary of Music and Musicians*, vol. 9, pp. 421–429, and in *A Temporary Mimeographed Catalogue of the Music Manuscripts and Related Materials of Charles Edward Ives 1874–1954* (New Haven: Library of the Yale School of Music, 1960; reprint ed., 1973).

CHAPTER TWO. THE AESTHETIC STANCE OF THE *ESSAYS*

1.   *Essays*, p. 18, referring to the ideas Emerson absorbed from the preacher William Ellery Channing, founder of Unitarianism.
2.   Ives also discusses the relationship between art and life in the "Postface to *114 Songs*," in *Essays, Majority*, pp. 124–129, and in a projected insert to the *Essays*, printed on pp. 253–254 of Boatwright's 1970 edition.
3.   "The intellect is never a whole. It is where the soul finds things. It is often the only track to the over-values."
4.   "That music must be heard is not essential—what it *sounds* like may not be what it *is*." Emphasis original.
5.   "The higher and more important value of this dualism is composed of what may be called reality, quality, spirit, or substance against the lower value of form, quantity, or manner."
6.   He credits Emerson and Thoreau with "the great transcendental doctrine of 'innate goodness' in human nature" (pp. 35 and 59–62), describes Bronson Alcott as a visionary idealist who tried to live out his ideals (pp. 46–48), and associates Hawthorne with "the idealism peculiar to his native land" (p. 41), although no more so than Emerson or Thoreau. Ives nowhere implies that Hawthorne was a Transcendentalist but rather associates him with the Puritan tradition of New England.
7.   "Universal mind" and "over-soul" are concepts borrowed from Emerson.
8.   For writings that pertain to the insurance business, see "The Amount to Carry," partially reprinted in *Essays, Majority*, pp. 232–242, and "Broadway" in *Memos*, Appendix 10, pp. 229–235; for writings in the field of politics, see the political essays gathered in *Essays, Majority*, pp. 134–231, and *Memos*, Appendix 9, pp. 205–228.
9.   By "rest" in this phrase, Ives means "the love of repose," which he opposes to "the activity of truth" (see above). In other words, Ives considers these composers to have sought not truth but merely a comfortable life.
10.   Salomon Jadassohn (1831–1902) was a German music theorist whose harmony textbook Ives had used while studying music theory with his father George Ives and again with Horatio Parker in college; see Ives's comment in the *Memos*, p. 49. Jadassohn became for Ives a symbol of academic pedantry and closed-mindedness, as authors of harmony texts have been for many a music

student. See Ives's comments in the *Memos*, p. 71; in a note on *Psalm 67*, ibid., Appendix 5, p. 178; and in a memo on the *Concord Sonata*, ibid., Appendix 7, p. 194. Of course, if Jadassohn were indeed incapable of analyzing Emerson's harmony, he would be equally stumped by the Emerson movement of the *Concord Sonata*. As is true at several other points in the Emerson essay, what Ives says of Emerson is equally apropos of his own work (and often more so).

11.   Ives gives two dates for the time period he means, 1845 in the preface to the *Essays*, 1840–1860 on the sonata's title page.

12.   The program is presented on p. 58 of the Arrow/Associated Music Publishers score and on pp. 67–69 of the *Essays*. The exact relationship of the program to the music is problematic, as is often the case with Ives's programs. It should not be assumed for any work that the program presents the only way to understand or approach the music. Indeed, Ives often worked out a program after the music was already written, sometimes offering several contradictory programs for the same piece. See J. Peter Burkholder, "The Evolution of Charles Ives's Music: Aesthetics, Quotation, Technique" (Ph.D. dissertation, University of Chicago, 1983), pp. 410–424, for a discussion of aspects of this issue.

13.   *Essays*, p. 48, score, p. 52: "We won't try to reconcile the music sketch of the Alcotts with much besides the memory of that home under the elms—the Scotch songs and the family hymns that were sung at the end of each day—though there may be an attempt to catch something of that common sentiment (which we have tried to suggest above)—a strength of hope that never gives way to despair—a conviction in the power of the common soul which, when all is said and done, may be as typical as any theme of Concord and its Transcendentalists." The "common sentiment" is the movement's main theme, gradually put together from fragments (including the opening motto of Beethoven's *Fifth Symphony* and melodically related hymn tunes) and presented whole in the closing bars of the first and third sections of the movement.

14.   Kirkpatrick has pointed out that both the Emerson essay and the Emerson movement are in three parts and has suggested that there is a relationship of structure and tone between the two, if not a program as such. Private communication, New Haven, 27 October 1981.

15.   On p. 79 of the *Essays*, Ives argues that music written by an American will be "American to the core" even if "chock-full of Scotch tunes" or devoid of any suggestion of old American tunes at all, so long as the composer's "interest, spirit, and character sympathize with, or intuitively coincide with that of the subject."

16.   See *Essays*, p. 73, and the comment of Ives's nephew Chester Ives, in Perlis, *Charles Ives Remembered*, pp. 87–88: "One evening, I talked with him [Ives] about Beethoven, and I said that I felt that what he was doing was what Beethoven would have done had he been able to keep on living. And he said that was the way he felt about it—a sort of continuing spirit."

17.   Ives uses the term *Geigermusik* (fiddle music) to connote music that is idiomatic, and therefore easy to play (or easier to play than it looks), but lacking in substance. The "windmills" refer to Strauss's tone poem *Don Quixote*, and the "human heads on silver platters" to the climactic final monologue of *Salome*. The "adventures of baby-carriages" refers to *Adventures in a Perambulator* (1914), by the American composer John Alden Carpenter.

18.   Peter J. Rabinowitz discusses Ives, among several other composers, in "Fictional Music: Toward a Theory of Listening," in *Theories of Reading, Looking, and Listening*, ed. Harry R. Garvin, *Bucknell Review*, vol. 26, no. 1 (Lewisburg, Penn.: Bucknell University Press, 1981), pp. 193–208. Lou Harrison was the first to compare Ives with Joyce, in his article "On Quotation," *Modern Music* 33 (Summer 1946): 168; see also Peter Dickinson, "A New Perspective for Ives," *Musical Times* 115 (October 1974): 836–838. Cowell and Cowell, *Ives*, p. 147, use the term *stream-of-consciousness*, and more recently Rosalie Sandra Perry has elaborated the idea, in *Charles Ives and the American Mind* (Kent, Ohio: Kent State University Press, 1974), especially on pp. 40–55. Christopher Ballantine, "Charles Ives and the Meaning of Quotation in Music," *The Musical Quarterly* 65 (April 1979): 167–184, and Stuart Feder, "Decoration Day: A Boyhood Memory of Charles Ives," *The Musical Quarterly* 66 (April 1980): 234–261, have written of the parallels between the experience of dreams and memories and the ways in which Ives's mature music presents myriad simultaneous familiar, distorted, and unfamiliar images.

19.   In the organ *Prelude and Postlude for a Thanksgiving Service*, which was later incorporated into *Thanksgiving* for orchestra and chorus; see *Memos*, p. 39.

20.   Ward, "Charles Ives: The Relationship Between Aesthetic Theories and Compositional Processes" (Ph.D. dissertation, University of Texas at Austin, 1974), pp. 132–133. Ward borrows the idea that certain smaller pieces served Ives as preparatory exercises for the development of the techniques he needed in his larger works from John McLain Rinehart, "Ives' Compositional Idioms: An Investigation of Selected Short Compositions as Microcosms of his Musical Language" (Ph.D. dissertation, Ohio State University, 1970).

21.   See Ward's comments in his third chapter, entitled "Aesthetic Conflicts in the Development of Style," particularly pp. 81 and 124–125.

22.   Ward, for instance, highlights this paradox; ibid., p. 75.

23.   J. Peter Burkholder, *The Evolution of Charles Ives's Music*, to be published by Yale University Press.

CHAPTER THREE. IVES AND TRANSCENDENTALISM

1.   Bellamann, "Charles Ives: The Man and His Music," *The Musical Quarterly* 19 (January 1933): 50. Bellamann includes in his statement more than just the *Concord Sonata*, but even for that work he goes beyond Ives's own claim for it as "an attempt to present (one person's) impression of the spirit of transcendentalism" (*Essays*, p. xxv); somehow Ives's sense of creating an impression has become for Bellamann a sense of creating an equivalent. On Bellamann's relationship with Ives, see Paul Parthun, "Concord, Charles Ives, and Henry Bellamann," *Student Musicologists at Minnesota* 6 (1975–1976): 66–86.

2.   Carter, "Ives Today: His Vision and Challenge," *Modern Music* 21 (May-June 1944): 199. On Carter's friendship with the Iveses, see his reminiscences of Ives in Perlis, *Ives Remembered*, pp. 131–145; in his "Documents of a Friendship with Ives," *Parnassus: Poetry in Review* 3, no. 2 (Spring-Summer 1975):

300–315, reprinted in *Tempo: A Quarterly Review of Modern Music*, no. 117 (June 1976): 2–10; and in his other writings.

3.   Typical is Perlis's summary in *Ives Remembered*, p. 52, repeating what has by now become common currency: "Emersonian transcendentalism and the ideas of the Concord group formed the core of Ives's philosophy. He lived as though Emerson were standing beside him, and this is reflected in his music and in his prose writings." See the similar comments in Wilfred Mellers, "Realism and Transcendentalism: Charles Ives as American Hero," in *Music in a New Found Land: Themes and Developments in the History of American Music* (London: Barrie and Rockliff, 1964), pp. 38–64; Audrey Davidson, "Transcendental Unity in the Works of Charles Ives," *American Quarterly* 22 (Spring 1970): 35–44; Perry, *Ives and the American Mind*, pp. 18–39; Rossiter, *Ives and His America*, pp. 93, 105, 108–109, and 202; Richard Schermer, "The Aesthetics of Charles Ives in Relation to his 'String Quartet No. 2' " (M.A. thesis, California State University, Fullerton, 1980); the works cited below in notes 11 and 12; and many other articles, theses, and papers.

4.   Bellamann's review appeared in the New Orleans literary journal *Double Dealer* 2 (October 1921): 166–169.

5.   See, for instance, Paul Rosenfeld's review of the first performance of the *Concord Sonata* in *Modern Music* 16 (1939): 109–112.

6.   Ives cites other sections of Bellamann's article with approval in the *Memos*, pp. 36–37 and 131. Carter's "Documents" include a letter from Ives to Carter about the latter's article "Ives Today," making several corrections of detail while passing over the passage about Transcendentalism without comment.

7.   See, for instance, the reminiscences in Perlis, *Ives Remembered*, by Chester Ives (p. 86), Charles Kauffman (p. 111), Louis Untermeyer (pp. 211–212), and John Kirkpatrick (pp. 218–219).

8.   According to Brewster Ives, the composer's nephew, Ives intended the correspondence to be quite exact in the case of the *Concord Sonata*. As Brewster Ives recalls in Perlis, *Ives Remembered*, p. 74, "He illustrated what he was attempting to do by reading passages from Emerson, the Alcotts, Hawthorne, and Thoreau and then playing passages [from the sonata] after he had read them to convince me that the music was expressing the words of the author." (My editorial insertion.)

9.   Cowell and Cowell, *Ives*, pp. 6–7.

10.   Boatwright, *Essays, Majority*, p. xiv. Boatwright has informed me that the Cowells' book, particularly pp. 6–7, was the sole source for his statement.

11.   For example, Dunja Dujmić, "The Musical Transcendentalism of Charles Ives," *International Review of the Aesthetics and Sociology of Music* 2 (June 1971): 89–95, and William Anson Call, "A Study of the Transcendental Aesthetic Theories of John S. Dwight and Charles E. Ives and the Relationship of These Theories to Their Respective Work as Music Critic and Composer" (D.M.A. dissertation, University of Illinois, 1971). See my Bibliography for other writings about Transcendentalism as an aspect of Ives's aesthetic.

12.   See, for instance, David Wooldridge, *From the Steeples and the Mountains: A Study of Charles Ives* (New York: Knopf, 1974), p. 4: "Transcendental propositions underlie almost the entire gamut of his music." Dujmić, "Musical Transcendentalism," p. 91, says of Ives's music that "American transcendentalism,

shaped by literature, was its continuous source." Similarly, Gianfranco Vinay, *L'America musicale di Charles Ives* (Torino: Giulio Einaudi, 1974), p. vi, considers Transcendentalism to be "the propulsive force and the constant point of reference for [Ives's] life as an artist and as a man" (il motore propulsore e il riferimento costante della sua vicenda artistica ed umana). In his text on twentieth-century music, Eric Salzman states that Ives and his father George Edward Ives are "the only important musical representatives" of the literary tradition of "Whitman, of Thoreau, Emerson and the New England 'transcendentalists,' and Ives set himself the job of creating, single-handed, a musical equivalent." Salzman regards the diversity of Ives's music as the result of this aspiration, asserting that Ives "had to compose out the entire tradition from one end to the other." *Twentieth-Century Music: An Introduction* (Englewood Cliffs, N.J.: Prentice-Hall, 1967), p. 147 (p. 131 of the 2nd ed. of 1974).

13.   *Memos*, Appendix 8, p. 201 (from a letter dated 11 October 1935 to Kirkpatrick from Harmony Ives, writing for her husband) and Appendix 13, p. 245. On an earlier occasion, citing the same letter from Harmony Ives, Kirkpatrick had described the entire Danbury Ives family as "enthusiastic transcendentalists," although he presented no evidence that any other family members shared the enthusiasm of Sarah Hotchkiss Wilcox Ives and her eldest son, Joseph. See John Kirkpatrick, "Ives's Transcendental Achievement," talk presented at Tanglewood, 4 July 1958; cited by Charles Ward, "The Use of Hymn Tunes as an Expression of 'Substance' and 'Manner' in the Music of Charles E. Ives, 1874–1954" (M.A. thesis, University of Texas at Austin, 1969), p. 6.

14.   That is, Wallach considers Transcendentalism to be fundamental to George Ives's approach to music and therefore to Charles Ives's approach as well. Laurence Wallach, "The New England Education of Charles Ives" (Ph.D. dissertation, Columbia University, 1973), p. 291. Rossiter, *Ives and His America*, pp. 126–127, comes to the same conclusion from the same evidence, citing the letter from Harmony Ives to John Kirkpatrick and asserting that Ives absorbed his Transcendentalism from Sarah Ives and from his father.

15.   On p. 96, in the Epilogue, Ives mentions "a part of Alcott's philosophy: that all occupations of man's body and soul in their diversity come from but one mind and soul!"

16.   Octavius B. Frothingham, in *Transcendentalism in New England: A History* (Boston: American Unitarian Association, [ca. 1876]), discusses Channing on pp. 110–113, describing him as "a Transcendentalist in feeling" (p. 113) though "certainly not a Transcendentalist in philosophy" (p. 111).

17.   Both Parker and Fuller had some connections with the Ives family (see Chapter 4), and both are mentioned in Edward Waldo Emerson's *Thoreau, As Remembered By a Young Friend* (Boston: Houghton Mifflin, 1917), a book Ives cites several times in *Essays Before a Sonata*.

18.   Some of the discussion that follows draws on Michael Moran's brief but insightful article, "New England Transcendentalism," in *The Encyclopedia of Philosophy*, ed. Paul Edwards et al., vol. 5, pp. 479–480.

19.   Frothingham, *Transcendentalism*, p. 355.

20.   He makes the same statement in the Thoreau essay (pp. 53–54 and 59), refers to the related "conviction in the power of the common soul" in the

Alcotts essay (p. 48), and cites the idea of man's innate goodness in other writings as well—for instance, in an early draft for "The Majority," in *Memos*, Appendix 9, p. 224. Hawthorne is not credited with this belief; Ives considered Hawthorne's "basic theme" to be "the influence of sin upon the conscience" (p. 41), suffusing Hawthorne's writings more with Puritan thought than with Transcendentalism. Ives never described Hawthorne or the Alcott children as Transcendentalists; they are included in the *Concord Sonata* because they lived in Concord.

21. Frothingham, *Transcendentalism*, p. 136.

22. For this interpretation I am indebted to James Miller of the University of Chicago, who helped clarify my view of Emerson.

23. For a discussion of this, see Ward, "Aesthetic Theories," p. 28.

24. With regard to Emerson's polarity, see Vivian C. Hopkins, *Spires of Form: A Study of Emerson's Aesthetic Theory* (Cambridge: Harvard University Press, 1951; reprint ed., New York: Russell & Russell, 1965), pp. 5, 17ff., and 40ff., especially pp. 43–45.

25. As Rossiter comments in *Ives and His America*, p. 105.

26. See *Essays*, pp. 41–42. Wooldridge, *From the Steeples*, pp. 286–293, points out the satirical side of much of Hawthorne's writing, the satirical nature of his story *The Celestial Railroad*, and the importance this has for the character of the Hawthorne music not only in the *Concord Sonata*, but also in the second movement of the Fourth Symphony, which is partly derived from the Hawthorne movement of the sonata. Around 1924–1925, Ives reworked the music from these two movements into a solo piano piece called *The Celestial Railroad*, based on this story by Hawthorne, which is a satire on Transcendentalism. Ives may have had the connection in mind for the earlier works as well.

27. "Emerson is more interested in what he perceives than in his expression of it. He is a creator whose intensity is consumed more with the substance of his creation than with the manner by which he shows it to others."

28. "The Transcendental Philosophy of Charles E. Ives as Expressed in 'The Second Sonata for Pianoforte, "Concord, Mass., 1840–1860" ' " (M.A. thesis, San Jose State College, 1966), p. 23; cited by Wallach, "Education," p. 99.

29. *Spires of Form*, p. 193. Hopkins discusses Emerson's attitudes towards music on pp. 190–193.

30. Roland Crozier Burton, "Margaret Fuller's Criticism of the Fine Arts," *College English* 6 (October 1944): 18–23, reprinted in Joel Myerson, ed., *Critical Essays on Margaret Fuller* (Boston: G. K. Hall, 1980), pp. 209–215; the quotation is on p. 212 of the reprint.

31. See Edward N. Waters, "John Sullivan Dwight, First American Critic of Music," *The Musical Quarterly* 21 (January 1935): 69–88. Waters's comments on Dwight's lack of training as a musician are on pp. 80–81 and rely on William Foster Apthorp's evaluation in his memorial essay, "John Sullivan Dwight," in *Musicians and Music Lovers* (New York: Charles Scribner's Sons, 1894), pp. 280–281.

32. Further on Dwight, see Walter L. Fertig, "John Sullivan Dwight, Transcendentalist and Literary Amateur of Music" (Ph.D. dissertation, University of Maryland, 1952).

33. Waters, "Dwight," pp. 73, 77, 80, and 85–88.

34. Quoted in George Willis Cooke, *John Sullivan Dwight: A Biography*

(Boston: Small, Maynard, 1898), p. 209. Chief among the startling new composers was Wagner, whom Dwight long opposed on philosophical grounds. Berlioz, Liszt, Brahms, and Joachim Raff were among the others (Apthorp, "Dwight," p. 281).

35.   Call, "A Study of the Transcendental Theories of Dwight and Ives," pp. 36–44.

36.   Ives described the *Concord Sonata* as "an attempt to present (one person's) impression of the spirit of transcendentalism" (*Essays*, p. xxv), and opened the Prologue of his *Essays* (p. 3) by asking, "How far is anyone justified, be he an authority or a layman, in expressing or trying to express in terms of music (in sounds, if you like) the value of anything, material, moral, intellectual, or spiritual, which is usually expressed in terms other than music?"

37.   The Alcotts lived in Orchard House in Concord.

38.   *Essays*, p. 48.

39.   See Ives's footnote in the *Essays*, p. 84, and the *Memos*, pp. 77 and 79–80 on *Emerson*, p. 81 on *Hawthorne*, and p. 82 on *The Alcotts* and *Thoreau*. On the Emerson and Hawthorne movements, see also Ives's letters to Kirkpatrick, in *Memos*, Appendix 8, pp. 199–204. In a 1923 memo, Ives wrote that "the Emerson movement started as a kind of piano concerto, the orchestra [representing] the world and people hearing, and the piano cadenza was Emerson" (*Memos*, Appendix 7, p. 189; my editorial insertion).

40.   These groupings appear on Ives's music manuscripts and are transcribed in Kirkpatrick's *Temporary Catalogue*, pp. 13–14. The group that eventually became the *Holidays Symphony* was also first jotted down on a manuscript (ibid., p. 10), suggesting that Ives considered these sets seriously.

41.   See Edward Waldo Emerson's note to the poem in *The Complete Works of Ralph Waldo Emerson*, Centenary Edition, biographical introduction and notes by Edward Waldo Emerson, vol. 9: *Poems* (Boston: Houghton Mifflin, [ca. 1903]), p. 470.

42.   Letter to John Tasker Howard, dated 30 June 1930, printed in *Memos*, Appendix 11, p. 240.

43.   See Taylor Stoehr's provocative discussion of these issues in *Nay-Saying in Concord: Emerson, Alcott, and Thoreau* (Hamden, Conn.: Archon Books, 1979), p. 15: "It is the very premise of fiction that it leave our daily lives alone." The same might be said for art music, even that of Ives. Ives by no means disdained novels; much of the reading he did all his life was fiction. During the Iveses' trip to Asheville, North Carolina, in early 1919, while Ives was recuperating from his heart attack of the previous autumn, they kept a list of their reading; half of Ives's reading was nineteenth-century English novels, especially Jane Austen, just the type for which Stoehr claims the Transcendentalists had such revulsion.

CHAPTER FOUR. THE PHILOSOPHICAL TRADITION OF THE IVES FAMILY

1.   Rossiter, *Ives and His America*, pp. 9–10; Kirkpatrick, *Memos*, Appendix 13, p. 245. The source for much of the information that both Rossiter and Kirkpatrick provide is an extended interview with Charles Ives's second cousin Amelia Van Wyck by Vivian Perlis, 7 and 21 November 1968, Tapes 2A, 2B, and

2C, Ives Oral History Project, in the Ives Collection. Excerpts from this interview are published in Perlis, *Ives Remembered*, pp. 3–12.

2. W. Bigelow Ives, interview with the author at his home in Southbury, Connecticut, 27 October 1981. I am very grateful to Mr. Ives for his information about the family and for letting William Brooks and me make a catalogue of the books from the Ives household, which were moved from Danbury to Charles and Harmony Iveses' country house in West Redding before the Second World War and are now housed in the family's old secretary in Bigelow Ives's house in Southbury. (Charles and Harmony Ives spent the warmer half of each year, beginning in 1913, in the West Redding house, staying in New York City during the winter.) For the history of the Ives residences in Danbury (and thus of the books, before they were moved to West Redding), see the interviews with Amelia Van Wyck and Philip Sunderland in Perlis, *Ives Remembered*, pp. 4–8 and 14–16, and Kirkpatrick, *Memos*, Appendix 13, pp. 245–249. For the catalogue, see William Brooks and J. Peter Burkholder, "Books in Bigelow Ives' Library and Identified by Him as Belonging to Charles Ives or His Family," compiled spring 1982, revised March 1984 (computer printout). I am also grateful to Vivian Perlis for providing me with a copy of a preliminary listing of the books that remain in the West Redding house, prepared by her students in 1979.

3. Among these are three volumes by Rev. Orville Dewey, a Unitarian who preached against the Transcendentalists. These are: *Discourses on Various Subjects*, 2nd ed. (New York: David Felt, 1835), *Moral Views of Commerce, Society and Politics, in Twelve Discourses*, 2nd ed. (New York: David Felt, 1838), and *Discourses on Human Life* (New York: David Felt, 1841). There are two copies of the first of these, one of them inscribed "Geo. W. Ives." The second and third are signed by William C. White, apparently a relative of George White Ives through his mother, née Sarah Amelia White (1773–1851); while these books may have been part of George and Sarah Ives's library, they may also have joined the collection at a later date. Dewey's views on the morality of politics are very like Charles Ives's, and there are some other startling similarities in their attitudes. Ives never mentions Dewey, and apparently there is no direct connection between them, but the coincidence that Ives's political philosophy seems to match that of Dewey, the anti-Transcendentalist, as well as it matches that of Emerson may serve to warn of the dangers of drawing parallels where no direct influence can be proven. The presence of Dewey's work in the collection may likewise make clear that the family's interest in religion and philosophy transcended the Transcendentalists to include most of the major figures of the time.

4. Boston: Little, Brown, 1856. The book was first issued in 1842, and this is a later edition.

5. Four volumes of the 1884 Riverside Edition of Emerson, including two copies of one of the volumes, are now on the bookshelf in Bigelow Ives's living room. Two of these volumes are inscribed by L. D. Brewster, Charles Ives's Uncle Lyman (Amelia Ives's husband), who lived in the Ives homestead from 1889 on. Presumably these are all from his set, rather than from the Ives family's own copies of Emerson, which would have dated from before the Civil War. The list prepared by Perlis's students includes sets of both Thoreau and Emerson but

records neither inscriptions nor publishing date, making it impossible to tell whether they could have belonged to Sarah Ives.

6. Interview, 27 October 1981. The slave incident would have taken place around 1831, the year Sarah and George were married. Sarah had moved to Danbury from her nearby hometown of Killingworth, according to Kirkpatrick, *Memos*, Appendix 13, p. 245.

7. Preface to *The Anti-Abolitionist Riots in the 1830's and 1840's* for piano solo (1908). In the first printing of this piece in 1949, Ives's grandfather was identified as an anti-abolitionist, an error that angered Ives so much that he corrected it with exclamation marks on his own printed copies of the piece. The brief program note in the preface describes the piece as "an attempt to reflect the spirit and courage of some Americans, like [William Lloyd] Garrison, [John Greenleaf] Whittier and others, who stood up and fought the Anti-Abolitionists in the 1830's and 1840's."

8. Bigelow Ives, interview, 27 October 1981.

9. Wooldridge, *From the Steeples*, pp. 27–29.

10. Ives's grandfather had died in 1862. Kirkpatrick describes Brooks's career and his relationship with the Ives family in the *Memos*, Appendix 14, pp. 250–252.

11. J. Moss Ives, *The "Ark" and the "Dove": The Beginning of Civil and Religious Liberties in America* (London: Longmans, Green, 1936). The *Ark* and the *Dove* were the ships that in 1633 brought Catholic and non-Catholic settlers to Maryland, sailing "under orders that proclaimed religious freedom for all who might seek sanctuary at the journey's end," in stark contrast to the complete absence of religious tolerance in the Puritan colonies of New England (ibid., p. vi).

12. Rossiter, *Ives and His America*, pp. 7, 140, and 177–178. Rossiter says of Moss Ives that "in doing perhaps more than any other member of the old Danbury families to give Catholics that sense of belonging, he earned their gratitude and respect" (p. 178).

13. Rossiter, ibid., pp. 10–11, mentions Joseph's acquaintance with Emerson, citing the interview with Amelia Van Wyck, 21 November 1968, Tape 2B, Ives Oral History Project (see note 1 above). Wooldridge, *From the Steeples*, pp. 26–27, provides further information; and Kirkpatrick, interviewed in Perlis, *Ives Remembered*, p. 218, mentions the family tradition that Emerson stayed at the Ives's house in Danbury during his visit there in the 1850s. Bigelow Ives, in an interview on 27 October 1981, confirmed both Joseph's link to Emerson and the story about Emerson staying with the Iveses. According to his pocket diaries, Emerson apparently visited Danbury twice, once on 19 or 21 November 1856 and again on 7 December 1859 (although the earlier visit is marked with question marks, perhaps to indicate a tentative date). *The Journals and Miscellaneous Notebooks of Ralph Waldo Emerson*, vol. 14, ed. Susan Sutton Smith and Harrison Hayford (Cambridge: Harvard University Press, Belknap Press, 1978), pp. 438 and 469.

14. The letter, about the *Concord Sonata*, dates from 1935 and is printed in the *Memos*, Appendix 8, pp. 199–202; the quotation is from p. 201. According to Kirkpatrick (personal communication, 27 October 1981), this was not the 1859 lecture at Danbury, which was on "Success." If Ives did not misremember the title, Sarah Ives may have heard Emerson speak twice.

15. Wooldridge, *From the Steeples*, p. 27. Like many of Wooldridge's interesting bits of information, this cannot be traced and should be accepted only with caution, if at all. John Kirkpatrick, in his review of Wooldridge's book in *HiFi/Musical America*, September 1974, pp. MA33–36, cites dozens of errors of fact and indicates that they are only a sampling.

16. *Memos*, Appendix 9, pp. 224–225.

17. The only books in the family collection in Bigelow Ives's possession that are identified as having belonged to George Edward Ives are the Rev. Albert Barnes's *Notes, Explanatory and Practical, on the Gospels* in 2 volumes (New York: Harper, 1856), inscribed "Geo E. Ives / Danbury / 2 May / 1858" (the first volume has the date missing) and very lightly annotated, and *Howe's New Flute Without a Master*, by Elias Howe (Boston: Elias Howe, 1863), stamped "Geo. E. Ives." In the house in West Redding, according to the list of books prepared by Perlis's students, there are also copies of *Edward & Miriam: A Tale of Iceland*, written for the American Sunday-school Union (Philadelphia: American Sunday-school Union, n.d. [ca. 1836]), inscribed "To George E Ives / from his cousin Harriet / July 1, 1850" (when he was five years old), and William H. Smith's *The Definer's Manual; Being a Dictionary on a New Plan* (New York: A. S. Barnes, 1859), inscribed "George E. Ives / Danbury, Conn." If George bought or was given books as an adult, they have not been located. It would have been contrary to the family custom not to sign them, making it unlikely that any of the books without inscriptions in the collections at West Redding or in Bigelow Ives's secretary could have come from George. George's books may have stayed with his wife, who died only in 1929, and may have been dispersed among his grandchildren on Moss's side of the family—or he may not have acquired many books as an adult. If George Ives had his own copies of Emerson and Thoreau, it would be surprising if Charles Ives had not acquired them at some point. George Ives would not have had the library of his parents George and Sarah Ives in his house; he died before his mother, and the family books would have remained in her possession.

18. Rossiter, *Ives and His America*, p. 22.

19. According to Bigelow Ives (interview, 27 October 1981), "Reading aloud was a family ritual, in our family and in Uncle Charlie's." The custom goes back at least to Charles Ives's childhood and probably further.

20. Ibid., p. 20.

21. The small number of books identified as belonging to George Edward Ives (see note 17 above) contrasts sharply with the many owned by his parents, by his sister and brother-in-law, Amelia and Lyman Brewster, and by Harmony Twichell's family that are contained in the collections at West Redding and in Bigelow Ives's home, and with the many inscribed by Charles Ives himself. There are no books in either place that seem to have come from Charles Ives's mother's family, the Parmalees. To judge both from the surviving family libraries and from descriptions by family members, George Edward Ives's household was in this respect unlike that of his mother Sarah, where, according to Charles Ives's cousin Amelia Van Wyck, people would stop by after church to discuss "what was going on in the world, men and books and so forth." Charles apparently did not take part in these sessions. Mrs. Van Wyck remembers Charles at the age of fourteen— ten years older than she and already a regular church organist—being as bored by adult talk as she. Interviewed in Perlis, *Ives Remembered*, pp. 8–9.

22.   According to Bigelow Ives, Moss learned the flute, which George Ives had also played as a boy (on George, see Kirkpatrick, *Memos*, Appendix 13, p. 246). Bigelow Ives still has the book of flute exercises that Moss used as a child, *Howe's New Flute Without a Master*; see note 17 above. The Ives brothers played together in an "orchestra" they organized, mentioned in Moss's diary for 1885 and in a letter from Charles to his aunt dated 14 September 1886. Both documents are preserved in the Ives Collection, the former catalogued as Diary D1, series V, box 45, folder 1, the latter in series III A, box 33, folder 1. For a catalogue of the holdings of the Ives Collection, other than the music itself (which is catalogued in Kirkpatrick's *Temporary Catalogue*), see Vivian Perlis, compiler, *Charles Ives Papers* (New Haven: Yale University Music Library, 1983). Moss also saw to it that his own children had an opportunity for music lessons.

23.   Interview, 27 October 1981. It is possible, given interpersonal dynamics between siblings, that if Charles Ives had been a strong Transcendentalist as a boy, Moss might have chosen not to be interested. (Thanks to Jean Burkholder for this point.) However, the two boys seem to have been quite close, sharing most other enthusiasms, and if anything, Moss seems to have been more literary than his brother, editing and publishing a newspaper for four years in collaboration with other Danbury teenagers. See Kirkpatrick, *Memos*, Appendix 13, p. 248.

24.   Cowell and Cowell, Ives, p. 7.

25.   The several exegeses of, concordances to, and commentaries on the Bible that were part of the Ives family's collection make clear the importance of the Bible as an object of study, not just a book to be read. It was the Bible, not Emerson, that Sarah Ives read and carefully explained to Henry Anderson Brooks (Kirkpatrick, quoting from a letter from Brooks to Sarah, 13 March 1876, in *Memos*, Appendix 14, p. 251). Both Moss's 1885 diary (Diary D1) and Charlie's from the following year (Diary D2, Ives Collection, series V, box 45, folder 2) frequently mention church attendance, sometimes both morning and evening, including Sunday-school classes. When one of the Ives boys did not attend church, it was worthy of comment, as in Charlie's letter to his father from the Connecticut shore, Sunday, 17 August 1890 (Ives Collection, series III A, box 33, folder 1).

26.   Sidney Cowell has kindly replied to a query about the source for the statement quoted above (letter, 21 November 1981), indicating that I may have taken her words more literally than she intended. She doubts that Ives studied Emerson or Thoreau "in an academic sense," says she does not know what Ives may have learned at home, and means only to suggest that the thinking of Emerson and Thoreau created a kind of "philosophical climate" in the same sense that the Bible or the Bill of Rights have done. I appreciate the clarification. As other scholars seem to rely on Cowell and Cowell for the idea that Ives learned his Transcendentalism at home, it now appears that no one knows what role Emerson and Thoreau played in Charles Ives's childhood and youth. None of the descriptions of Ives's family background that were written during his lifetime make any mention of Transcendentalism in the Ives family. This includes the most complete look at Ives's boyhood to be completed during his life, in an article by Lucille Fletcher, "A Connecticut Yankee in Music," intended for *The New Yorker* but never published. Fletcher's article is a particularly useful source because Ives went over it carefully, making suggestions. Three typed drafts, two with corrections by Charles Ives, plus earlier notes by Fletcher and jottings by Ives, are preserved with

the Fletcher correspondence in the Ives Collection, series III A, box 29, folder 8. Cowell and Cowell, *Ives*, p. vii, credit this article for much of their information on Ives's boyhood. If there is evidence for a steady diet of the Transcendentalist writers in the Danbury Ives family, I have yet to see it.

27. In the letter just cited, Sidney Cowell mentions these readings and notes that they continued into the 1950s.

28. Spoken by the character George in Ives's sketch towards an early version of "The Majority," in *Memos*, Appendix 9, p. 224.

29. Interview, New Haven, 26 October 1981.

30. *Memos*, Appendix 9, p. 227. George can be assumed to be articulating Ives's own thoughts throughout most of the piece.

31. *Memos*, p. 83. Since his grandmother lived until 1899, it is even possible, though perhaps unlikely, that she and Charles did not discuss Emerson until his own enthusiasm for the essayist had been enkindled in his senior American Literature class in 1897–1898. See the section on William Lyon Phelps, Ives's literature professor at Yale, in Chapter 6 below.

32. *Essays*, pp. 63–64. The "schoolteacher in English literature" dismissed Thoreau as "a kind of a crank who styled himself a hermit-naturalist and who idled about the woods because he didn't want to work." Ives comments, "If this teacher had had more brains, it would have been a lie." This teacher is obviously not Ives's Yale literature professor, William Lyon Phelps, who thought highly of Thoreau and whom Ives regarded affectionately. See the discussion of Phelps in Chapter 6 below.

33. Ibid., note n, p. 67.

34. Wooldridge, *From the Steeples*, pp. 144–145, confirmed by Kirkpatrick in his exchange with Wooldridge, "The New Ives Biography: A Disagreement," *HiFi/Musical America*, December 1974, p. MA20.

35. Eight volumes published in the 1870s by J. R. Osgood of Boston, according to Perlis's list; the smallest set Osgood published was twelve volumes total.

36. Boston: James Munroe, 1836–1837, in 2 volumes. Both volumes lack annotations and inscriptions but are presumably from G. W. Ives's collection.

37. Ives uses stories drawn from Edward Waldo Emerson, *Thoreau*, and Henry A. Beers, "A Pilgrim in Concord," *Yale Review*, n.s. 3 (July 1914): 673–688.

CHAPTER FIVE. EARLY MUSICAL TRAINING (1874–1894)

1. Kirkpatrick, *Memos*, Appendix 13, p. 246; Rossiter, *Ives and His America*, pp. 11–12. The best discussion of George Ives's background and career is that by Laurence Wallach in his dissertation, "Education," pp. 37–94. Wallach discusses George Ives's studies with Foeppl on pages 73–77. Little is known about Foeppl himself.

2. See Ives's letter to John Tasker Howard, in *Memos*, Appendix 11, p. 237.

3. Ives also mentions the "family prejudice" for quarter-tones in "Some 'Quarter-tone' Impressions," in *Essays, Majority*, pp. 110–111.

4. *Memos*, p. 47; Kirkpatrick's editorial insertions.

5. Wallach, "Education," p. 50.

6. David Eiseman, "George Ives as Theorist: Some Unpublished Documents," *Perspectives of New Music* 14 (Fall-Winter 1975): 141, confirms this.

7. *Memos*, p. 115.

8. Ibid., pp. 38 and 115.

9. Kirkpatrick, *Temporary Catalogue*, p. 106.

10. The development of Ives's compositional methods and the dichotomy between his experimental and concert music are both discussed at length in my book *The Evolution of Charles Ives's Music* (forthcoming from Yale University Press), a companion volume to this one.

11. From the letter to John Tasker Howard, 30 June 1930, in *Memos*, Appendix 11, p. 237.

12. Paraphrased by Charles Ives, *Memos*, p. 132. The last sentence sounds less like George Ives than like his son, who once sketched a mocking poem beginning "Nice little easy sugar-plum sounds" to the tune of the adagio from Haydn's *Surprise Symphony*; see item 7C22 of Kirkpatrick's *Temporary Catalogue*, p. 221. But the gist is similar to another maxim of George's, quoted in the letter to Howard (*Memos*, Appendix 11, p. 240): "If a poet knows more about a horse than he does about heaven, he might better stick to the horse, and some day the horse may carry him into heaven." Since these and others of George Ives's colorful sayings are preserved only through Charles Ives's memory, it is impossible to ascertain how accurately Ives is reporting a conversation of forty or fifty years earlier, and how much of the color is his own embroidery.

13. Emphasis original. This passage has been subject to misinterpretation; Ives is insisting only on the primacy of the musical idea over its realization or ease of performance, as did Beethoven and other composers a century before.

14. *Memos*, p. 133.

15. Letter of 28 May 1931, printed in Nicolas Slonimsky, *Music Since 1900*, 4th ed. (New York: Charles Scribner's Sons, 1971), p. 1327. Slonimsky had conducted the piece six months earlier at a concert with the Boston Chamber Orchestra in Town Hall, New York.

16. In a letter of 11 October 1935 to Kirkpatrick, in *Memos*, Appendix 8, pp. 200–201. Emphasis original.

17. Wallach, "Education," pp. 41–42, suggests that George Ives's musical tastes were both relatively simple and consonant with his environment.

18. *Symphony No. 4*, performance score, ed. Theodore A. Seder, Romulus Franceschini, and Nicholas Falcone, with a preface by John Kirkpatrick (New York: Associated Music Publishers, 1965), p. 14. Also printed as "Music and Its Future," in *American Composers on American Music*, ed. Henry Cowell (Stanford: Stanford University Press, 1933; reprint ed., New York: Frederick Ungar, 1962), p. 198.

19. Memo dated 5 June 1914, copied into a miscellaneous diary in the Ives Collection, series V, box 45, folder 12. Quoted in Kirkpatrick, *Memos*, Appendix 13, p. 247.

20. *Essays*, *Majority*, p. 111.

21. Described in *Memos*, pp. 42–43.

22. In *Psalm 150* (ca. 1894), verse 3, trumpets are evoked by a melody built of fourths and octaves.

23. Set to static pianissimo augmented triads in *Crossing the Bar* (1890).
24. From Ives's note to *Central Park in the Dark*, ed. Jacques-Louis Monod, with notes by John Kirkpatrick (Hillsdale, N.Y.: Boelke-Bomart, 1973), p. 31.
25. Hopkins, *Spires of Form*, p. 192, writes: "His journal of 1841 mentions the violent effect upon the nerves of country orchestras in their first stages of practicing—chiefly, he says, because of their loud volume."
26. *The Writings of Henry David Thoreau*, Walden Edition (Boston: Houghton Mifflin, 1906), vol. II, p. 136. Ives quotes part of this in the *Essays*, p. 68, and Boatwright supplies the full text, p. 249.
27. Rossiter, *Ives and His America*, p. 29, mentions piano lessons with Miss Ella Hollister; Cowell and Cowell, *Ives*, pp. 24–25, drum lessons with a barber named Slier; and Kirkpatrick's "Chronological Index of Dates," in *Memos*, pp. 325–326, organ lessons with J. R. Hall and Alexander Gibson and organ posts at the Second Congregational Church and, eight months later, at the Baptist Church in Danbury. Kirkpatrick's annotations depend on Ives's own diaries, D2 and D4 in the Ives Collection, series V, box 45, folders 2 and 4.
28. Rossiter, *Ives and His America*, pp. 17–19.
29. In "Postface to *114 Songs*," in *Essays, Majority*, pp. 124–129, and other writings discussed in Chapter 2.
30. Rossiter, *Ives and His America*, pp. 24–26. The first chapter in Wallach, "Education" ("Ives' Musical Background and Its History," pp. 1–36), is excellent in tracing the origins and progress of this schism in the musical life of nineteenth-century New England. The terms *cultivated* and *vernacular* are borrowed from H. Wiley Hitchcock, *Music in the United States: A Historical Introduction*, 2nd ed. (Englewood Cliffs, N.J.: Prentice-Hall, 1974), p. x.
31. Wallach, "Education," pp. 37–94, emphasizes both the friction between these two musical traditions and George Ives's activities in both.
32. Rossiter, *Ives and His America*, pp. 41–43, sums up this integration nicely.
33. Wallach, "Education," pp. 231–232, makes a similar point.

CHAPTER SIX. YEARS OF APPRENTICESHIP (1894–1902)

1. The sole exception is his reconstruction (or recomposition) in 1923–1924 of *Psalm 90*, for church choir, organ, and bells, after the earlier version, written sometime between 1894 and 1902, was lost.
2. *Memos*, pp. 48–49, 115–116, and Appendix 6, pp. 180–183. On p. 49, Ives mentions going through Salomon Jadassohn's harmony textbook under Parker. Since this was the required text in Parker's Harmony course (see the list of music courses, with descriptions, in ibid., Appendix 6, p. 182), which was presumably a prerequisite for the more advanced courses Ives took as an upperclassman, it seems probable that Ives audited the course during his first two years. Parker's History of Music course was delivered as a series of public lectures, and Ives must certainly have attended them at some point during his time at Yale; see Kirkpatrick's comments in ibid., p. 183.
3. Kirkpatrick shows Ives's college transcript in *Memos*, Appendix 6, pp.

180–182, and lists the enrollments for each of the courses Parker taught during those years on p. 182.

4.   There are several polytonal fugues, mostly fragmentary. Ives had begun some of these while his father was alive, but the most substantial was the *Fugue in Four Keys on "The Shining Shore"*, for flute, cornet, and strings, written in 1897 while at Yale.

5.   Kirkpatrick's editorial insertions. I have removed the italic parentheses that Kirkpatrick uses to indicate a later insertion.

6.   William Kay Kearnes, "Horatio Parker 1863–1919: A Study of His Life and Music" (Ph.D. dissertation, University of Illinois, 1965), pp. 2, 21, 7, and 4–5.

7.   Address presented in 1899 to the Episcopal Club of Massachusetts, quoted in Isabel Parker Semler's reminiscence of her father, *Horatio Parker* (New York: G. P. Putnam's Sons, 1942; reprint ed., New York: AMS Press, 1975), pp. 74–75.

8.   See Parker's statements about music in college education in Kearnes, "Parker," pp. 105–106, and his opinions on aesthetics expressed in his lectures on music history, ibid., pp. 114–115.

9.   Ibid., p. 7: "He mistrusted that music which he felt gratified only the senses. He insisted that music should have deeper, abiding values, but he never analyzed these in any detail."

10.   Rosalie Sandra Perry, *Ives and the American Mind*, pp. 7–12, was the first to point out this relationship between the ideals of teacher and student, although she does so somewhat differently and makes errors, such as claiming that Parker thought "the art of absolute music was exhausted" (p. 8) when he said exactly the opposite (passages quoted in Kearnes, "Parker," p. 186, and Semler, *Parker*, p. 163).

11.   Kearnes, "Parker," p. 188, citing Parker's unpublished "Miscellaneous notes for Addresses," in the John Herrick Jackson Music Library, Yale University.

12.   Kearnes, "Parker," pp. 7–8, 105–106, 114–115, 186–188, and 249.

13.   Perry, *Ives and the American Mind*, p. 11, citing as her source Kearnes, "Parker," p. 8.

14.   There is no mention of Emerson in Parker's available writings or lecture notes or in the biography by his daughter. Classroom lecture notes do not survive (Kearnes, "Parker," p. 122), but his classes were almost solely concerned with the technical aspects of music. Notes do survive for his History of Music course, which was open to the public. I have not examined these notes or scoured Parker's diaries and letters, but Kearnes has, and he surely would have offered documentation for his argument had he found any direct Transcendentalist influence on Parker. While Parker claims preeminence for New England in American literature (ibid., pp. 87–88), his citations are primarily European (e.g., the European historians of music cited in his lectures, ibid., p. 115), and his interests in literature are purely classical (ibid., p. 684).

15.   "Impressions of a Year in Europe" (Address to the Episcopal Club of New Haven), quoted at length in Semler, *Parker*, pp. 155–165; the quotation is from p. 164.

16.   *Essays*, p. 75, where he contrasts the "higher and more important value . . . of what may be called reality, quality, spirit, or substance against the lower value of form, quantity, or manner."

17.   Ibid., p. 4: "Is not all music program music? Is not pure music, so called, representative in its essence? Is it not program music raised to the nth power, or, rather, reduced to the minus nth power?"

18.   Semler, *Parker*, p. 164.

19.   *Memos*, p. 49.

20.   Ibid., p. 73.

21.   The present first movement, later adapted as the third movement of the *Fourth Symphony*, is derived from a fugue written for Parker, according to a note on the quartet's manuscript title page; Kirkpatrick, *Temporary Catalogue*, p. 57.

22.   Apparently, during Ives's years at Yale, Parker had no respect for popular music, although his views mellowed somewhat later in life; see Kearnes, "Parker," p. 249.

23.   Kearnes, "Parker," pp. 682–683 and 686, points out that Parker's compositions were by no means all rigidly conservative, and several had novel features.

24.   As Wooldridge points out, *From the Steeples*, p. 79. Parker's teaching style did not encourage self-confidence in his students. John Tasker Howard, in *Our American Music: Three Hundred Years of It* (New York: Thomas Y. Crowell, 1931), p. 337, described him as "something of the bully" in class. See also Rossiter, *Ives and His America*, p. 57. One wonders how much of Ives's own later bluster on musical subjects he owed to Parker's example.

25.   Rossiter, *Ives and His America*, p. 64.

26.   Ibid., pp. 64–66. On George Felsburg, see *Memos*, pp. 56–57; on Frank Fichtl, see ibid., p. 40, note 6.

27.   Included in John Kirkpatrick's typed transcriptions of Ives family letters, which he graciously permitted me to consult, is a note dated August 1892 from a New York publisher suggesting possible cuts in the *Variations* and a letter of 4 February 1894 from Charles to his father mentioning that the publisher had sent the score back to Danbury without offering to print it.

28.   Rossiter, *Ives and His America*, p. 65.

29.   According to one of Ives's lists of his works, *Memos*, Appendix 2, p. 148.

30.   Kirkpatrick lists these performances in *Memos*, Appendix 15, pp. 254–255.

31.   I have changed to normal roman type the italic parentheses Kirkpatrick uses to indicate a later insertion.

32.   The letter is printed in *Memos*, Appendix 15, pp. 257–258.

33.   Griggs saw Ives in New York in 1899 and 1902, according to memos on music manuscripts; see Kirkpatrick, *Memos*, Appendix 15, pp. 254–255, and Appendix 17, p. 264. The only surviving correspondence with Griggs between 1898 and the publication of the *Essays* is an exchange of letters from the summer of 1916, in which Ives writes, "You must come to Redding again this summer. Mrs. Ives and I are counting on another visit." (Carbon copy of letter from Ives to Griggs, 19 May 1916, in the Ives Collection, series III A, box 29, folder 14. This note is printed in *Memos*, Appendix 15, p. 255.) Their cordiality is clear, but the course of their relationship between 1902 and 1916 cannot be traced. It is not clear

whether the contact between Griggs and Ives remained unbroken or whether they renewed their friendship after a lapse of some years.

34. Kirkpatrick's comment, *Memos*, Appendix 15, p. 255; Griggs's letter, printed on pp. 255–257, is dated 27 August 1921, and was sent from Canton, China, where he was a professor of English at Canton Christian College (later Lingnan University) from 1919 to 1927. Griggs is briefly mentioned in Charles Hodge Corbett's *Lingnan University: A Short History Based Primarily on the Records of the University's American Trustees* (New York: Trustees of Lingnan University, 1963), but no mention is made of his musical interests or activities, if any. While in China, Griggs published several articles in *Current History* and *China Review* about the political revolution in China. Citations for these articles, as well as all his known writings on music and other subjects, are given in the Bibliography to this volume.

35. *Memos*, Appendix 15, p. 256.

36. "Claude Debussy," *Yale Review*, n.s. 1 (April 1912): 484–494; quotation from p. 493.

37. *Yale Literary Magazine* 53 (November 1887): 62–67; quotation from p. 63. In the vita he appended to his dissertation on American music, submitted to the University of Leipzig in 1893, Griggs mentions that this essay won him an editorship of the *Literary Magazine* during his senior year at Yale in 1888–1889.

38. *Memos*, Appendix 15, p. 256.

39. Ibid., p. 257.

40. Ives cites Griggs's article (*Essays*, p. 81) only in respect to this central issue, though he seems to rely on it for much of his discussion of Debussy, pp. 81–82. What little of Debussy's music Ives knew he probably learned through Griggs.

41. Ives Collection, series II A, box 24, folder 1.

42. *The Musical Quarterly* 3 (October 1917): 552–561. Griggs resigned as a singing teacher at Vassar College in 1919 and almost immediately took the position at Canton, ending his professional association with music. The articles mentioned here and below are probably, but not certainly, all of the important articles Griggs published in music journals. In addition to consulting standard indexes such as the *Reader's Guide to Periodical Literature, Poole's Index to Periodical Literature*, and the *International Index to Periodicals*, I have combed through a card-file index to American and European music periodicals that was made prior to 1942 by employees of the Works Projects Administration at Chicago's Newberry Library (and in 1982 was in the library of DePaul University in Chicago) and have found no additional articles by or references to Griggs. Since the index was never completed, it is possible that other articles exist that were not indexed. Griggs may have published articles in German periodicals or newspapers during his student days in Germany, but this seems unlikely; such publication would have been a rare achievement for an American student, and Griggs would most likely have listed any such articles in the vita attached to his dissertation, where he mentions his other publications on music before 1893.

43. *Music* (Chicago) 5 (April 1894): 688–692.

44. "Possibilities of a Pure Toned Organ," *Music* (Chicago) 2 (September 1892): 483–490. In *Memos*, Appendix 15, p. 254, Kirkpatrick quotes a passage from Griggs's dissertation with comments similar to those in the above article.

45.   Compare Griggs's arguments in "Possibilities," p. 486, with Ives's acid comments on the "true, fundamental, natural laws of tone," in *Memos*, pp. 48 and 50.

46.   Ives's Yale transcript appears in *Memos*, Appendix 6, pp. 180–182.

47.   See the reminiscences of two of Ives's classmates, in Perlis, *Ives Remembered*: "We all had Billy Phelps and loved him" (p. 21). "Everyone studied with Billy Phelps. He attended all our reunions, and was probably the most popular professor in our day" (p. 24). See also Phelps's own reminiscences in his *Autobiography With Letters* (New York: Oxford University Press, 1939), pp. 281–287, where he discusses his close relationships with his students in his first years of teaching at Yale, beginning in 1892.

48.   Ives was a sorry student, but his grades for his three classes with Phelps are generally higher than for any of his other classes except those with Parker, according to the transcript in *Memos*, Appendix 6, pp. 180–182.

49.   Typed draft of this letter to Phelps, dated 6 January 1937, in the Ives Collection, series III A, box 31, folder 6.

50.   Phelps, *Autobiography*, p. 308.

51.   The transcript on p. 181 of the *Memos*, Appendix 6, lists these works.

52.   New York: Thomas Y. Crowell, 1907.

53.   *Memos*, p. 76.

54.   The list of books in the Ives household at West Redding, prepared by Perlis's students in the late 1970s, mentions on p. 28 a volume of *Prayers from Plymouth Pulpit* by Henry Ward Beecher, dated 5 November 1894 (the day after George Ives's sudden death), with Charles Ives's name and Yale address and a dedicatory note from his grandmother. As there is no other book of Beecher's in the Redding house or in the secretary at Bigelow Ives's home, presumably it was this gift from Sarah Ives that inspired Ives to include Beecher in his "Men of Literature" series.

55.   Ives mentions the incident in *Memos*, p. 83. It is unlikely that such a paper would have been written for any other course—possibly sophomore Rhetoric, but certainly not senior Philosophy—and almost certain that Ives would not have written it on the side, outside the classroom, since his extracurricular time seems to have been so heavily involved in music; see Kirkpatrick's comment, *Memos*, Appendix 6, p. 182. Perhaps it was Griggs, who had been an editor of and frequent contributor to the *Literary Magazine* during his years as an undergraduate, who encouraged Ives to submit the paper. The paper apparently does not survive, but Ives says in the *Memos*, pp. 82–83, that some of the Emerson essay in *Essays Before a Sonata* was adapted from it.

56.   "The American Philosopher: Ralph Waldo Emerson" and "Nathaniel Hawthorne and Puritanism," in *Some Makers of American Literature* (Boston: Marshall Jones, 1923), pp. 129–162 and 97–128 respectively, and "Thoreau," in *Howells, James, Bryant, and Other Essays* (New York: Macmillan, 1924), pp. 66–95.

57.   *Autobiography*, pp. 207–208. There are more than seven times as many citations of Browning in the index as of Emerson.

58.   Phelps, "Emerson," p. 135.

59.   Rossiter, *Ives and His America*, p. 185. Rossiter considers the review as "hardly more than an act of personal friendship," but this is not borne out by

Phelps's consistent enthusiasm for it, both in the review ("This is a brilliant and provocative book, full of challenging ideas, and marked by chronic cerebration. I enjoyed every page of it, and I heartily recommend it to those who have minds, and wish to use them") and in his letters to Ives acknowledging receipt of the book ("Your book is full of thought and inspiration—it came out of a rich, active mind—I can see how happy you must be and how you must enjoy living"—letter of 17 June 1920, in the Ives Collection, series III A, box 31, folder 6). Ives later sent Phelps the *Concord Sonata* and *114 Songs*, and after Kirkpatrick's first performance of the complete sonata in 1939, Phelps arranged for him to repeat it in New Haven so that he and his wife could attend. While Phelps's style is a little effusive, the enthusiasm for both essays and music seems genuine.

60. There are some suggestive passages in Phelps's essay that seem to incorporate some of Ives's thinking—for instance, the following from p. 142, on the disconnectedness of Emerson's writing style: "As a friend suggests, although the sentences were not always connected with one another, they were all connected with God." Could this friend be Ives? Compare this with pp. 22–23 of the *Essays*, which also discuss Emerson's epigrammatic style.

61. Rossiter, *Ives and His America*, p. 110.

62. As in the "Postface to *114 Songs*" and Ives's letter to Henry Bellamann, quoted in the latter's article "Charles Ives: The Man and His Music," *The Musical Quarterly* 19 (January 1933): 47–48.

63. In *Memos*, p. 131, Ives writes that a single man "might write music that no one would play, publish, listen to, or buy. *But*—if he has a nice wife and some nice children, how can he let the children starve on his dissonances [?] . . . If a man has, say, a certain ideal he's aiming at in his art, and has a wife and children whom he can't support (as his art products won't sell enough unless he lowers them to a more commercial basis), should he let his family starve and keep his ideals? No, I say—for if he did, his 'art' would be dishonestly weakened, his ideals would be but vanity."

64. Cowell and Cowell, *Ives*, pp. 36–39, seem to have been the first to fix this decision at the point of Ives's graduation from Yale and to suggest that both the decision to give up music and the idea of serving mankind through insurance came easily to Ives because of his Transcendentalist background. The choice of insurance seems to have depended upon personal contacts, chiefly Granville White, however, rather than upon altruistic motivations. As has been shown in Chapter 3 above, Transcendentalism explains rather less about Ives's life and thought than has been assumed.

65. Rossiter, *Ives and His America*, p. 84.

66. According to Wallach, "Education," p. 42.

67. Rossiter, *Ives and His America*, p. 20.

68. Letter of 29 March 1894, taken from a transcription by Kirkpatrick. Gustave J. Stoeckel, organist, voice teacher, composer, and German immigrant, was Parker's predecessor as Battell Professor of Music and was instrumental in establishing a department of music at Yale in 1890; Kearnes, "Parker," pp. 99–104.

69. Kearnes, "Parker," pp. 96–97, points out that Yale had throughout

the nineteenth century "stressed mental discipline rather than training for a professional field."

70. Kirkpatrick, *Memos*, Appendix 13, pp. 245-246; Rossiter, *Ives and His America*, pp. 9-12; Wooldridge, *From the Steeples*, pp. 25-27.

71. Rossiter discusses George Ives's status as a poor relation at some length in *Ives and His America*, pp. 12-23.

72. Kirkpatrick, *Memos*, Appendix 13, p. 248.

73. In his "Chronological Index of Dates," in *Memos*, p. 327, Kirkpatrick suggests 26 June 1898, the Sunday before Yale's commencement, as the probable date of Ives's first service as organist at the Bloomfield Presbyterian Church.

74. Interview with Amelia Van Wyck, in Perlis, *Ives Remembered*, p. 45; Kirkpatrick, *Memos*, Appendix 13, p. 246; and Rossiter, *Ives and His America*, pp. 11-12.

75. From a conversation with Kirkpatrick, 1963, in *Memos*, p. 103, note 7.

76. Rossiter, *Ives and His America*, p. 29.

77. The best of the surviving recordings, made in New York City in 1938 and 1943, have been released on *Charles Ives: The 100th Anniversary*, Columbia M4 32504 (1974), Record IV.

78. Rossiter, *Ives and His America*, p. 29.

79. Kearnes, "Parker," p. 129.

80. The first and third of these chorales also exist in arrangements for instrumental ensembles and choir.

81. Parker, introduction to *Music and Public Entertainment* (Boston: Hall and Locke, 1911; reprint ed., New York: AMS Press, 1980), p. xvi. Besides teaching at Yale, Parker worked as an organist and choirmaster in Boston and New York until 1910 (Kearnes, "Parker," pp. 156, 194, and 218), conducted the New Haven Symphony and choral groups in New Haven, Philadelphia, and smaller cities in Massachusetts and Connecticut from 1894 until a few months before his death in 1919 (ibid., pp. 156, 157, 181, 193, 207-210, and 250), and was often paid for lectures as well (ibid., pp. 158 and 233). Parker continued his teaching and conducting activities even after winning two substantial prizes of $10,000 each for his operas *Mona* and *Fairyland* in 1911 and 1914 respectively (ibid., pp. 214-219 and 229-230).

82. Unlike the Cowells and others, Ives himself considered 1902, and not 1898, as the pivotal year when he gave up music as a career and turned wholeheartedly to business, composing only for himself.

83. Review of the first recording of *The Celestial Country*, *The Musical Quarterly* 60 (July 1974): 500-508; quotation from p. 506. The rest of this paragraph summarizes Yellin's argument.

84. The cantata was premiered on Friday evening, 18 April 1902, and the *Musical Courier* reviewed the concert in its issue of 23 April 1902, p. 34, noting that the cantata "shows undoubted earnestness in study and talent for composition, and was fairly creditably done." A week after the performance, a news item in the *Danbury Evening News* (Saturday, 26 April 1902) told of Ives's resignation (see Kirkpatrick, "Chronological Index of Dates," in *Memos*, pp. 327-328; see also *Memos*, p. 68, note 3). According to Wooldridge, *From the Steeples*, pp. 111-112, the resignation was "completely unexpected," and the pastor had to persuade Ives

to stay until a replacement could be found. The suddenness of Ives's departure supports Yellin's argument for the importance of this concert to Ives's career hopes and the impact of its failure.

85.   Kearnes, "Parker," p. 8, discusses the conformism among American composers of the time, which derived from uniformity of background and purpose.

CHAPTER SEVEN. INNOVATION AND SYNTHESIS (1902–1908)

1.   Stuart Feder, in his psychological study of Ives, emphasizes the private nature of many of his compositions, especially those that draw on his boyhood experiences. See Feder, "Decoration Day."

2.   *Memos*, Appendix 2, p. 148. It was subsequently disposed of and presumably destroyed when the church changed location.

3.   The concept of fictional music and its applicability to Ives in particular have been discussed by Peter Rabinowitz in his excellent article on "Fictional Music."

4.   Ives notes in the *Memos*, p. 61, and elsewhere that some of the pieces from the period 1902–1908 were indeed "played—or better tried out—usually ending in a fight or hiss." In some cases, the pieces were simply tried out in private (pp. 64, 74, and 90–91), but two pieces, including one of the *Ragtime Dances*, were played in 1904 in New Haven at the Sexennial Reunion of the Yale class of 1898 (p. 58), and some were even played in New York theatres during shows "somewhere between 1903 and 1906" (p. 119). They may not have fit in very well in the New York theatres ("At the second afternoon performance, the manager of the theater came out and stopped them, saying it made too much of a disturbance"), but they were presented as if they were vernacular music rather than art music. These performances were probably Ives's last attempts to present his remarkable amalgamation of vernacular styles with classical aspirations in the guise of entertainment music. See also Rossiter's discussion of performances in this period, in *Ives and His America*, pp. 150–151.

William Brooks has suggested that a search through the archives of Tams (now Tams-Witmark), where Ives often had his music copied and where most of these trial runs were staged, might turn up scores and parts to some of these pieces, perhaps even for some that have been lost.

5.   Ives used this form in the outer movements of the *Third Symphony*, most movements of the sonatas for violin and piano and for piano solo, *Thanksgiving*, *The Fourth of July*, *From Hanover Square North*, and other works. The procedure of gradually building a theme out of fragments and presenting it whole only at the end of a movement or section is not unique to Ives; it also appears in the music of other composers of the late nineteenth and early twentieth centuries, notably Tchaikovsky, Mahler, and Sibelius. For a discussion of cumulative form in relation to Ives's uses of borrowed musical material, see J. Peter Burkholder, "The Evolution of Charles Ives's Music: Aesthetics, Quotation, Technique" (Ph.D. dissertation, University of Chicago, 1983), pp. 385–407.

6.   Ives described the piece in the *Memos*, p. 62, as "but a trying to take off,

in sounds and rhythms, a very common thing in a back lot—a foul ball—and the base runner on 3rd has to go all the way back to 1st."

7.   Ives discusses some of these pieces and their character as "stunts" or "jokes" in the *Memos*, pp. 61–64.

8.   From a memo on a music manuscript, transcribed in *Memos*, Appendix 3, p. 158.

9.   *Halloween, All the Way Around and Back,* and *Central Park in the Dark* are examples of pieces that fall into all three categories.

10.   Kirkpatrick's listing in his *New Grove Dictionary* article gives 1903–1914 as the date for the composition of the *Scherzo*, following Ives's own list (*Memos*, Appendix 3, p. 157). Ives's list dates the whole *Scherzo* to 1903, noting that the middle section, the trio, was "finished later, some time before 1914." But the sketch of the outer scherzo section is dated 1904 (*Temporary Catalogue*, p. 66), and Ives's account below makes clear that the middle section was written separately, probably in 1903.

11.   Kirkpatrick's editorial insertion.

12.   See Kirkpatrick, *Memos*, Appendix 17, pp. 262–267.

13.   Ibid., p. 266.

14.   See, for instance, Sondra Rae Clark, "The Elements of Choice in Ives's *Concord Sonata,*" *The Musical Quarterly* 60 (April 1974): 167–186.

15.   My editorial insertions. Some italic parentheses, which Kirkpatrick uses to indicate Ives's hand-written insertions to the typescript prepared by a stenographer from Ives's dictation, have been changed to normal parentheses, and others have been omitted, in order to make the passage as readable as possible. Jadassohn is the author of the harmony text Ives used as a student under both his father and Parker.

16.   Emphasis original.

17.   "Ives, Charles E(dward)," in *New Grove Dictionary*, vol. 9, pp. 416–417.

CHAPTER EIGHT. YEARS OF MATURITY (1908–1917)

1.   Interview, 27 October 1981. "Harmony was the queen of the Yale prom that year. The wonder to me was that he worked up the courage to ask her."

2.   Bigelow Ives tells the story with some humor, relating that Twain reviewed Ives's appearance front and back before giving his approval.

3.   Harmony once commented to John Kirkpatrick that Ives had never told her what he was composing.

4.   Letter of Tuesday, 18 October 1910, from Kirkpatrick's transcriptions of "Ives Family Letters etc., 1910–1923," p. 2. This excerpt and others in the following pages from letters transcribed by Kirkpatrick are printed here with his permission.

5.   Perlis, *Ives Remembered*, p. 95. In 1920, T. Findlay MacKenzie became the tutor of Ives's nephew Moss White Ives, then living with Charles and Harmony, and eventually became a family friend.

6.   Lucille Fletcher, "A Connecticut Yankee in Music," unpublished article intended for *The New Yorker*, p. 12; in the Ives Collection, series III A, box 29, folder 8, with the Fletcher correspondence.

7. Letter from p. 8 of Kirkpatrick's folder of transcriptions, labelled "Additional Ives Letters, mostly 1907–1908." Dated a Tuesday before 12 March (possibly 25 February?) 1908 and addressed to Ives at 34 Gramercy Park, New York (the current location of Poverty Flat), probably from Harmony's parents' home in Hartford. My ellipses. Emphasis and details of style are original.

8. She sent the first draft to Ives in a letter dated Sunday-Monday, 27–28 October 1907, asking, "Do you think it seems like last Tuesday at all—from the cliff?" That "last Tuesday," 22 October, was the day of their engagement is clear from other letters partially transcribed by John Kirkpatrick. There is a change in tone in Harmony's letters at that point. In her first letter after that day (Friday, 25 October), she writes, "I never wrote a love letter & I don't know how." In the following letter (Saturday-Sunday, 26–27 October), she muses about "the happenings of the past blessed week." Later (Tuesday, 12 November), she admits telling her Aunt Sally Dunham Twichell that she is engaged; apparently Harmony and Charles kept the engagement secret for a time. In his first letter to Harmony that survives, Charles writes, "This is Nov 22—a month after Oct 22 and the greatest event in the history of this country though the populace doesn't know it—poor souls!" These letters are all transcribed in Kirkpatrick's first (untitled) folder of transcriptions of Ives family letters, pp. 5–11.

9. The last movement of the *Holidays Symphony, Thanksgiving*, was written earlier than the others (in 1904) and is concerned not with Danbury's celebration of the holiday, as are the other three movements, but with the character of the early Puritans themselves. Although it is descriptive, it is not an attempt to represent life experiences in music.

10. Sunday-Monday, 27–28 October 1907; p. 6 of Kirkpatrick's transcriptions of Ives letters. Ellipsis original.

11. Tuesday, 4 February 1908; p. 21 of Kirkpatrick's transcriptions. Kirkpatrick's ellipsis.

12. Cowell and Cowell, *Ives*, p. 12.

13. Feder, "Decoration Day." Feder is a psychoanalyst, interested in the psychology of Ives's composing and compositions. He concludes, "In general, Ives's life-long 'collaboration' with George was part of his mourning process. In *Decoration Day*, we have an unusually specific instance. It was a process which was destined to be incomplete and which approached arrest as Charles neared George's age at death. Ives's reconstruction of the idealized memory of George, in music, results in a representation intended for the composer himself to experience and the responsive listener to share" (p. 256).

14. Letter of Tuesday, 24 December 1907, from Hartford to Ives in Danbury; p. 16 of Kirkpatrick's transcriptions.

15. Letter of Thursday, 30 January 1908, from Harmony in Danbury to Ives in New York; p. 20 of Kirkpatrick's transcriptions.

16. Robert Gould Shaw (1837–1863), from a prominent Boston family, commanded the Fifty-fourth Massachusetts Regiment, the first regiment of black soldiers in the Union army, and died along with half of his men in the assault they led on Fort Wagner in South Carolina on 18 July 1863. For more on Shaw and his troops, see Peter Burchard, *One Gallant Rush: Robert Gould Shaw and his Brave Black Regiment* (New York: St. Martin's Press, 1965). The memorial, dedicated in 1897, stands at the northeast corner of Boston Common, facing the State House across

Beacon Street. The sculpture by Saint-Gaudens (1848–1907), the most prominent American sculptor of his time, is a large bronze bas-relief depicting the
regiment on the march, with the free-standing figure of Shaw on horseback in the
foreground. The same statue inspired Robert Lowell's poem *For the Union Dead*,
written half a century after Ives's orchestral picture. The bravery of Shaw and his
men had earlier moved other poets, including James Russell Lowell, whose words
are inscribed beneath the bas-relief, and Ralph Waldo Emerson, whose poem on
the subject, *Voluntaries*, includes the only four lines of Emerson's poetry that
Charles Ives ever set to music (in the brief song *Duty*).

    17.   Wendell Phillips (1811–1884) was an abolitionist, an important mem-
ber of William Lloyd Garrison's Anti-Slavery Society and eventually its president.
Phillips was a young Harvard-educated lawyer when, on 8 December 1837, there
was a public meeting at Boston's Faneuil Hall concerning the recent murder of a
newspaper publisher in Illinois as he defended his press from a pro-slavery mob.
After the attorney general of Massachusetts had defended the crowd's action and
compared it to the Boston Tea Party, Phillips took the stage to condemn the
comparison as slander against the founders of the nation. The speech carried the
day, brought Phillips a reputation as a speaker, and inaugurated his career as an
orator. The incident is described in Lorenzo Sears, *Wendell Phillips, Orator and
Agitator* (New York: Doubleday, Page, 1909). Perhaps the publication of this book
suggested the piece to Ives.

    The projected movement based on Phillips's speech, to be titled "The
abolishionists [sic] (allegro) Wendell Phillips—Faneuil Hall," is mentioned in a
memo on a sketch towards *The 'St. Gaudens' in Boston Common* as the middle
movement of a projected set, to begin with "The common (Largo) (Emerson &
Park church)"—presumably the Emerson music—and conclude with *The 'St.
Gaudens'*; Kirkpatrick, *Temporary Catalogue*, p. 14. Since each of the three projected
movements was associated with a well-known place in Boston, this may have been
intended as a set commemorating places in Boston, as a Civil War set, or as both.
Ives still had the Faneuil Hall incident in his mind when he wrote the *Essays*, where
he mentions it on p. 79.

    18.   Conversation recalled by Kirkpatrick, in his interview with Perlis, *Ives
Remembered*, p. 225.

    19.   From a copy made by Edith Ives Tyler, the Ives's only child, of a letter
from February 1908; quoted from Kirkpatrick's file of "Additional Ives Letters,
mostly 1907–1908," p. 9; quoted at length in Rossiter, *Ives and His America*, p. 173.

    20.   The *Orchard House Overture*, from which the Alcotts movement was
adapted, was of course written in 1904 and is the only untexted piece prior to the
Emerson Concerto to have anything whatsoever to do with literature. By Ives's own
admission (*Essays*, p. 48), it is in a different class from the other music inspired by
literature, as it aims only to evoke "the memory of that home under the elms," not
the writings of either Louisa May Alcott or her father—except perhaps to the
extent that Louisa wrote of her own family. *The Alcotts* is closer in style and
structure to other works of around 1904, such as *Thanksgiving*, the *Third Symphony*,
and the *Trio* for violin, cello, and piano, than to the other movements of the
Concord Sonata.

    21.   According to Perlis's list of books at Redding, there is a collection of

Selected Poems of Matthew Arnold inscribed to "Meg" (Harmony's childhood name) from her parents, dated 1898. The other volume of Arnold's poems in the collection has no inscription, and the book list does not provide a date of publication.

22. On that day, Charles and Harmony were with her brother Dave Twichell and his wife Ella at Saranac Lake, where Twichell worked at a sanatorium. Of the three, Harmony is the only one likely to have inscribed the book "to Charlie, with love, Oct 20 1908"; Wooldridge, *From the Steeples*, pp. 280 and 142. This book was at the Redding house when Wooldridge saw it, but it does not appear on Perlis's list. Ives used words from the last scene of *Paracelsus* for a later arrangement for voice and piano of some of the music from the *Browning Overture*.

23. From an undated memo after reading John Tasker Howard's *Our American Music*, transcribed on p. 5 of a miscellaneous collection of memos, in the Ives Collection, series V (Diaries), box 45, folder 12.

24. Kearnes, "Parker," pp. 16–18.

25. In his dissertation for the University of Leipzig, "Studies in America's Music," 1893. I am grateful to Kirkpatrick for furnishing me with a photocopy of Griggs's handwritten English-language original; the dissertation was published in German in 1894.

26. Letter of Monday, 6 January 1908; from Kirkpatrick's transcriptions of "Additional Ives Letters, mostly 1907–1908," p. 8; printed in *Memos*, Appendix 21, p. 324. Kirkpatrick summarizes the projected plot of this opera and the progress of its planning in Appendix 21, pp. 318–324.

27. The *Second Symphony* was copied at Tams in 1909 or 1910, after Ives had made revisions, and the *Third Symphony* was rescored in 1909 and copied in 1910 or 1911. See Kirkpatrick, *Temporary Catalogue*, pp. 3–9, and *Memos*, pp. 51–52 and 55.

28. "Father died just at the time I needed him most. It's been years since I've had an older man that I felt like going to when things seem to go wrong or a something comes up when it's hard to figure out which is the best or right thing to do." Letter from Ives to Twichell, late 1907, printed in *Memos*, Appendix 16, pp. 260–261.

29. Kirkpatrick gives a brief summary of Twichell's life in the *Memos*, Appendix 16, pp. 259–261, based on the more comprehensive account in Leah A. Strong's biography, *Joseph Hopkins Twichell: Mark Twain's Friend and Pastor* (Athens, Ga.: University of Georgia Press, 1966).

30. "He is probably in the same amiable state of mind that the Jesuit priest said God was in when He looked down upon the camp ground and saw the priest sleeping with a Congregationalist chaplain." The chaplain of course is Twichell, and the priest was Father Joseph O'Hagan, the other chaplain of Twichell's regiment. Strong, *Twichell*, pp. 32–33, tells a version of the same story as recollected by O'Hagan. According to Strong, Twichell's service alongside O'Hagan was an important experience in his development of religious tolerance. Twichell probably told the story many times to make a point about Christian unity beyond sectarian divisions.

31. Strong, *Twichell*, pp. 24, 55–56, 59, 61, and 61–62.

32. Ibid., pp. 7–9, 46–48, and 58. Twichell "adopted Bushnell's theology

almost in its entirety" (p. 58). Bushnell was accused of heresy but never tried.

33. He mentions Bushnell together with Unitarian minister William Ellery Channing on p. 20 of the Emerson essay, cites Bushnell's sermon on "Unconscious Influence" in the Thoreau essay, p. 60, and cites the same sermon again eleven years later in a letter of January 1930 to Griggs, printed in *Memos*, Appendix 15, p. 257. Griggs apparently was a model for Ives of the type of person who exerts the "unconscious influence" Bushnell discusses. The sermon is printed in Bushnell's collection of *Sermons for the New Life*, rev. ed. (New York: Scribner, Armstrong, 1876), pp. 186–205. Ives may have known of Bushnell from his uncle Lyman D. Brewster, whose copy (inscribed "L. D. Brewster / Nov. / 1858") of Bushnell's *Nature and the Supernatural* (New York: Chas. Scribner, 1858) is with the Ives books in the secretary in Bigelow Ives's house. However, Brewster does not seem to have been impressed with Bushnell, if one may judge by his annotations in the book, many of them critical.

34. Letter of Friday, 31 January 1908, on p. 21 of Kirkpatrick's first set of transcriptions of Ives family letters. In a letter of a month earlier, Monday, 30 December 1907, Harmony wrote to Ives, "I've read one of Mr. Bushnell's sermons—that just fitted in with some thoughts I'd been having." ("Additional Ives Letters, mostly 1907–1908," p. 6.)

35. Exemplified in the sermons "Every Man's Life a Plan of God" and "Dignity of Human Nature Shown from its Ruins," in *Sermons for the New Life*, pp. 9–28 and 50–70.

36. *Memos*, Appendix 19, p. 275. The whole essay is printed on pp. 275–276.

37. Ibid., p. 277. Other witnesses have made similar comments; see that of their nephew Brewster Ives, in Perlis, *Ives Remembered*, p. 80.

38. *Memos*, Appendix 19, pp. 277–278.

39. In Perlis, *Ives Remembered*, p. 219.

40. For instance, according to Strong, *Twichell*, p. 59, Twichell could readily incorporate biological evolution into his religious views as proof of the inevitability of progress in society as well as biology, yet there is a letter from Harmony to Ives (Monday, 11 May 1908, on p. 27 of Kirkpatrick's first set of transcriptions of Ives family letters) in which she says she "felt horribly" after reading an article on evolution.

41. See his comments in the *Essays*, p. 80.

CHAPTER NINE. THE IMPORTANCE OF TRANSCENDENTALISM

1. See the letter of February 1908 from Harmony to Ives cited above in Chapter 8, note 19.

2. See the writings on insurance and politics in *Essays, Majority*, pp. 134–242, and in *Memos*, Appendices 9–10, pp. 205–235. See also Gordon A. Schultz, "A Selected Bibliography of Ives's Insurance Writings," *Student Musicologists at Minnesota* 6 (1975–1976): 272–279. The formation of Ives's own agency coincides with this period as well: Ives & Co. was inaugurated 1 January 1907, and the more successful Ives & Myrick, for whose classes for agents Ives wrote his philo-

sophical and educational tracts on insurance and sales, was founded exactly two years later.

3. *The Complete Works of Ralph Waldo Emerson*, Centennial Edition, vol. 1: *Essays, First Series* (Boston: Houghton Mifflin, [ca. 1903]), pp. 45–46. Ives knew this essay and cited it in a newspaper advertisement for Ives & Myrick in 1929; reprinted in Perlis, *Ives Remembered*, p. 53. This essay is not cited or paraphrased anywhere in the *Essays*.

4. Phelps, "Emerson," p. 129.

5. *Wittgenstein's Vienna* (New York: Simon and Schuster, 1973), p. 32.

CHAPTER TEN. THE WRITING OF THE *ESSAYS* AND AFTER

1. Boatwright, in his introduction to the *Essays*, pp. xvi–xvii; Cowell and Cowell, *Ives*, p. 53.

2. Diary D8, now in the Ives Collection, series V, box 45, folder 8. Entries for Monday, 20 January (Harmony's hand: "Charlie finishing up copy of Sonata 'Prologue' "), Wednesday, 22 January (Ives's hand: "C. worked on Thoreau. —trying to write something to make people think Thoreau movement sounds like Thoreau."), Tuesday, 4 February (Harmony's hand: "Day spent writing (C.) & reading (H.)"), and Wednesday, 5 February (Ives's hand: "C. finishes 'Thoreau' ").

3. Entries for Saturday, 15 February (Harmony's hand: "C. reading 'Pride & Prejudice'—& copying music.") and Thursday, February 20 (Ives's hand: "Emerson, Alcott & Thoreau all [or 'are'?] finished & copied 3 movements—"). The latter entry clearly refers to the music, not the essays.

4. Edward Waldo Emerson, *Thoreau*, and Mark Van Doren, *Henry David Thoreau: A Critical Study* (Boston: Houghton Mifflin, 1916), both cited in the Thoreau essay.

5. Ives Collection, series II A, box 24, folder 1.

6. The drafts are in the Ives Collection, box 24, and are listed in Perlis, *Charles Ives Papers*, p. 7.

7. Kirkpatrick, in Perlis, *Ives Remembered*, p. 224, reporting information he had been told by Mrs. Ives.

8. Perlis, *Ives Remembered*, p. 138.

9. Kirkpatrick's note, *Memos*, Appendix 3, p. 155. I have also seen the manuscript of the original ending in the Ives Collection and much prefer it. In my opinion, performing this work of 1902 with an ending from the 1940s is an absolute travesty. The new ending would not have been added had Ives received recognition for this symphony at the time he wrote it and would not have stayed in use this long had performers and scholars understood the logic and evolution of his music. Ives's original, tonal ending belongs to his original, tonal symphony.

10. Letter to Nicolas Slonimsky, 6 July 1936, copy by Kirkpatrick, in the Ives Collection; cited by Rossiter, *Ives and His America*, p. 156.

11. "Ives, Charles E(dward)," in *New Grove Dictionary*, vol. 9, p. 419, col. 2, and in the interview with Perlis, in *Ives Remembered*, p. 224.

12. "Winston Churchill and Charles Ives: The Progressive Experience in Literature and Song," *Student Musicologists at Minnesota* 4 (1970–1971), pp.

175–176. This Winston Churchill is the American novelist, not the British statesman. For an opposing view of Ives's attitude towards the war, see Rossiter, *Ives and His America*, p. 132.

13. On pp. 112–113, he writes: "In 1917 the War came on, and I did but little in music. I didn't seem to feel like it." Ives is obviously referring to the United States' entry into the war, as the years from the onset of the war to the spring of 1917 were among his most productive.

14. Rossiter, *Ives and His America*, pp. 186–187.

15. Feder, "Decoration Day."

16. *From the Steeples*, pp. 187 and 182–183. Kirkpatrick hotly disagreed with Wooldridge's idea in his review of the book in *Hi Fi/Musical America*, September 1974, p. MA34. In his rebuttal, printed in the December 1974 issue of the same periodical, Wooldridge asked how Kirkpatrick knew his theory to be false and suggested that it could be confirmed by looking at Ives's income tax returns. I have looked at copies of Ives's returns, which are in the Ives Collection at Yale, and there is not the slightest support for Wooldridge's view. Ives's income was substantial and gradually rose as the firm of Ives & Myrick grew, but there was no radical jump in income to suggest that Ives made a killing in the stock market. See also Rossiter, *Ives and His America*, p. 120.

SELECTED BIBLIOGRAPHY

IVES STUDIES AND DOCUMENTS

Albert, Thomas Russel. "The Harmonic Language of Charles Ives' Concord Sonata." D.M.A. dissertation, University of Illinois, 1974.

Argento, Domenick. "A Digest Analysis of Ives' 'On the Antipodes'." *Student Musicologists at Minnesota* 6 (1975–1976): 192–200.

Austin, William W. "Ives and Histories." In *Bericht über den internationalen musik-wissenschaftlichen Kongress Bonn 1970*, edited by Carl Dahlhaus et al., pp. 299–303. Kassel: Bärenreiter, 1971.

Babcock, Michael J. "Ives' 'Thoreau': A Point of Order." *American Society of University Composers Proceedings* 9 and 10 (1976): 89–102.

Bader, Yvette. "The Chamber Music of Charles Edward Ives." *The Music Review* 33 (November 1972): 292–299.

Badolato, James Vincent. "The Four Symphonies of Charles Ives: A Critical, Analytical Study of the Musical Style of Charles Ives." Ph.D. dissertation, Catholic University of America, 1978.

Ballantine, Christopher. "Charles Ives and the Meaning of Quotation in Music." *The Musical Quarterly* 65 (April 1979): 167–184.

Banfield, Stephen. Review of *An Ives Celebration*, edited by H. Wiley Hitchcock and Vivian Perlis. *Music and Letters* 60 (April 1979): 216–217.

Bellamann, Henry. "Charles Ives: The Man and His Music." *The Musical Quarterly* 19 (January 1933): 45–58.

———. "Reviews: 'Concord, Mass., 1840–1860' (A Piano Sonata by Charles E. Ives)." *Double Dealer* 2 (October 1921): 166–169.

Bernlef, J., and de Leeuw, Reinbert. *Charles Ives*. Amsterdam: De Bezige Bij, 1969.

Blum, Stephen. "Ives's Position in Social and Musical History." *The Musical Quarterly* 63 (October 1977): 459–482.

———. Review of *Charles Ives and His America*, by Frank R. Rossiter. *The Musical Quarterly* 62 (October 1976): 597–603.

Boatwright, Howard. "Ives' Quarter-tone Impressions." *Perspectives of New Music* 3, no. 2 (Spring-Summer 1965): 22–31.

Bonham, Robert John. "Some Common Aesthetic Tendencies Manifested in Examples of Pioneer American Cabins and Old Harp Music and in Selected Works of H. H. Richardson and Charles E. Ives." Ph.D. dissertation, Ohio University, 1981.

Brooks, William. "Ives Today." In *An Ives Celebration: Papers and Panels of the Charles Ives Centennial Festival-Conference*, edited by H. Wiley Hitchcock

and Vivian Perlis, pp. 209–223. Urbana: University of Illinois Press, 1977.
———. "Sources and Errata List for Charles Ives' Symphony No. 4, Movement II." D.M.A. dissertation, University of Illinois, 1976.
———. "Unity and Diversity in Charles Ives's Fourth Symphony." *Yearbook for Inter-American Musical Research* 10 (1974): 5–49.
Brooks, William, and Burkholder, J. Peter. "Books in Bigelow Ives' Library and Identified by Him as Belonging to Charles Ives or His Family." Computer printout. Compiled Spring 1982, revised March 1984.
Bruce, Neely. "Ives and Nineteenth-Century American Music." In *An Ives Celebration: Papers and Panels of the Charles Ives Centennial Festival-Conference*, edited by H. Wiley Hitchcock and Vivian Perlis, pp. 29–43. Urbana: University of Illinois Press, 1977.
Budde, Elmar. "Anmerkungen zum Streichquartett Nr. 2 von Charles E. Ives." In *Bericht über den internationalen musikwissenschaftlichen Kongress Bonn 1970*, edited by Carl Dahlhaus et al., pp. 303–307. Kassel: Bärenreiter, 1971.
Burkholder, J. Peter. "The Evolution of Charles Ives's Music: Aesthetics, Quotation, Technique." Ph.D. dissertation, University of Chicago, 1983.
———. "'Quotation' and Emulation: Charles Ives's Uses of His Models." *The Musical Quarterly*, in press.
Cage, John. "Two Statements on Ives." In *A Year From Monday: New Lectures and Writings*, pp. 36–42. Middletown, Conn.: Wesleyan University Press, 1967.
Call, William Anson. "A Study of the Transcendental Aesthetic Theories of John S. Dwight and Charles E. Ives and the Relationship of These Theories to Their Respective Work as Music Critic and Composer." D.M.A. dissertation, University of Illinois, 1971.
Cameron, Janet. "An Analysis of the First Movement of the First Piano Sonata by Charles Ives." Seminar paper, University of Illinois, n.d.
Carter, Elliott. "The Case of Mr. Ives." [Part of "Forecast and Review."] *Modern Music* 16 (March-April 1939): 172–176.
———. "Documents of a Friendship with Ives." *Parnassus: Poetry in Review* 3, no. 2 (Spring-Summer 1975): 300–315. Reprinted in *Tempo: A Quarterly Review of Modern Music*, no. 117 (June 1976): 2–10.
———. "Ives Today: His Vision and Challenge." *Modern Music* 21 (May-June 1944): 199–202.
———. "Shop Talk by an American Composer." *The Musical Quarterly* 46 (April 1960): 189–201. Reprinted in *Problems of Modern Music*, edited by Paul Henry Lang, pp. 51–63. New York: W. W. Norton, 1962.
Charles, Sydney Robinson. "The Use of Borrowed Materials in Ives' Second Symphony." *The Music Review* 28 (May 1967): 102–111.
Chase, Gilbert. "Composer from Connecticut." In *America's Music: From the Pilgrims to the Present*, rev. 2nd ed., pp. 403–428. New York: McGraw-Hill, 1966.
Childs, Barney. "Some Anniversaries." *American Society of University Composers Proceedings* 9 and 10 (1976): 13–27.
Clark, Sondra Rae. "The Elements of Choice in Ives's *Concord Sonata*." *The Musical Quarterly* 60 (April 1974): 167–186.
———. "The Evolving *Concord Sonata*: A Study of Choices and Variants in the

Music of Charles Ives." Ph.D. dissertation, Stanford University, 1972.

———. "The Transcendental Philosophy of Charles E. Ives As Expressed in 'The Second Sonata for Pianoforte, "Concord Mass., 1840–1860."' " M.A. thesis, San Jose State College, 1966.

Clarke, Henry Leland. Review of *Essays Before a Sonata*, by Charles E. Ives. *The Musical Quarterly* 50 (January 1964): 101–103.

Conn, Peter. "Innovation and nostalgia: Charles Ives." In *The Divided Mind: Ideology and Imagination in America, 1898–1917*, pp. 230–250. Cambridge: Cambridge University Press, 1983.

Copland, Aaron. "One Hundred and Fourteen Songs." *Modern Music* 11 (January-February 1934): 59–64.

Cowell, Henry. "American Composers. IX: Charles Ives." *Modern Music* 10 (1932): 24–33.

———. "Charles E. Ives." In *American Composers on American Music: A Symposium*, edited by Henry Cowell, pp. 128–145. Stanford: Stanford University Press, 1933. Reprint. New York: Frederick Ungar, 1962.

———. Review of Second Symphony, first performance. *The Musical Quarterly* 37 (1951): 399–402.

Cowell, Henry, and Cowell, Sidney. *Charles Ives and His Music*. 2nd ed. New York: Oxford University Press, 1969.

Crunden, Robert M. "Charles Ives' Innovative Nostalgia." *The Choral Journal* 15, no. 4 (December 1974): 5–12.

———. "Charles Ives's Place in American Culture." In *An Ives Celebration: Papers and Panels of the Charles Ives Centennial Festival-Conference*, edited by H. Wiley Hitchcock and Vivian Perlis, pp. 4–15. Urbana: University of Illinois Press, 1977.

Cyr, Gordon. "Intervallic Structural Elements in Ives' Fourth Symphony." *Perspectives of New Music* 9, no. 2 and 10, no. 1 (1971): 291–303.

Davenport, Guy. "Ives the Master." *Parnassus: Poetry in Review* 3, no. 2 (Spring-Summer 1975): 374–380.

Davidson, Audrey. "Transcendental Unity in the Works of Charles Ives." *American Quarterly* 22 (Spring 1970): 35–44.

Davidson, Colleen. "Winston Churchill and Charles Ives: The Progressive Experience in Literature and Song." *Student Musicologists at Minnesota* 3 (1968–1969): 168–194, and 4 (1970–1971): 154–180.

de Leeuw, Reinbert. "Charles Ives, Zijn Muziek: Inleidung, Ives' Gebruik van Muzikaal Materiaal." [From J. Bernlef and Reinbert de Leeuw, *Charles Ives*.] Translated by Bertus Polman. *Student Musicologists at Minnesota* 6 (1975–1976): 128–191.

De Lerma, Dominique-René. *Charles Ives, 1874–1954: A Bibliography of His Music*. Kent, Ohio: Kent State University Press, 1970.

Dickinson, Peter. "Charles Ives: 1874–1954." *Musical Times* 105 (July 1964): 347–349.

———. "A New Perspective for Ives." *Musical Times* 115 (October 1974): 836–838.

Dujmić, Dunja. "The Musical Transcendentalism of Charles Ives." *International Review of the Aesthetics and Sociology of Music* 2 (June 1971): 89–95.

Eiseman, David. "Charles Ives and the European Symphonic Tradition: A Historical Reappraisal." Ph.D. dissertation, University of Illinois, 1972.
———. "George Ives as Theorist: Some Unpublished Documents." *Perspectives of New Music* 14 (Fall-Winter 1975): 139–147.
Elkus, Jonathan. "Charles Ives and the American Band Tradition: A Centennial Tribute." Exeter: American Arts Documentation Centre, University of Exeter, 1974.
Feder, Stuart. "Charles and George Ives: The Veneration of Boyhood." *The Annual of Psychoanalysis* 9 (1981): 265–316.
———. "Decoration Day: A Boyhood Memory of Charles Ives." *The Musical Quarterly* 66 (April 1980): 234–261.
———. "The Nostalgia of Charles Ives: An Essay in Affects and Music." *The Annual of Psychoanalysis* 10 (1982): 301–332.
Fletcher, Lucille. "A Connecticut Yankee in Music." Article intended for *The New Yorker* but never published. With Fletcher correspondence. New Haven. Yale University, John Herrick Jackson Music Library, Ives Collection.
Forte, Allen. "Ives and Atonality." In *An Ives Celebration: Papers and Panels of the Charles Ives Centennial Festival-Conference*, edited by H. Wiley Hitchcock and Vivian Perlis, pp. 159–186. Urbana: University of Illinois Press, 1977.
Ghander, Ann. "Charles Ives: Organisation in *Emerson*." *Musicology: The Journal of the Musicological Society of Australia* 6 (1980): 111–127.
Gilman, Lawrence. "Music: A Masterpiece of American Music Heard Here for the First Time." *New York Herald Tribune*, 21 January 1939, p. 9.
Grantham, Donald. "A Harmonic 'Leitmotif' System in Ives's Psalm 90." *In Theory Only* 5, no. 2 (May-June 1979): 3–14.
Gratovich, Eugene. "The Sonatas for Violin and Piano by Charles Ives: A Critical Commentary and Concordance of the Printed Editions and the Autographs and Manuscripts of the Yale Ives Collection." D.M.A. dissertation, Boston University School of Fine and Applied Arts, 1968.
Green, Douglass M. "*Exempli gratia*: A Chord Motive in Ives's *Serenity*." *In Theory Only* 4, no. 5 (October 1978): 20–21.
Hansen, Chadwick. "One Place in New England: The Fifty-Fourth Massachusetts Volunteer Infantry as a Subject for American Artists." *Student Musicologists at Minnesota* 6 (1975–1976): 250–271. Reprinted as "The 54th Massachusetts Volunteer Black Infantry as a Subject for American Artists." *Massachusetts Review* 16 (Autumn 1975): 745–759.
Harrison, Lou. "On Quotation." *Modern Music* 23 (Summer 1946): 166–169.
Helms, Hans G. "Charles Edward Ives—Ideal American or Social Critic?" *Current Musicology*, no. 19 (1975): 37–44.
———. "Charles Ives—Hommage zur 100. Geburtstag; 1. Zur Physiognomie eines revolutionären Komponisten und Citoyen; 2. Zum Phänomen der Ungleichzeitigkeit kompositorischer Konzeptionen und ihrer technischen Realiserbarkeit." *Student Musicologists at Minnesota* 6 (1975–1976): 95–127.
Henderson, Clayton Wilson. "Quotation as a Style Element in the Music of Charles Ives." Ph.D. dissertation, Washington University, 1969.
———. "Structural Importance of Borrowed Music in the Works of Charles Ives: A Preliminary Assessment." *Report of the Eleventh Congress of the International*

Musicological Society held at Copenhagen, 1972, ed. Henrik Glahn et al., vol. I, pp. 437–446.

Herrmann, Bernard. "Four Symphonies by Charles Ives." *Modern Music* 22 (May-June 1945): 215–222.

Hitchcock, H. Wiley. "Charles E. Ives." In *Music in the United States: A Historical Introduction*, 2nd ed., pp. 149–172. Englewood Cliffs, N.J.: Prentice-Hall, 1974.

———. "Charles Ives's Book of 114 Songs." In *A Musical Offering: Essays in Honor of Martin Bernstein*, edited by Edward H. Clinksdale and Claire Brook, pp. 127–135. New York: Pendragon Press, 1977.

———. *Ives*. London: Oxford University Press, 1977.

———, ed. *Charles Ives Festival-Conference*. Program booklet. New York: G. Schirmer and Associated Music Publishers, 1974.

Hitchcock, H. Wiley, and Perlis, Vivian, eds. *An Ives Celebration: Papers and Panels of the Charles Ives Centennial Festival-Conference*. Urbana: University of Illinois Press, 1977.

Isham, Howard. "The Musical Thinking of Charles Ives." *Journal of Aesthetics and Art Criticism* 31 (Spring 1973): 395–404.

Ives, Charles E. *The Anti-Abolitionist Riots in the 1830's and 1840's*, for piano solo. Edited by Henry Cowell. New York: Mercury Music, [1949]. Reprint, with corrected preface. Bryn Mawr: Mercury Music, n.d.

———. *Central Park in the Dark*. Edited by Jacques-Louis Monod, with notes by John Kirkpatrick. Hillsdale, N.Y.: Boelke-Bomart, 1973.

———. *Essays Before a Sonata*. New York: Knickerbocker Press, 1920.

———. *Essays Before a Sonata and Other Writings*. Edited by Howard Boatwright. New York: W. W. Norton, 1964.

———. *Essays Before a Sonata, The Majority, and Other Writings*. Edited by Howard Boatwright. New York: W. W. Norton, 1970.

———. *Memos*. Edited and with appendices by John Kirkpatrick. New York: W. W. Norton, 1972.

———. "Music and Its Future." [Excerpted from Conductor's Note to *Fourth Symphony*, second movement.] In *American Composers on American Music: A Symposium*, edited by Henry Cowell, pp. 191–198. Stanford: Stanford University Press, 1933. Reprint. New York: Frederick Ungar, 1962.

———. *114 Songs*. Redding, Conn.: By the author, 1922.

———. [Sonata No. 2 for Piano.] *Second Pianoforte Sonata ("Concord, Mass., 1840–1860")*. Redding, Conn.: By the author, 1920.

———. [Sonata No. 2 for Piano.] *Piano Sonata No. 2 ("Concord, Mass., 1840–1860")*. Second edition, prepared by Ives with the assistance of George F. Roberts. New York: Arrow Music Press, 1947. Reprint. Associated Music Publishers, n.d.

———. *Symphony No. 4*. Performance score edited by Theodore A. Seder, Romulus Franceschini, and Nicholas Falcone. Preface by John Kirkpatrick. New York: Associated Music Publishers, 1965.

Ives, Charles E., and Phelps, William Lyon. Manuscript correspondence. New Haven. Yale University, John Herrick Jackson Music Library, Ives Collection.

Johnson, Russell I. "A View of Twentieth-Century Expression." *Journal of Aesthetics and Art Criticism* 28 (Spring 1970): 361–368.

Josephson, Nors S. "Charles Ives: Intervallische Permutationen im Spätwerk." *Zeitschrift für Musiktheorie* 9, no. 2 (1978): 27–33.

————. "Zur formalen Struktur einiger später Orchester-werke von Charles Ives (1874–1954)." *Die Musikforschung* 27 (1974): 57–64.

Joyce, Mary Ann. "The Three-Page Sonata of Charles Ives: An Analysis and a Corrected Version." Ph.D. dissertation, Washington University, 1970.

Kavanaugh, James Vincent. "Music and American Transcendentalism: A Study of Transcendental Pythagoreanism in the Works of Henry David Thoreau, Nathaniel Hawthorne and Charles Ives." Ph.D. dissertation, Yale University, 1978.

Kirkpatrick, John. "Ives, Charles E(dward)." In *The New Grove Dictionary of Music and Musicians*, vol. 9, pp. 414–429.

————. Review of *From the Steeples and the Mountains*, by David Wooldridge. *HiFi/Musical America*, September 1974, pp. MA33–36.

————. *A Temporary Mimeographed Catalogue of the Music Manuscripts and Related Materials of Charles Edward Ives 1874–1954*. New Haven: Library of the Yale School of Music, 1960. Reprint, 1973.

————. "Thoughts on the Ives Year." *Student Musicologists at Minnesota* 6 (1975–1976): 218–224.

————, ed. "Additional Ives Letters, mostly 1907–1908." Compiled July 1964. Typewritten. In John Kirkpatrick's possession. Microfilm copy. New Haven. Yale University, John Herrick Jackson Music Library, Ives Collection.

————, ed. "Ives Family Letters etc. 1910–1923." Typewritten. In John Kirkpatrick's possession. Microfilm copy. New Haven. Yale University, John Herrick Jackson Music Library, Ives Collection.

————, ed. [Transcriptions of Ives family letters.] Typewritten. In John Kirkpatrick's possession. Microfilm copy. New Haven. Yale University, John Herrick Jackson Music Library, Ives Collection.

Koller, Horst. "Zur Kompositionstechnik von Charles Edward Ives." *Neue Zeitschrift für Musik* 133, no. 10 (1972): 559–567.

Kolosick, J. Timothy. "A Computer-Assisted, Set-Theoretic Investigation of Vertical Simultaneities in Selected Piano Compositions by Charles E. Ives." Ph.D. dissertation, University of Wisconsin, Madison, 1981.

Koppenhaver, Allen J. "Charles Ives, Winslow Homer, and Thomas Eakins: Variations on America." *Parnassus: Poetry in Review* 3, no. 2 (Spring-Summer 1975): 381–393.

Kumlien, Wendell Clarke. "The Sacred Choral Music of Charles Ives: A Study in Style Development." D.M.A. dissertation, University of Illinois, 1969.

Larson, Gary O. "Charles Ives and American Studies." *Student Musicologists at Minnesota* 6 (1975–1976): 237–249.

Magers, Roy V. "Aspects of Form in the Symphonies of Charles E. Ives." Ph.D. dissertation, Indiana University, 1975.

Mandel, Alan. "Charles Ives's Music for the Piano." *Student Musicologists at Minnesota* 6 (1975–1976): 201–217.

Marshall, Dennis. "Charles Ives's Quotations: Manner or Substance?" *Perspectives of New Music* 6, no. 2 (1968): 45–56.

Maske, Ulrich. *Charles Ives in seiner Kammermusik für drei bis sechs Instrumente.* Kölner Beiträge zur Musikforschung, vol. 64. Regensburg: G. Bosse, 1971.

Mead, Rita H. "Cowell, Ives, and New Music." *The Musical Quarterly* 66 (October 1980): 538–559.

———. *Henry Cowell's New Music 1925–1936: The Society, the Music Editions, and the Recordings.* Studies in Musicology, no. 40. Ann Arbor: UMI Research Press, 1981.

Mellers, Wilfred. "Realism and Transcendentalism: Charles Ives as American Hero." In *Music in a New Found Land: Themes and Developments in the History of American Music*, pp. 38–64. London: Barrie and Rockliff, 1964.

Middleton, Richard. "Ives and Schoenberg: An English View." *Saturday Review/World*, 21 September 1974, pp. 39–41.

Moor, Paul. "On Horseback to Heaven: Charles Ives." *Harper's* 197 (September 1948): 65–73.

Morelli, Giovanni. Review of *L'America musicale di Charles Ives*, by Gianfranco Vinay. *Rivista Italiana di Musicologia* 9 (1974): 316–322.

Morgan, Robert P. "American Music and the Hand-Me-Down Habit." *High Fidelity*, June 1976, pp. 70–72.

———. "Ives and Mahler: Mutual Responses at the End of an Era." *19th Century Music* 2 (1978): 72–81.

———. Review of *Charles Ives and His America*, by Frank Rossiter. *Yearbook for Inter-American Musical Research* 11 (1975): 225–228.

———. "Rewriting Music History: Second Thoughts on Ives and Varèse." *Musical Newsletter* 3, no. 1 (January 1973): 3–12 and 3, no. 2 (April 1973): 15–23, 28.

———. "Spatial Form in Ives." In *An Ives Celebration: Papers and Panels of the Charles Ives Centennial Festival-Conference*, edited by H. Wiley Hitchcock and Vivian Perlis, pp. 145–158. Urbana: University of Illinois Press, 1977.

Muser, Frani. Review of *Charles Ives and the American Mind*, by Rosalie Sandra Perry. *The Musical Quarterly* 61 (July 1975): 489–490.

Nelson, Mark D. "Beyond Mimesis: Transcendentalism and Processes of Analogy in Charles Ives' *The Fourth of July*." Typewritten. University of Illinois, n.d.

New Haven. Yale University. John Herrick Jackson Music Library. Ives Collection. Complete extant sketches and scores. In particular, final scores or sketches of the following unpublished works: *Decoration Day*, manuscript score by Emil Hanke, with two versions of the postface; *The General Slocum*, sketch; *Second Orchestral Set*, manuscript score by Emil Hanke; *Third Orchestral Set*, sketches; *Overture in G*, sketches; *Postlude in F*, orchestral score; *Thanksgiving and Forefathers Day*, manuscript score by George F. Roberts; *Universe Symphony*, sketches; *Yale-Princeton Football Game*, sketches. Ives's annotated copies of his own published works, particularly the early printings of the *Second Pianoforte Sonata* (1920), *114 Songs* (1922), and *The Anti-Abolitionist Riots*. Ives family personal papers and correspondence. In particular, all correspondence up to 1920 of Charles Ives, Harmony Twichell, and the Danbury Ives family; later correspondence of Charles Ives with

John C. Griggs and William Lyon Phelps; diaries of Charles Ives, Moss Ives, Moss White Ives, Harmony Twichell, and Charles and Harmony Ives; Charles Ives's scrapbooks; sketches for *Essays Before a Sonata* and for other program notes; and Charles Ives's other memoranda on all subjects.

Newman, Philip Edward. "The Songs of Charles Ives." Ph.D. dissertation, University of Iowa, 1967.

Parthun, Paul. "Concord, Charles Ives, and Henry Bellamann." *Student Musicologists at Minnesota* 6 (1975–1976): 66–86.

Perison, Harry. "The Quarter-tone System of Charles Ives." *Current Musicology*, no. 18 (1974): 96–104.

Perlis, Vivian. *Charles Ives Remembered: An Oral History*. New Haven: Yale University Press, 1974. Reprint. New York: W. W. Norton, 1976.

———. "Ives and Oral History." *Notes* 28 (June 1972): 629–642.

———, compiler. *Charles Ives Papers*. New Haven: Yale University Music Library, 1983.

———, ed. [A manuscript list of books in the Charles Ives family home in West Redding, Connecticut.] Handwritten by many hands and photocopied.

Perry, Rosalie Sandra. *Charles Ives and the American Mind*. Kent, Ohio: Kent State University Press, 1974.

Prausnitz, Frederik. Review of *Memos*, by Charles E. Ives, and books on Ives by Vivian Perlis, David Wooldridge, Jonathan Elkus, and Gianfranco Vinay. *Tempo: A Quarterly Review of Modern Music*, no. 114 (September 1975): 28–30, 33.

Rabinowitz, Peter J. "Fictional Music: Toward a Theory of Listening." In *Theories of Reading, Looking, and Listening*, edited by Harry R. Garvin, pp. 193–208. *Bucknell Review*, vol. 26, no. 1. Lewisburg: Bucknell University Press, 1981.

Rinehart, John McLain. "Ives' Compositional Idioms: An Investigation of Selected Short Compositions as Microcosms of his Musical Language." Ph.D. dissertation, Ohio State University, 1970.

Robinson, David B. "Children of the Fire: Charles Ives on Emerson and Art." *American Literature* 48 (January 1977): 564–576.

Rosa, Alfred F. "Charles Ives: Music, Transcendentalism, and Politics." *New England Quarterly* 44 (September 1971): 433–443.

Rosen, Lee Cyril. "The Violin Sonatas of Charles Ives." B.Mus. paper, University of Illinois, 1965.

Rosenfeld, Paul. "Ives." In *Discoveries of a Music Critic*, pp. 315–324. New York: Harcourt, Brace, 1936.

———. "Ives's Concord Sonata." [Part of "Forecast and Review."] *Modern Music* 16 (1939): 109–112.

Rossiter, Frank R. *Charles Ives and His America*. New York: Liveright, 1975.

———. "Charles Ives: Good American and Isolated Artist." In *An Ives Celebration: Papers and Panels of the Charles Ives Centennial Festival-Conference*, edited by H. Wiley Hitchcock and Vivian Perlis, pp. 16–28. Urbana: University of Illinois Press, 1977.

———. Review of *Memos*, by Charles E. Ives. *Yearbook for Inter-American Musical Research* 9 (1973): 182–185.

Schermer, Richard. "The Aesthetics of Charles Ives in Relation to his 'String Quartet No. 2'." M.A. thesis, California State University, Fullerton, 1980.

Schoffman, Nachum. "Charles Ives's Song 'Vote for Names'." *Current Musicology*, no. 23 (1977): 56–68.

———. "Serialism in the Works of Charles Ives." *Tempo: A Quarterly Review of Modern Music*, no. 138 (September 1981): 21–32.

———. "The Songs of Charles Ives." Ph.D. dissertation, Hebrew University of Jerusalem, 1977.

Schrade, Leo. "Charles E. Ives: 1874–1954." *Yale Review*, n.s. 44 (June 1955): 535–545.

Schultz, Gordon A. "A Selected Bibliography of Charles Ives' Insurance Writings." *Student Musicologists at Minnesota* 6 (1975–1976): 272–279.

Siegmeister, Elie. Review of *From the Steeples*, by David Wooldridge. *Notes* 31 (December 1974): 291–293.

Starr, Lawrence. "Charles Ives: The Next Hundred Years—Towards a Method of Analyzing the Music." *The Music Review* 38 (May 1977): 101–111.

———. "The Early Styles of Charles Ives." *19th Century Music* 7 (Summer 1983): 71–80.

———. "Style and Substance: 'Ann Street' by Charles Ives." *Perspectives of New Music* 15, no. 2 (Spring-Summer 1977): 23–33.

Stein, Alan. "The Musical Language of Charles Ives' Three Places in New England." D.M.A. dissertation, University of Illinois, 1975.

Sterne, Colin. "The Quotations in Charles Ives's Second Symphony." *Music and Letters* 52 (January 1971): 39–45.

Stone, Kurt. "Ives's Fourth Symphony: A Review." *The Musical Quarterly* 52 (January 1966): 1–16.

Stravinsky, Igor, and Craft, Robert. *Expositions and Developments*. Garden City, N.Y.: Doubleday, 1962.

———. *Retrospectives and Conclusions*. New York: Knopf, 1969.

Taruskin, Richard. Letter in reply to Hans G. Helms, "Ives—Ideal American or Social Critic?" *Current Musicology*, no. 20 (1975): 33–40.

Taubman, Howard. "Posterity Catches Up With Charles Ives." *The New York Times Magazine*, 23 October 1949, pp. 15, 34–36.

Thomson, Virgil. "The Ives Case." In *American Music Since 1910*, pp. 22–30. New York: Holt, Rinehart and Winston, 1971. Reprinted in *A Virgil Thomson Reader*, pp. 460–467. Boston: Houghton Mifflin, 1981.

Tick, Judith. "Ragtime and the Music of Charles Ives." *Current Musicology*, no. 18 (1974): 105–113.

Tonietti, Tito. Review of *L'America musicale di Charles Ives*, by Gianfranco Vinay. *Nuova Rivista Musicale Italiana* 9 (January-March 1975): 137–140.

Trimble, Lester. Review of *Robert Browning Overture*, by Charles E. Ives. In "Current Chronicle." *The Musical Quarterly* 43 (January 1957): 90–93.

Vinay, Gianfranco. *L'America musicale di Charles Ives*. Torino: Giulio Einaudi, 1974.

———. "Charles Ives e i musicisti europei: anticipazioni e dipendenze." *Nuova Rivista Musicale Italiana* 7 (July-December 1973): 417–429.

Walker, Donald R. "The Vocal Music of Charles Ives." *Parnassus: Poetry in Review* 3, no. 2 (Spring-Summer 1975): 329–344.

Wallach, Laurence. "The Ives Conference: A Word from the Floor." *Current Musicology*, no. 19 (1975): 32–36.

———. "The New England Education of Charles Ives." Ph.D. dissertation, Columbia University, 1973.

———. Review of *Memos*, by Charles E. Ives. *The Musical Quarterly* 60 (1974): 284–290.

Ward, Charles. "Charles Ives: The Relationship Between Aesthetic Theories and Compositional Processes." Ph.D. dissertation, University of Texas at Austin, 1974.

———. "Charles Ives's Concept of Music." *Current Musicology*, no. 18 (1974): 114–119.

———. "The Use of Hymn Tunes as an Expression of 'Substance' and 'Manner' in the Music of Charles E. Ives, 1874–1954." M.A. thesis, University of Texas at Austin, 1969.

Warren, Richard. *Charles E. Ives: Discography*. New Haven: Historical Sound Recordings, Yale University Library, 1972.

Wasson, Jeffrey. "The Organ Works of Charles Ives: A Research Summary." *Student Musicologists at Minnesota* 6 (1975–1976): 280–289.

Wooldridge, David. *From the Steeples and the Mountains: A Study of Charles Ives*. New York: Knopf, 1974. Republished as *Charles Ives: A Portrait*. London: Faber & Faber, 1975.

Wooldridge, David, and Kirkpatrick, John. "The New Ives Biography: A Disagreement." [Exchange about Kirkpatrick's review of Wooldridge's book.] *HiFi/Musical America*, December 1974, pp. MA18–MA20.

Yates, Peter. "Charles Ives: An American Composer." *Parnassus: Poetry in Review* 3, no. 2 (Spring-Summer 1975): 318–328.

———. "An Introduction to Charles Ives." In *Twentieth Century Music: Its Evolution from the End of the Harmonic Era into the Present Era of Sound*, pp. 252–270. New York: Pantheon Books, 1967.

Yellin, Victor Fell. Review of first recording of *The Celestial Country*, by Charles E. Ives. *The Musical Quarterly* 60 (July 1974): 500–508.

———. Review of *Essays Before a Sonata*, by Charles E. Ives. *Journal of the American Musicological Society* 17 (Summer 1964): 229–231.

OTHER WORKS

Allen, Gay Wilson. *Waldo Emerson: A Biography*. New York: Viking Press, 1981.

Apthorp, William Foster. "John Sullivan Dwight." In *Musicians and Music Lovers*, pp. 277–286. New York: Charles Scribner's Sons, 1894.

Austin, William. *Music in the 20th Century from Debussy through Stravinsky*. New York: W. W. Norton, 1966.

Beers, Henry A. "A Pilgrim in Concord." *Yale Review*, n.s. 3 (July 1914): 673–688.

Burkholder, J. Peter. "Museum Pieces: The Historicist Mainstream in Music of the Last Hundred Years." *The Journal of Musicology* 2 (Spring 1983): 115–134.

————. "Brahms and Twentieth-Century Classical Music." *19th Century Music* 8 (Summer 1984): 75–83.

Burton, Roland Crozier. "Margaret Fuller's Criticism of the Fine Arts." *College English* 6 (October 1944): 18–23. Reprinted in *Critical Essays on Margaret Fuller*, edited by Joel Myerson, pp. 209–215. Boston: G. K. Hall, 1980.

Bushnell, Horace. *Sermons for the New Life*. Rev. ed. New York: Scribner, Armstrong, 1876.

Cooke, George Willis. *John Sullivan Dwight: A Biography*. Boston: Small, Maynard, 1898.

Corbett, Charles Hodge. *Lingnan University: A Short History Based Primarily on the Records of the University's American Trustees*. New York: Trustees of Lingnan University, 1963.

Drew, James. "Information, Space, and a New Time-Dialectic." *Journal of Music Theory* 12 (1968): 86–103.

Emerson, Edward Waldo. *Thoreau, As Remembered by a Young Friend*. Boston: Houghton Mifflin, 1917.

Emerson, Ralph Waldo. *The Complete Works of Ralph Waldo Emerson*. Biographical introduction and notes by Edward Waldo Emerson. Centenary Edition. Boston: Houghton Mifflin, [ca. 1903].

————. *The Journals and Miscellaneous Notebooks of Ralph Waldo Emerson*. Edited by Susan Sutton Smith and Harrison Hayford. Cambridge: Harvard University Press, Belknap Press, 1978.

Fertig, Walter L. "John Sullivan Dwight, Transcendentalist and Literary Amateur of Music." Ph.D. dissertation, University of Maryland, 1952.

Frothingham, Octavius B. *Transcendentalism in New England: A History*. Boston: American Unitarian Association, [ca. 1876].

Gillespie, Don. "John Becker, the Musical Crusader of St. Thomas College." *Student Musicologists at Minnesota* 6 (1975–1976): 31–65. Revised and printed as "John Becker, Musical Crusader of Saint Paul." *The Musical Quarterly* 62 (April 1976): 195–217.

Griggs, John C. "An Amateur Hermit." *Yale Literary Magazine* 53 (October 1887): 32–35.

————. "Canton's Contribution to the Chinese Revolution." *Current History* 24 (September 1926): 872–876.

————. "Chopin and George Sand." *Yale Literary Magazine* 52 (June 1887): 362–365.

————. "The Church Choir: Its Origins, Its Needs, Its Possibilities." *The Congregationalist* 77, no. 16 (21 April 1892): 124 (p. 2); 77, no. 17 (28 April 1892): 134 (p. 2); 77, no. 18 (5 May 1982): 142 (p. 2).

————. "Claude Debussy." *Yale Review*, n.s. 1 (April 1912): 484–494.

————. "Contacts with China." *China Review* 6 (April 1924): 102–104.

————. "Growth vs. Intermittent Reform." *Yale Literary Magazine* 53 (May 1888): 337–342.

————. "The Influence of Comedy Upon Operatic Form." *The Musical Quarterly* 3 (October 1917): 552–561.

————. "An Interview." *Yale Literary Magazine* 54 (January 1889): 161–164.

———. "The Literary Work of Richard Wagner." *Yale Literary Magazine* 53 (November 1887): 62–67.

———. [Part of "Portfolio," on Poe.] *Yale Literary Magazine* 52 (June 1887): 383–384.

———. [Part of "Portfolio."] *Yale Literary Magazine* 53 (November 1887): 89–90, and 54 (January 1889): 182–183.

———. "The Pastor and His Choir." *Music* (Chicago) 5 (April 1894): 688–692.

———. "Possibilities of a Pure Toned Organ." *Music* (Chicago) 2 (September 1892): 483–490.

———. "Relation of College Men to Politics." *Yale Literary Magazine* 54 (December 1888): 99–102.

———. *Studien über die Musik in Amerika.* Leipzig: Breitkopf & Härtel, 1894.

———. "Studies in America's Music." Ph.D. dissertation, University of Leipzig, 1893. [English-language longhand manuscript draft.]

———. "Sun Yat-sen and Chinese Unity." *Current History Magazine of The New York Times* 17 (October 1922): 133–137.

———. "What South China is Fighting For." *Current History Magazine of The New York Times* 15 (January 1922): 637–643.

[Griggs, S.C.] "Higher Music Education in America: The Metropolitan College of Music." *Music* (Chicago) 6 (August 1894): 381–390. (Includes information on John C. Griggs, p. 388, with a portrait.)

Hopkins, Vivian C. *Spires of Form: A Study of Emerson's Aesthetic Theory.* Cambridge: Harvard University Press, 1951. Reprint. New York: Russell & Russell, 1965.

Howard, John Tasker. *Our American Music: Three Hundred Years of It.* New York: Thomas Y. Crowell, 1931.

Ives, J. Moss. *The "Ark" and the "Dove": The Beginning of Civil and Religious Liberties in America.* London: Longmans, Green, 1936.

Janik, Allan, and Toulmin, Stephen. *Wittgenstein's Vienna.* New York: Simon & Schuster, 1973.

Kearnes, William Kay. "Horatio Parker, 1863–1919: A Study of His Life and Music." Ph.D. dissertation, University of Illinois, 1965.

Lowens, Irving. "Writings about Music in the Periodicals of American Transcendentalism (1835–1850)." *Journal of the American Musicological Society* 10 (Summer 1957): 71–85.

Moran, Michael. "New England Transcendentalism." In *The Encyclopedia of Philosophy*, ed. Paul Edwards et al., vol. 5, pp. 479–480.

Nagel, Stuart, and Burkholder, Kathleen, eds. *Policy Publishers and Associations Directory.* N.p.: Policy Studies Organization, 1980.

Parker, Horatio, ed. *Music and Public Entertainment.* Boston: Hall and Locke, 1911. Reprint. New York: AMS Press, 1980.

Phelps, William Lyon. *Autobiography with Letters.* New York: Oxford University Press, 1939.

———. *Howells, James, Bryant, and Other Essays.* New York: Macmillan, 1924.

———. *The Pure Gold of Nineteenth Century Literature.* New York: Thomas Y. Crowell, 1907.

———. *Some Makers of American Literature.* Boston: Marshall Jones, 1923.

Salzman, Eric. *Twentieth-Century Music: An Introduction.* Englewood Cliffs, N.J.: Prentice-Hall, 1967. 2nd ed. 1974.

Semler, Isabel Parker, in collaboration with Pierson Underwood. *Horatio Parker: A Memoir for his Grandchildren compiled from Letters and Papers.* New York: G. P. Putnam's Sons, 1942. Reprint. New York: AMS Press, 1975.

Slonimsky, Nicolas. *Music Since 1900.* 4th ed. New York: Charles Scribner's Sons, 1971.

Stoehr, Taylor. *Nay-Saying in Concord: Emerson, Alcott, and Thoreau.* Hamden, Conn.: Archon Books, 1979.

Strong, Leah A. *Joseph Hopkins Twichell: Mark Twain's Friend and Pastor.* Athens, Ga.: University of Georgia Press, 1966.

Thoreau, Henry David. *The Writings of Henry David Thoreau.* Walden Edition. Boston: Houghton Mifflin, 1906.

Van Doren, Mark. *Henry David Thoreau: A Critical Study.* Boston: Houghton Mifflin, 1916.

Waters, Edward N. "John Sullivan Dwight, First American Critic of Music." *The Musical Quarterly* 21 (January 1935): 69–88.

Zuck, Barbara A. *A History of Musical Americanism.* Studies in Musicology, no. 19. Ann Arbor: UMI Research Press, 1980.

Index

References to works by Charles Ives are indexed under the composer's name rather than by title.

161

(continued)